Walking in Truth™

A Biblical Worldview and Bible Survey Curriculum for Grades 6–8

Christianity in Action

Student Textbook
Grade 8

Summit Ministries

Acknowledgements

Vice President of Program Services: Jason Graham

Managing Curriculum Editor: Macki Jones

Authors
Kevin Bywater
Chuck Edwards
Mike Hamel
Macki Jones
Pat Maloy
Kim Pettit
Keith Robinson
Lorraine Wadman

Editorial Team
John Conaway
Macki Jones
Kim Pettit
Nancy Sutton
Lisa Tamayo
Lorraine Wadman

Design Team
Claire Coleman
Mike Riester

Illustrators
Aline Heiser

Published by Summit Press, P.O. Box 207, Manitou Springs, CO 80829
Third Printing (2023)
Printed in India

ISBN: 978-1-7330256-7-6

Walking in Truth Table of Contents—Student Textbook

Worldview

Getting Started—Maps

"Any of you guys know how to read a map?" Evan dropped his geography textbook on the table and plopped down next to his friends.

This earned him a scowl and a "shhh" from the librarian.

"Who reads maps anymore?" Mark said. "Just ask your phone for directions."

"Not allowed," Evan replied. "My teacher wants us to learn how to read maps, whether they're digital or paper."

Phillip laughed. "Good luck finding a paper map. They're in the museum next to the typewriters and rotary phones."

"That's a dumb assignment," Rob said.

"It's an excellent assignment."

They all turned to see the librarian, who had been listening to their conversation. The young lady looked fresh out of college.

"Maps provide much more than just a location," she said as she came over. "They give a sense of perspective and show you your place in the world, provided you have a good one."

"What makes a map good?" Evan asked.

"It has to accurately represent the terrain it pictures. A poor map will get you lost. Or get you killed." She added that last part to spark their interest.

That definitely got their attention.

"A map represents something larger than you can see with the naked eye." She pointed to a globe on the information desk. "The circumference of the earth is 2,400 miles. The circumference of that globe is 24 inches. You can find your place on the big globe by using the little globe."

Her next comment caught them by surprise. "Have any of you been to Peru?"

The boys looked at each other in confusion. *What was up with this lady?*

"So, none of you have been to Europe?"

"Peru's not in Europe," Evan said. "It's in South America."

"How do you know?" the librarian challenged.

"I learned it in school."

"How do you know what you learned is true?"

Evan got an idea. He went to the information desk and returned with the globe. He found Peru and pointed. "South America."

"Do you trust that globe?"

Evan thought for a moment, then said, "Sure. It's in a library, and you wouldn't have a faulty globe."

"Good." The librarian smiled. "To determine if your map is accurate, you should find out who trusts it, and who made it in the first place. This globe was made by the National Geographic Society. Now, would you like a few tips on map reading?"

What Is a Worldview?

A worldview is like a map. It represents a reality larger than what the naked eye can see. Some worldviews are better than others. Some do a superior job of accurately picturing what is real. The more accurate the worldview, the better guide it will be through life.

A worldview is simply the way we see the world. It's *a pattern of ideas and beliefs that help us make sense of the world and that guide our decisions and actions.*

In this lesson you will learn the answers to these questions:
> *What are you using to guide you through life?*
> *How do you know it's trustworthy?*
> *Who else do you know who's using the same map (worldview)?*
> *What other worldviews are there, and why do so many others use different maps?*

A leading Christian author gives this helpful explanation:

> A worldview is not the same thing as a formal philosophy; otherwise, it would be only for professional philosophers. Even ordinary people have a set of convictions about how reality functions and how they should live. Because we are made in God's image, we all seek to make sense of life. Some convictions are conscious, while others are unconscious, but together they form a more or less consistent picture of reality.[1]

> **Worldview**
> A pattern of ideas and beliefs that help us make sense of the world and that guide our decisions and actions

Topic 1—Ideas, Beliefs, and Actions

Let's look a bit closer at what makes up a worldview. An *idea* is *a thought, plan, or suggestion about what to do; something you imagine or picture in your mind*. Ideas naturally give rise to a system of beliefs that becomes the basis for our decisions and actions. A *belief* is *a certainty that something exists or is true*.

A worldview begins with ideas. Ideas have consequences, both good and bad. Ideas form our beliefs, shape our convictions, and solidify into habits of behavior. Jesus explained the connection by using the example of a fruit tree. A fruit tree has a root system that draws nutrients from the soil and channels sap up the trunk to the branches and produces fruit. If there were no roots, there would be no fruit.

Our unseen ideas and beliefs about God and the world nourish and shape our choices and actions. Good roots result in good fruit, as Jesus said: "You can identify them by their fruit, that is, by the way they act. Can you pick grapes from thorn bushes, or figs from thistles? A good tree produces good fruit, and a bad tree produces bad fruit. A good tree can't produce bad fruit, and a bad tree can't produce good fruit" (Matthew 7:16–18).

The connection between root ideas and the resulting fruit can easily be seen in whether people believe in God or not. Those who do not believe he exists cannot look to him for answers when facing moral dilemmas or deciding what's right or wrong. They can only look within themselves or to others. The answers they come up with will change from person to person or culture to culture. On the other hand, those who believe God exists have a clear basis for moral choices based on his unchanging character, as revealed in the Bible.

Another metaphor we could use to understand worldviews more clearly is eyeglasses. They can bring the world into clearer focus, provided the lenses have the correct prescription. If you've ever put on someone else's glasses, you probably saw a distorted view of your surroundings because the prescription wasn't right for you. Glasses either help or hinder our sight, just as a worldview either helps or hinders our understanding of reality.

Would you want an airplane pilot who was nearsighted—unable to see things clearly unless they are close up? Or a surgeon who was farsighted—unable to see things clearly unless they are far away? The right glasses can correct the distortions of nearsightedness and farsightedness and lead to a safer, healthier life. The right worldview can correct the distorted way we see reality as finite and fallen human beings.

© Walking in Truth Grade 8

What's true for individuals is also true for societies and nations. People will help or harm others based on their ideas about God, themselves, and others. And if a whole society begins to believe wrong ideas, it will move in the wrong direction.

Take Germany in the 1930s and 1940s, for example. Prior to World War II, German society was built for the most part on a biblical Christian worldview. This was the home of Martin Luther and the birthplace of the Reformation! But when Adolf Hitler and the Nazis took over, they quickly substituted their own ideas for God's. They would decide what was right and wrong and who would live or die. Since Hitler hated both Judaism and Christianity, as he and the Nazis became more powerful, the German people failed to take a stand for God's truth. Many remained silent, including many Christians, as Hitler plunged the world into war and sought to exterminate the Jews. His bad ideas had horrendous consequences for everyone!

JEWISH PRISONERS IN A NAZI CONCENTRATION CAMP

Or take India in 1928, when an 18-year-old young woman went there for the first time. She was shocked to see people being left in the streets to die. Once she understood more about the Hindu worldview, with its belief in karma and reincarnation, she realized that Hindus saw the world very differently from Christians. Her belief that every human being had value, because each one is made in God's image, led her eventually to open the Home for the Dying.

Today we know this woman as *Mother Teresa*. She went on to minister to thousands of sick and dying Hindus, and her love for the poor went on to influence thousands more. Her life was so inspiring that the anniversary of her death has been designated the International Day of Charity by the United Nations.[2]

Both Adolf Hitler and Mother Teresa had a profound impact on the world because of their worldviews. They had very different answers to life's biggest questions: Is there a God? Who am I? Why am I here? What happens when I die? What is the meaning and purpose of life? Is there a difference between right and wrong? Their lives had very different outcomes as a result.

Topic 2—Popular Worldviews

Everyone has a worldview, even the people who don't realize that they have one. There are hundreds of different worldviews. Religions are worldviews. A *religion* is *a set of beliefs about the existence and nature of God*. Some major religious worldviews include Christianity, Islam, Judaism, Hinduism, and Buddhism. Some popular nonreligious worldviews include secularism, Marxism, new spirituality, and postmodernism. Here's a bird's-eye view of five leading worldviews:

Christianity believes in a personal God who has made himself known through creation and the Bible. He made human beings in his image to have fellowship with him. Instead, humans chose to sin, which affected all creation. Jesus Christ, God in the flesh, paid the penalty for sin and made reconciliation possible through his death and resurrection.

 **Secularism** believes humans are the center of reality and rejects belief in God, the afterlife, and anything beyond what we can perceive with our five senses. Secularism is atheistic (no God) and materialistic (no soul or spirit) and anti-religious (advocating a society free from religion). Secularists say we should live for the here and now, not for eternity.

 **Marxism** sees history as a struggle between the haves (the owners) and the have-nots (the workers). The ideal state humans can achieve is called *communism*. To reach this state, the poor must revolt against the wealthy, who keep them from living meaningful lives. Marxism rejects God, promotes socialism, and insists on the scientific method as the basis for knowledge and morality.

 **New spirituality** is a mix of Eastern religions, paganism, and pseudoscience. It teaches that the world is spiritual but not governed by a personal, all-powerful God. God is "consciousness," and since we are all a part of this consciousness, we are all god. New spiritualists believe in a continuous cycle of life, death, and reincarnation, and in karma (the total of a person's good and bad actions which result in good or bad consequences in this life or in a reincarnated life).

 **Postmodernism** denies the existence of God and absolute truth. Belief in universal moral principles must be replaced with reverence for unique individuals and cultures. Postmodernism contends that when humans believe their worldview is true and others are false, it only leads to disagreement, war, and destruction. The solution to this problem is just to declare that no one can truly know how the world actually is.

In this course, we will show why we believe the Christian worldview:
- provides the best answers for life's biggest questions.
- does the best job of explaining the world in which we find ourselves.
- gives the best instructions for living a meaningful and joyous life.

Topic 3—The Biblical Christian Worldview

The biblical Christian worldview explains how God designed and created the universe and the beings who live in it. It is based on the unchanging character and Word of God. The Bible introduces us to God, his plan for creation, and his continued involvement with everything he's made. The big picture it presents could be called *a metanarrative*.

A metanarrative is similar to a worldview. It is *an overarching story of events that provides a structure for people's beliefs and gives meaning to their experiences.*

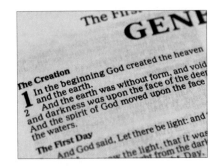 The biblical metanarrative is the overall structure or storyline of the Bible. The many stories in Scripture tell one big story that has four parts: creation, the fall, redemption, and restoration.

The framework of this metanarrative is that in the beginning, creation was "good" and became "very good" with the creation of human beings as God's image-bearers. And, in the end, God will establish his image-bearers in a beautiful city forever, the crown jewel of a renewed Earth. But between

Genesis 1 and Revelation 22, things went horribly wrong. Humans chose to believe the serpent instead of God (Genesis 3). Thankfully, God does not leave us in our idolatry and injustice; he is restoring us and his creation. He is rescuing and redeeming the world that will one day be our eternal home.

> **Metanarrative**
> An overarching story of events that provides a structure for people's beliefs and gives meaning to their experiences

Part 1—The Metanarrative

Creation

The Bible begins with the beginning of everything—everything, that is, except God. He was already in the beginning and he brought all things into existence through his living Word. As John 1:1–4 says: In the

beginning the Word already existed. The Word was with God, and the Word was God. He existed in the beginning with God. God created everything through him, and nothing was created except through him. The Word gave life to everything that was created, and his life brought light to everyone.

Colossians 1:16 also affirms for through him God created everything in the heavenly realms and on earth. He made the things we can see and the things we can't see—such as thrones, kingdoms, rulers, and authorities in the unseen world. Everything was created through him and for him.

God created humans in his image (Genesis 1:27) to live in harmony with him and to take charge of the earth (Genesis 1:28–30). Everything that God created was "very good" (Genesis 1:31).

The Fall

The perfection of creation didn't last long. Soon there was trouble in paradise. Our first human parents chose to disobey God and death entered the world as the result of their sin, just as God had warned (Genesis 2:16). This disobedience became known as *the fall*. Genesis 3 gives the costly results. There would be pain in childbirth and tension in marital relationships. The ground was cursed and work would be hard. After a life of toil, humans would return to dust through physical death (Genesis 3:16–19). All Adam's descendants would also share his spiritual death and separation from God: When Adam sinned, sin entered the world. Adam's sin brought death, so death spread to everyone, for everyone sinned" (Romans 5:12).

Adam and Eve were immediately expelled from the garden of Eden (Genesis 3:22–24). The curse of sin passed along to their children. Cain killed his brother Abel. Violence and evil spread until God decided to wipe the world clean and start over with Noah (Genesis 6–9).

Redemption

But God did not leave his creation in this fallen condition. He had a plan to bring us back into a special relationship with himself and restore the relationships we were meant to have with others and the world. He

did this by sending his own Son to be born of a woman so he could pay the penalty for our sin: He is so rich in kindness and grace that he purchased our freedom with the blood of his Son and forgave our sins (Ephesians 1:7). This part of God's plan is called redemption, meaning that God paid in full for our sins and restored us to fellowship with him: For he has rescued us from the kingdom of darkness and transferred us into the Kingdom of his dear Son, who purchased our freedom and forgave our sins (Colossians 1:13–14).

When we are in a right relationship with God, we can better understand who we are and how to relate to others. We can be agents of his kingdom here on Earth until the time when that kingdom is fully revealed.

Restoration

The Bible looks ahead to a restored creation; believers will have a new body, and they will live for eternity with God in an unbroken fellowship with him: Then I saw a new heaven and a new earth, for the old heaven and the old earth had disappeared. And the sea was also gone. And I saw the holy city, the new Jerusalem, coming down from God out of heaven like a bride beautifully dressed for her husband. I heard a loud shout from the throne, saying, "Look, God's home is now among his people! He will live with them, and they will be his people. God himself will be with them. He will wipe every tear from their eyes, and there will be no more death or sorrow or crying or pain. All these things are gone forever" (Revelation 21:1–4).

Until that time, all creation struggles in the tension between the sinful "now" and the glorious "then" (Romans 8:19–22). We know how the story ends, and that's exciting!

Part 2—The Four Relationships

The metanarrative outlined above impacts all of us every day. We are created in God's image but we have been warped by sin. Christ has redeemed those who believe in him and will one day restore all things (Ephesians 1:10). For now, we are in the middle of this story, and understanding what God is doing can help us with the four relationships he has placed us in from the beginning: our relationship with God, with ourselves, with others, and with the earth.

First, we are in a relationship with God, our Creator. This is the most important relationship we have, since our very existence depends on him daily (Acts 17:28). He desires a relationship of authentic obedience and love from everyone he's made.

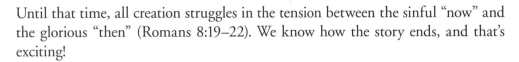

Second, we are in a relationship with ourselves. This may sound strange but being self-aware is what makes us different from animals. We both have physical bodies, but only humans have a soul. (See Lesson 6 for more details.) Because we have souls and were created in his image, we have intrinsic value and an eternal purpose. We should see ourselves as God sees us and rejoice (Psalm 139:14–16).

Third, all of us are in relationships with others who also bear God's image. We have family, friends, teachers, and acquaintances. The relationships between humans are the key ingredients of families, churches, and governments—the three primary social institutions. How we manage these relationships determines the kind of culture we live in.

Finally, every human is in a relationship with the rest of creation. From the beginning God charged us to look after the world he made for us (Genesis 1:28, 2:15–20). We are to care for the animals and environment as his stewards. A *steward* is *a person who manages another's property: one who administers anything as the agent of another.* Part of being made in God's image is being his representatives and managing his creation in a way that reflects his glory.

Our relationship with God has the most impact on how we live each day. This relationship is restored by trusting in Jesus Christ as Lord and Savior (John 3:16). God then breathes his Holy Spirit into his children (Galatians 4:6). The Spirit guides and enables us to treat ourselves and others as image-bearers. We are to be salt and light in a dark world (Matthew 5:13–16) and live as citizens of God's kingdom. We have a sacred duty to influence the culture around us.

Topic 4—Influencing Culture

When we talk about culture, we mean *the way of life of a particular people as shown in their ordinary behavior, habits, attitudes toward others, and their moral and religious beliefs.*

Culture is shaped over time and its foundations often go unnoticed and unexamined. As one modern thinker puts it: "Cultural legacies are powerful forces. They have deep roots and long lives. They persist, generation after generation, virtually intact, even as the economic and social and demographic conditions that spawned them have vanished, and they play such a role in directing attitudes and behavior that we cannot make sense of our world without them."[3]

We are more aware of what's happening on the surface, or what we might call "popular" culture. Popular culture is *a collection of values, themes, ideas, and behavior popularized mainly through media and technology* such as movies, video games, music, television, books, advertising, and the internet.

The ideas and beliefs of popular culture can be heard in sound bites and seen on social media. And the more often they are repeated, the more people think they are true. Popular ideas become memes. A *meme* is *an idea, behavior, style, or usage that spreads from person to person within a culture.* Memes are to culture what genes are to life.

But not all memes are created equal. Many have become generally accepted as cultural truth, regardless of whether they are actually based in reality. For instance:
"That may be true for you, but not for me."
"I can do whatever I want as long as it doesn't hurt anyone else."
"All religions are the same."
"I am the master of my fate. I am the captain of my soul."[4]

The apostle Paul warned believers to not allow false ideas to influence their thinking, no matter how popular they are: Don't let anyone capture you with empty philosophies and high-sounding nonsense that come from human thinking and from the spiritual powers of this world, rather than from Christ (Colossians 2:8). He told Timothy to guard what God has entrusted to you. Avoid godless, foolish discussions with those who oppose you with their so-called knowledge (1 Timothy 6:20). The apostle Peter repeated the same message: so be on guard; then you will not be carried away by the errors of these wicked people and lose your own secure footing (2 Peter 3:17).

We are also told to understand the truth so that we can help others see where their ideas are wrong: We destroy every proud obstacle that keeps people from knowing God. We capture their rebellious thoughts and teach them to obey Christ (2 Corinthians 10:5).

Our idea of truth comes from a biblical Christian worldview. Without this foundation, Christians are as likely as anyone to adopt the beliefs and practices of those around them. Francis Schaeffer, a Christian philosopher, blamed the Christian community for the church's shift away from God. He saw how Christians had moved away from a comprehensive biblical worldview to focusing on their private relationship with Jesus. They lost sight of the importance of shining the light of a Christian worldview into philosophy, ethics, politics, economics, science, art, entertainment, and other areas.

Schaeffer explained how Christians had very gradually "become disturbed over permissiveness, pornography, the public schools, the breakdown of the family, and finally abortion. But they have not seen this as a totality—each thing being a part, a symptom of a much larger problem. They have failed to see that all of this has come about due to a shift in worldview—that is, through a fundamental change in the overall way people think and view the world and life as a whole."[5]

But Schaeffer's warnings came too late. Christianity had embraced a series of postures in the past several decades that didn't help very much. They were content to remain isolated and not get involved in the larger culture. They became known for condemning, critiquing, and judging culture. This caused many people to reject the Christian worldview. As a result, Christians today have an uphill battle in trying to regain a positive influence in society.

If we want to change our culture for the better, then we must understand and apply a biblical worldview. We have to become like the men of Issachar in ancient Israel, who understood the signs of the times and knew the best course for Israel to take (1 Chronicles 12:32). They provided leadership for the entire nation because they understood God and what he was doing in their culture. They saw the events of the day through the lens of God's truth—a biblical worldview.

A biblical worldview not only helps us see the world as it truly is, it tells us what the world should be like. "Our worldview not only *describes* reality, it *prescribes* how we act and respond to every aspect of life. Because our ideas do determine how we behave, the bottom line is that our ideas do have consequences."[6]

Culture
The way of life of a particular people as shown in their ordinary behavior, habits, attitudes toward others, and their moral and religious beliefs

Topic 5—Developing Your Worldview

The challenge for Christians today is not to accept the worldview of the culture around us but to have a biblical worldview: Don't copy the behavior and customs of this world, but let God transform you into a new person by changing the way you think. Then you will learn to know God's will for you, which is good and pleasing and perfect (Romans 12:2). This isn't an easy task when there are so many different versions of "truth" clamoring for attention. So many proposed answers to life's biggest questions. So many false memes being pushed by popular culture.

This course will be your map through hostile territory. It will lay out the ideas and beliefs that should shape our thinking and behavior in seven disciplines, asking and answering the key questions in each:

- Theology—*What about God?*
  Every serious worldview begins with this question. Christianity says he exists and can be known through general revelation (creation) and special revelation (his Word).
- Philosophy—*What is true and how do we know?*
  How we think affects our view of knowledge, wisdom, and truth. Faith and reason are meant to work together to give us an accurate view of reality.
- Ethics—*How should we behave?*
  God is concerned about our attitudes and actions. We discover what is moral by learning about God's character and how he has made us and the world.
- Biology—*What is the origin of life?*
  Life's origin and design display the work of an intelligent designer.
  Human beings and creation are not the result of a cosmic accident but the result of a divine plan.
- Psychology—*What does it mean to be human?*
  Humans have a physical body made from the dust of the earth, and a spiritual soul. We also have a sin nature that causes problems in our relationships with God, ourselves, others, and our world.
- Sociology—*What makes a healthy society?*
  God has ordained the social institutions of family, church, and state so that each would foster love, respect, discipline, and harmonious community.
- History—*What is the meaning of history?*
  God is sovereign over history, and it is moving according to his plan.

The answers to these questions are interconnected and come together to form an overall system of beliefs—a worldview—that shapes our thoughts, dictates our actions, and influences our impact on culture. This isn't a journey we take on our own: For God is working in you, giving you the desire and the power to do what pleases him (Philippians 2:13). He has given us his Word as a lamp to guide my feet and a light for my path (Psalm 119:105). And we have fellow Christians to teach and encourage us (1 Corinthians 14).

The foundation for everything to follow—in this book and in life—depends on how you answer the question tackled in Lesson 2: What about God?

ENDNOTES:
1 Nancy Pearcey, *Total Truth* (Wheaton, Illinois: Crossway Books, 2004), 23.
2 "International Day of Charity 5 September," United Nations, accessed January 18, 2021, https://www.un.org/en/observances/charity-day#:~:text=The%20date%20of%205%20September,constitute%20a%20threat%20to%20peace.
3 Malcolm Gladwell, *Outliers: The Story of Success* (New York: Back Bay Books, 2011), 175–76.
4 William Ernest Henley, "Invictus," in *Poems* (London, David Nutt, 1907), 119.
5 Francis A. Schaeffer, *A Christian Manifesto* (Westchester, IL: Crossway Books, 1981), 17.
6 Jeff Myers, *Understanding the Times: A Survey of Competing Worldviews* (Manitou Springs, CO: Summit Ministries, 2015), 6.

Application Story: Stalling Tactics

"Navin, you've got the green light. The security measures in the room are deactivated. You may proceed with the mission. Good luck."

My pulse quickened as the words spilled out of my earpiece. "Copy that. I'm moving in."

The hardest part—the waiting—was over. Now was the time to let my spy training kick in. I checked the connection between my harness and the cable one last time, then climbed onto the edge of the hotel roof. My jet-black hair and clothing made me blend in perfectly with the darkness of the night. I had considered wearing a black mask to cover my face, but I was confident the dark brown skin tones of my Indian ancestry would be enough to hide me from wandering eyes.

I checked the tension on the cable and lowered myself over the edge of the hotel in the city of Mumbai, India. The penthouse suite was only a few stories from the roof. Within a matter of heartbeats, I cut a hole in the glass with my laser cutter and slipped through it. Once my feet were firmly on the carpet inside the suite, I unhooked my harness and anchored it to the floor.

"I'm in," I said into the commlink on my lapel.

"Copy that."

Like a shadow, I crossed the room and entered the office. Resting on the desk was a computer used by one of India's wealthiest business owners—and crooked underworld kingpin—Jayesh Burman.

I inserted the special flash drive into the computer and downloaded enough info to bring down his entire organization. Once the download was complete, I grabbed the drive, stuffed it into a pocket, and headed for the window to make my exit.

A click was the only warning I got. A second later the main door opened, and the lights blazed to life. Caught in the middle of the room, I dove behind the couch.

"I'm compromised! Need backup!" I whispered into my commlink.

"Copy. We're sending—"

I missed the rest of the sentence as a high-pitched squeal erupted from my earpiece. The explosion of sound made my head swim until I managed to rip the small device out of my ear. When the pain subsided, I looked up into the barrel of a pistol.

"Get up."

The owner of the gun was a burly man in a dark suit. He slipped a small device into his pocket—no doubt the source of my new headache. I rose slowly to my feet. My stomach flipped as I recognized the man standing behind him.

"Hello, Agent Patel. We meet at last."

"The pleasure's all yours, Burman."

"Please, call me Jayesh. Your team was clever in shutting off my security. But your intel failed to discover the infrared scanners I had placed around the suite. Now, give me the flash drive."

My mind reeled as I desperately searched for a way out of this. Help was on the way, if only I could stall him long enough. But how? I scanned the room for inspiration. A book on the nearby table caught my eye. The title sparked a memory of something I read in Burman's file. Maybe . . .

I reached into my pocket and pulled out the drive. "Help me to understand something," I said, putting a warm, curious tone to my voice, "aren't you worried about all the bad karma you're getting? I mean, your business dealings alone have ruined the lives of hundreds, if not thousands of people. Aren't you worried about being reincarnated as a rat or something?"

Burman smiled broadly as his bodyguard snatched the flash drive from me and handed it to his boss. He stowed it into the inside pocket of his expensive business suit before responding. "Only if you believe in reincarnation. I don't buy into that nonsense."

"Don't let your mother hear you say that," I replied.

The corner of Burman's lip curled slightly. "I respect my parents' beliefs, but don't share them. I'm a man of science. Evolution has shown we evolved from lower life-forms over billions of years. There's no need to believe in the ultimate Brahman, or the multitude of 'gods' of the Hindu religion. And there is definitely no reason to believe in your Christian God or a Jewish Messiah. In fact, let me turn your question back on you. Aren't you worried about your own soul? Doesn't the Bible say something about, "You shall not steal. You shall not lie. You shall not . . . murder"?

While I was thankful he had taken the bait, his question hit too close to home. I, too, abandoned the faith of my parents. Since then, I've made all sorts of compromises. I've done many horrible things that I later regretted. What if there was a God? An untimely death was always a possibility in my line of work. Why was the prospect bothering me so much now?

"That may be true, but I'm sure God will be willing to negotiate," I said, putting more confidence into my voice than I truly felt. "After all, I'll just remind him of all the good I've done."

Burman laughed. "Somehow I don't believe a God of justice can be bribed quite that easily."

"What about you?" I asked, hoping to deflect his comment. "If you're wrong and there is a God, what will you tell him? How will you convince him to let you into heaven?"

His smile suddenly evaporated and he glared at me. "Enough of this. While I've enjoyed our little discussion, duty calls. Farewell, Agent Patel. For your sake, I hope your beliefs about God are correct." He turned to his bodyguard. "Take her downstairs and dispose of her."

I felt the icy grip of terror squeeze the air from my lungs as the man motioned for me to move toward the door. I needed to stall just a little longer!

Light suddenly flooded through the outer window. The bodyguard reacted by turning his weapon toward it.

My instincts kicked in once more. Literally.

I swung my right foot up and knocked the gun out of his grasp. He turned toward me and threw a punch. I dodged to the side and prepared to throw a punch of my own when he fell to the floor and began shaking. The sight of a thin taser wire snaking from his body to the window solved the riddle.

With the bodyguard out of commission, I turned my attention toward the crime lord who was making a dash for the door. My smaller frame and speed allowed me to catch him just as he reached for the handle. I swept his legs out from under him and he fell to the floor. A well-placed kick knocked him unconscious.

I paused long enough to catch my breath, then reached into Burman's pocket and grabbed the flash drive. I sprinted for the opening in the window and reattached the cable to my harness. A drone hovered outside the window, waiting for me like a lost puppy.

"Thanks for the assist, Ravi. Your timing is impeccable. I owe you one."

"Anytime," the remote operator said through its built-in speaker. "Now get back to the roof. The helicopter is almost here."

"On my way." I practically leaped through the hole in the window and activated the winch. I could hear shouts coming from below as I climbed onto the roof seconds later. A whirlwind from above announced the arrival of the helicopter. I grabbed the lowered ladder and clipped my harness to it. I was still dangling from the ladder as the helicopter pulled away from the building.

I had made it. But even as I drew comfort from the fact that I'd lived to see another day, I couldn't help but be haunted by the conversation with Burman. My stalling kept me alive this time. But death will eventually catch me. I can't stall forever.

Getting Started—Chaos or Creator?

"I saw a documentary last night called *The Secret Life of Chaos*," Manny told his friend Eli as they waited for the rain to stop so they could go outside. He pulled up a video clip on his tablet. "Watch this."

It began with a question: "How does a universe that starts off as dust end up with intelligent life? How does order emerge from disorder?"

The host, Professor Khalili, talked about the science behind the beauty and structure in the natural world. Far from being an act of God, they were just the laws of physics in action. The professor cited the work of very smart people who programmed very advanced computers to run very detailed simulations. These simulations showed that unplanned, self-repeating patterns created the universe. There was no need for a divine creator.

"I'm impressed," Eli said when the clip was done.

"Does that mean you're going to become an atheist?" Manny asked.

"Just the opposite. It strengthens my belief in God."

Manny scratched his head. "What? I'm confused."

"Think about it," Eli challenged. "The hardware and software used for the simulation took thousands of logical minds and skilled hands to invent and build. It required an organized, intelligent effort to come up with a simple set of rules that could shape chaos into order."

"Now *you* sound like a professor," Manny said. "What's your point?"

"My point," Eli replied, "is that the video shows the best minds and most sophisticated machines doing an experiment to prove there's no intelligence or design involved in nature. It took a lot of brainpower to reproduce the random chaos that supposedly produced everything else by chance."

Manny got what Eli was saying. "Yeah, there certainly was a lot of intelligence involved in proving there was no intelligence involved in creation."

Eli smiled. "Yup, ironic, huh?"

What Is Theology?
In Lesson 1 we talked about how important it is to develop a well-thought-out worldview. A strong worldview can help us make sense of the world and the part we play in it. Every serious worldview begins with this basic question: *What about God?* So, as we develop a Christian worldview, the place to start is with theology.

What is theology? The word comes from two Greek words—*theos*, meaning *God*, and *logos*, meaning *knowledge* or *word*. Theology is *the study of God*. Theology answers key questions like these:

Does God exist?

Does it make sense to believe in God?

Can we trust what the Bible says about God?

What is God like?

Theology
The study of God

Topic 1—Does God Exist?

If you ask someone this question—Does God exist?—you'll get one of three answers: *no*, *yes*, or *not sure*. A person who says *no* is an atheist. A person who says *yes* might be a theist or a pantheist. A person who is not sure is an agnostic. Here's what these words mean.

Atheism is *the belief that there is no God*. The term comes from the word *theos*, which means *God*, and the Greek prefix *a*, which means *no*. A person who doesn't believe in God is called *an atheist*. Atheists don't think about God when making life choices. Since they believe we're alone in the world, humans can decide what's right and wrong. There's no appeal to a higher power.

Theism is *the belief in the existence of a god or gods*. *Polytheism* is *the belief that there are many gods*. *Monotheism* is *the belief that there is only one God* who exists. Monotheists believe that God is complete in himself. This means he created the universe and everything in it, but he is separate from his creation. Because the universe has one Creator, everything in creation points to God, but only God is God. Monotheists believe that God has something to say about how they live. God created everything according to his own order and plan, so things and people have a purpose. Because God created people, he has the right to tell them what's right and wrong.

POLYTHEISM—HINDUS BELIEVE
IN 33 MILLION GODS

MONOTHEISM—JEWS, CHRISTIANS,
AND MUSLIMS BELIEVE IN ONE GOD

Pantheism is *the belief that God is everything and everything is God*. This word comes from the word *theos* and the Greek prefix *pan*, which means *all* or *everything*. Their idea of God influences how pantheists live. Their motive for taking care of the environment is that everything in nature is part of God. Their motive for being kind to others is that every person is part of God. Some pantheists will even say that individual things don't really exist. There is only one thing—God. So when we die, we are absorbed into God.

PANTHEISM—NEW SPIRITUALISTS BELIEVE THAT EVERYTHING IS GOD

AGNOSTICISM—AGNOSTICS ARE UNSURE ABOUT THE EXISTENCE OF GOD

Some people don't know whether there is a God, or if we can ever know God. They are called *agnostics*, from the Greek word *gnosis*, meaning *knowledge*, and the Greek prefix *a*. An atheist doesn't believe in God whereas an agnostic doesn't believe we can know for sure. In the end, both wind up living as if God doesn't exist.

English writer and philosopher G. K. Chesterton once quipped, "The worst moment for the atheist (or agnostic) is when he is really thankful and has no one to thank." How do Christians know whom to thank at such a time?

Christians believe that we are able to know about God because he has made it possible for us to know him. He has given people the ability to perceive reality and to think about what we perceive. He has also deliberately shown himself to people through two main types of revelation: *general* and *special*.

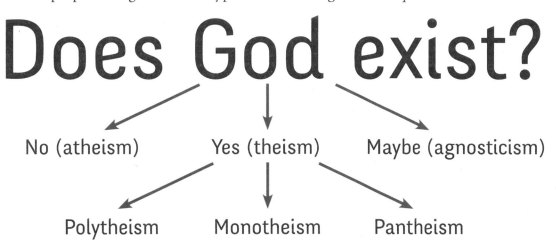

Does God exist?

No (atheism)　　Yes (theism)　　Maybe (agnosticism)

Polytheism　　Monotheism　　Pantheism

Part 1—General Revelation

General revelation refers to *knowledge about God that can be discovered through the natural creation*. For example: The heavens proclaim the glory of God. The skies display his craftsmanship. Day after day they continue to speak; night after night they make him known (Psalm 19:1–2). We are able to perceive things in nature with our five senses. Our senses tell us the world is full of things that are not us—things we didn't create or cause.

God reveals quite a lot about himself in nature, and this revelation is available to every person on Earth: They know the truth about God because he has made it obvious to them. For ever since the world was created, people have seen the earth and sky. Through everything God made, they can clearly see his invisible qualities—his eternal power and divine nature. So they have no excuse for not knowing God (Romans 1:19–20).

In addition to the messages from our senses, we have the ability to think about what that information means. We can detect patterns, differences, similarities, and categories. We can decide what to focus on, what to ignore, what's harmful, what's pleasant, what's important, and so on. We can process all we've learned and come up with ideas about what it all means. And if we're open to following our observations and thoughts, we can begin to understand that God is behind it all.

But God doesn't force his general revelation on anyone. It's possible for people to deliberately choose not to see what God is revealing. They can foolishly make up their minds to shut out any ideas about God (Psalm 14:1). In a sense, that's understandable. People who are determined to do whatever they want and don't want to be responsible to a higher authority are not open to thinking about God. If God exists, they know that they should submit to his will.

> **General Revelation**
> Knowledge about God that can be
> discovered through the natural creation

Part 2—Special Revelation

Special revelation refers to *the knowledge of God and spiritual matters that can be discovered only through supernatural means, such as the Bible and miracles.* When it comes to the Bible, God miraculously guided its authors to accurately record his Word while using their own words. Moreover, all Scripture is inspired by God and is useful to teach us what is true and to make us realize what is wrong in our lives. It corrects us when we are wrong and teaches us to do what is right. God uses it to prepare and equip his people to do every good work (2 Timothy 3:16–17).

General revelation tells us God exists, while special revelation tells us more about what God is like and what he expects of us. In addition to revealing himself through nature, God has communicated to people in special ways—sometimes by an audible voice, sometimes by dreams and visions, sometimes by specific actions, such as miracles. Our main source of information about these communications is the Bible. God the Holy Spirit moved people to write God's great story, which begins before creation and extends into the endless future.

The Bible draws our attention to Jesus—God's most accurate, complete, and wonderful communication about himself: Long ago God spoke many times and in many ways to our ancestors through the prophets. And now in these final days, he has spoken to us through his Son. God promised everything to the Son as an inheritance, and through the Son he created the universe (Hebrews 1:1–2).

In fact, the Bible calls Jesus *the Word of God*. John 1:1–18 tells how the Word of God became human and made God's glory known. When we pay attention to what Jesus said and did, we are learning about what God is like: No one has ever seen God. But the unique One, who is himself God, is near to the Father's heart. He has revealed God to us (John 1:18).

For thousands of years, the people of God have studied nature and Scripture. They've discussed and compared and argued and reached agreement about what God has said about himself. No matter how much people study, we can never know everything. But we can know enough about God to trust him and live for him and tell others about him.

God doesn't intend for us to figure all this out by ourselves. He has given us the Holy Spirit to help us think and understand: When the Spirit of truth comes, he will guide you into all truth. He will not speak on his own but will tell you what he has heard. He will tell you about the future (John 16:13). He has also given us other Christians—the community of faith, past and present—to help us grow in our knowledge of God.

Special Revelation
Knowledge about God and spiritual matters that can only be discovered through supernatural means, such as the Bible and miracles

Topic 2—Does It Make Sense to Believe in God?

There are lots of opinions about God as we've noted above. Christians are theists who have very specific beliefs about God and his Son, Jesus Christ. There are those who think that whatever anyone believes about God and Jesus is just fine—it's a matter of personal opinion. They don't think it's possible to decide whether beliefs about God and Jesus are true or not.

But Christians have always insisted there are very good reasons for believing God exists and that Jesus is who he says he is. Jesus' followers have told us what he was like, what he said, and what he did. These eyewitnesses saw him die on the cross, and they spent time with him after his resurrection (1 John 1:1–4). They received the Holy Spirit at Pentecost and began spreading the Good News to everyone they met. They didn't talk about Jesus in order to give people just another option. They had heard Jesus say, "I am the way, the truth, and the life. No one can come to the Father except through me" (John 14:6). They had very good reasons for believing that, and we can believe it too.

Early Christians lived in a world where people had different ideas about the divine. Many believed there were a multitude of gods. But Christians insisted there was only one God, and Jesus was the only Savior and Lord. In their teaching, preaching, writing, discussing, and evangelizing, they tried to persuade others to put their faith in Jesus.

The apostle Peter gave this advice to Christians: And if someone asks about your hope as a believer, always be ready to explain it (1 Peter 3:15). What does it mean to "explain" what we believe? The Greek word is *apologia*, which means *an answer, defense,* or *reason*. It's also the root for the English word *apologetics*. Apologetics is *a defense of one's faith*. Apologetics involves knowing what you believe, why you believe, and how to defend it. The purpose of apologetics is to answer doubt, to build confidence, and to change lives.

Every worldview lesson in this course has an apologetics section. By the end of this course you will be equipped with strong reasons for believing in Christianity and Jesus Christ.

Apologetics
A defense of one's faith

Topic 3—Can We Trust What the Bible Says about God?

The Bible is our main source of information about Jesus and is the foundation for our beliefs. We don't have to rely on our opinions or feelings about God. God inspired writers to communicate his teachings for us to read and study: Such things were written in the Scriptures long ago to teach us. And the Scriptures give us hope and encouragement as we wait patiently for God's promises to be fulfilled (Romans 15:4).

Are there good reasons to trust what the Bible says about God? Is it a reliable guide to this life and the next? Here are four reasons to have confidence in Scripture:

Part 1—A Unique Book

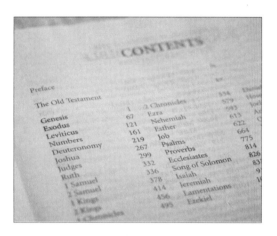

Pick up a Bible and look at the table of contents. If it were any other book, you might think you were looking at a list of chapters. But those aren't chapter titles—they are books. The Bible is a library, and each book is an independent work of literature. Some are history books, some are poetry books, some are law books, some are letters, some are prophecies. They were originally written in different languages—Hebrew, Aramaic, and Greek—in different parts of the world over a period of more than 1,500 years by more than 40 authors. But with all that diversity, there is unity. Each book provides part of one big story—the story of God and his relationship with his creation, especially human beings.

These books are linked in ways that no other literary collection can pull off. For example, some books contain predictions about future events. Many of the Old Testament prophecies gave facts about what would happen to certain nations—prophecies that have already come true. Old Testament writers also told about a deliverer—the Messiah—whom God would send to redeem his people. Hundreds of years later, the Gospel writers gave us facts about the life of Jesus that fulfilled those prophecies and verified that he was that Messiah. Interestingly, there are more than 300 different prophecies regarding the birth, crucifixion, and resurrection of the Lord Jesus Christ. The probability is 1 in

1,017 that just eight of these prophecies would be fulfilled in only one human being. The odds of 16 prophecies being fulfilled are 1 in 1,045. For 48 prophecies to be fulfilled, the probability is 1 in 10,157! With more than 300 prophecies, it would be virtually impossible for one person to fulfill them all. Yet Jesus did fulfill them. The most reasonable conclusion is that God led the Old Testament writers to write those prophecies.

The Bible is God's Word, and we can rely on it to tell us about God and his purpose for the world, and for us. It is unique in its scope, accuracy, and trustworthiness. One theologian puts it this way:

> The Bible is not a book like any other. It makes a claim that God spoke and speaks through its message. It argues that as his creatures, we are accountable to him for what he has revealed. The trustworthiness of Scripture points to its authority as well. Scripture is far more than a history book, as good and trustworthy as that history is. It is a book that calls us to examine our lives and relationship to God. Beyond the fascinating history, it contains vital and life-transforming truths about God and us.[1]

Part 2—A Reliable Text

A common view of the Bible is that it's not reliable. After all, it was written thousands of years ago and copied so many times that there must have been errors and changes along the way. How would you answer someone who believes that?

As in other areas of dispute, we can ask the experts. Scholars who study ancient texts have a number of tests to decide authenticity. Here's how the Bible stands up to these tests.

1. Number of manuscripts: Modern translations of many ancient documents are based on very few manuscripts. There are only about a dozen manuscripts of Greek writers such as Plato and Aristotle, and Roman writers such as Julius Caesar. Compare that with about 14,000 Old Testament manuscripts and fragments as well as about 25,000 New Testament manuscripts, fragments, and translations.

2. Date of manuscripts: For many ancient writings, the manuscripts we have were made more than 1,000 years *after* the original work was written. Because ancient manuscripts were composed on fragile materials such as papyrus, they had to be copied again and again. Some of the copying wasn't very good. By contrast, we have a number of New Testament manuscripts from around 100 to 150 years after the originals, raising confidence that these manuscripts match the originals. Another benefit of an early date is that there were still people around who would have read the originals and would have known if something had changed.

DEAD SEA SCROLLS FROM QUMRAN CAVES IN ISRAEL

3. Consistency of manuscripts: Many ancient manuscripts have major differences in wording. In some cases, translators have to provide several possible versions. By contrast, biblical manuscripts have only minor differences, such as variations in spelling or unclear markings. In ancient times, temple scribes were responsible for safeguarding Scripture texts. In addition to preserving the manuscripts, they were official copiers of the Scriptures. We have records of the strict rules they had to ensure that there were no changes in the text. Their work was carefully inspected by others and any manuscripts with copying errors were destroyed so that only accurate manuscripts were kept.

Part 3—A Historically Accurate Book

A number of ancient writers, some of whom didn't believe in God or the Bible, wrote about biblical people and events. The Jewish historian Josephus and Roman writers Tacitus and Suetonius mention Jesus. Early church leaders such as Irenaeus, Tertullian, and Clement of Rome provide evidence that the New Testament descriptions of life in those times are accurate.

A PAGE FROM A MANUSCRIPT DEPICTING FLAVIUS JOSEPHUS, THE JEWISH HISTORIAN WHO WROTE ABOUT JESUS

ARCHAEOLOGICAL SITE BELIEVED TO
BE THE REMAINS OF BEERSHEBA

Another source of historical evidence is archaeology. Archaeologists explore ancient ruins and study items from past cultures in order to build an accurate history of ancient peoples. Experts who have studied Egypt, Assyria, Babylon, Persia, and other areas where biblical events happened have concluded that biblical descriptions are accurate. For example, for many years some experts said the book of Daniel was untrue because they couldn't find any record of the Babylonian king Belshazzar. But later on, archaeological evidence forced those experts to change their minds. Of course, there are many statements in Scripture that haven't been confirmed by other sources, but there is enough evidence that we can trust the historical accuracy of the Bible.

Part 4—A Powerful Book

The Bible is the bestselling book of all time. Today, the Bible, or parts of it, are available in more than half the languages in the world. As of 2019, the full Bible has been translated into almost 700 languages, the New Testament has been translated into over 1,500 additional languages, and Bible portions or stories into more than 1,100 other languages. Thus, at least some portions of the Bible have been translated into 3,385 languages.[2]

The Bible has influenced literature and the arts throughout history. In fact, there are many historical documents and works of art that can't even be understood without knowledge of the Bible. Early scientists such as Newton, Kepler, Copernicus, and Galileo found support for their work in the Bible.

The Bible is the main source for beliefs about human dignity, human rights, equal representation under the law, and many other ideas that we, today, take for granted. It has motivated the abolishment of slavery, the establishment of hospitals and schools, and compassionate care for the poor. It is also the main source for moral and ethical standards in modern societies. Over the centuries, people from many cultures and people groups have pointed to the Bible as the power that changed their lives. They show that the word of God is alive and powerful. It is sharper than the sharpest two-edged sword, cutting between soul and spirit, between joint and marrow. It exposes our innermost thoughts and desires (Hebrews 4:12).

Author Alex McFarland makes a strong case for the trustworthiness of the Bible, noting it is internally consistent, externally validated, miraculously preserved, and comprehensively accurate. When we look closely at the Bible, the most reasonable conclusion is that we can trust what it says. Most importantly, we can confidently commit our lives to Jesus Christ, who is the main subject of this amazing book.

Topic 4—What Is God Like?

The Bible does more than tell us that God exists; it provides us with reliable information about who God is. Many people believe in God, but there can be big differences in what they mean when they say "God." Because we're not God and can't totally wrap our minds around who God is, it's very tempting to settle for what we'd like God to be. The Bible tells us that human beings are made in God's image, but many people turn that around and create a God in their own image.

Many books have been written about God. Theology is a huge subject. In this lesson we'll talk about just a few characteristics of God. This is only the beginning. There will always be more to learn, but this is a good place to start.

Part 1—God Is Personal

While pantheists believe that God is the universe and everything in the universe is God, Christians believe that God is separate from his creation. Other theists, however, take this separation to an extreme, as is the case with deism. Deism is *the belief in the existence of a supreme Creator who does not intervene in the universe or interact with humankind.* Human reason is sufficient to establish God's existence, but this belief in God doesn't come with any expectation that we can personally know him.

Contrary to deism, the Bible describes God as personal and active in his creation. He made human beings in his image and relates with us personally and individually. One New Testament scholar puts it this way:

> So the God of the Bible in the very first chapter [of Genesis] is not some abstract "unmoved mover," some spirit impossible to define, some ground of all beings, some mystical experience. He has a personality and dares to disclose himself in words that human beings understand. Right through the whole Bible, that picture of God constantly recurs. However great or transcendent he is, he is a talking God.[3]

God shows personal characteristics such as love, patience, anger, joy, determination, grief, concern; characteristics we share because we are made in his image. He is infinite, we are finite, but we can know and relate to God because we have personhood in common.

> **Deism**
> The belief in the existence of a supreme Creator who does not intervene in the universe or interact with humankind

Part 2—God Is Triune

God is one God in three persons: Father, Son, and Holy Spirit. Each person is fully God. Each person is distinct. We call this truth *the doctrine of the Trinity.* This belief is difficult to understand, but for almost 2,000 years, Christians have taken it seriously because they see it in Scripture passages like Luke 3:21–22, One day when the crowds were being baptized, Jesus himself was baptized. As he was praying, the heavens opened, and the Holy Spirit, in bodily form, descended on him like a dove. And a voice from heaven said, "You are my dearly loved Son, and you bring me great joy," and Matthew 28:19, therefore, go and make disciples of all the nations, baptizing them in the name of the Father and the Son and the Holy Spirit.

The doctrine of the Trinity can be confusing, but it is the conclusion we have to draw given what the Bible clearly teaches:

- There is only one God. All other "gods" are idols created by human beings (Deuteronomy 4:35, 39; Isaiah 43:10; Mark 12:29).

- The Father is God. The apostle Paul said there is "one God and Father of all" (Ephesians 4:6).

- The Son is God. John 1:1 says, "In the beginning the Word already existed. The Word was with God, and the Word was God."

- The Holy Spirit is God. Peter tells Ananias that by lying to the Holy Spirit, he lied to God (Acts 5:3–4). We are the temple of God because God's Spirit lives in us (1 Corinthians 3:16).

- The three persons are distinct but act in perfect unity (1 Peter 1:2, 1 Corinthians 13:14).

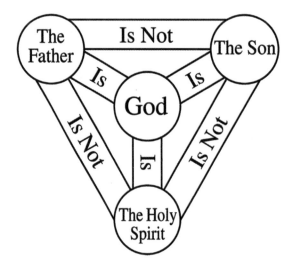

Part 3—God Is Involved

The Bible clearly tells us that God has always been closely involved with the world and its inhabitants—and always will be. For instance, when God sent Moses to Egypt to lead the chosen people to safety, he described himself this way: I have certainly seen the oppression of my people . . . I have heard their cries of distress . . . I am aware of their suffering. So I have come down to rescue them . . . and lead them out of Egypt (Exodus 3:7–8).

The Bible is full of hundreds of interactions between God and individuals. He is in control of history and is moving everything to accomplish his original purpose. The ultimate display of his involvement is his provision for our deliverance from sin. He loves his creation so much that he sent his Son to become a human being who suffered, died, and was raised from the dead to redeem us. God is not aloof. He is involved with us and will never leave us.

Part 4—God Is Just

Adam and Eve cast out of Paradise.

As Creator and Ruler of everything, God established laws. The material world follows the natural laws he set in place. God also made human beings. We were given a moral sense and moral laws, along with the ability to decide whether we would obey those laws. When sin came into the world through the disobedience of Adam and Eve, it brought tragic consequences for humanity and the rest of creation.

In judgment for sin, God expelled humans from the garden, judged Cain for murder, destroyed Sodom and Gomorrah, defeated Pharaoh's armies at the Red Sea, sent Israel and Judah into exile—the examples go on and on. And God still judges sin, which is why we are called to repent and turn to God. We are to rely on the Holy Spirit to become more like Jesus.

God is determined to eradicate sin and restore all creation to the goodness that was there at the beginning. The last chapter in the book of Revelation describes the culmination of God's judgment. The result will be a new heaven and earth, a good and perfect world with Jesus as King.

Part 5—God Is Merciful and Gracious

Yes, the Bible tells us that God is perfectly righteous in judging people for sin, but he often holds back his judgment: He does not punish us for all our sins; he does not deal harshly with us, as we deserve (Psalm 103:10). This is because he does not want anyone to be destroyed, but wants everyone to repent (2 Peter 3:9).

God doesn't just hold back his judgment; he goes much further by generously giving us what we don't deserve. The Bible calls this *grace*. God keeps us alive, provides food and clothing, gives us positive relationships with others, protects us from harm, gives us the ability to think and feel—the list is endless! The most amazing example of his grace is giving his Son to save us from sin. God is so rich in kindness and grace that he purchased our freedom with the blood of his Son and forgave our sins (Ephesians 1:7).

There is only one God. He is real and powerful and personal and loving and just and good and merciful and gracious. He calls us to trust him, live for him, and share him with others.

Part 6—God Matters

Because God created us, we owe him everything we are and have. Because he has a purpose for us, what we do matters. Because he loves his creation, we must care for it. Because he loves all people, we must love them too—even those who don't love us, and even those who hate us.

Because he gave his life for us, we must give our lives to him and serve him wherever he places us. Because we are part of his body on Earth, we must live in community with others in the church so that the world will see what it means to love one another. Because he has sent the Holy Spirit to live in us, we must follow where he leads and depend on his power for righteous living.

The more we know about God, the more obvious it becomes that he must be the foundation of our worldview, which gives us answers to important questions such as *Why am I here?* and *Where am I going?*

Jesus clearly answered the first question in Matthew 22:37–38: "You must love the Lord your God with all your heart, all your soul, and all your mind.' This is the first and greatest commandment. A second is equally important: 'Love your neighbor as yourself." We are here to love, glorify, and praise God. We are also here to love and serve others. "Let your good deeds shine out for all to see, so that everyone will praise your heavenly Father" (Matthew 5:16). God wants us to keep these things in mind no matter what we're doing.

The second question, *Where am I going?*, also touches on our purpose. No two lives are the same. We all develop differently. Our relationships and experiences will vary. Most of these differences aren't as important as people think. What's important is what Jesus told his disciples as he prepared to return to his Father, "And be sure of this: I am with you always, even to the end of the age" (Matthew 28:20). And he promised that one day, "When everything is ready, I will come and get you, so that you will always be with me where I am" (John 14:3).

Where we are going ultimately depends on whether we accept Jesus as our Lord and Savior. Those who believe and trust in him have everlasting life (John 3:16, 5:24) and will spend eternity with him. Those who do not believe do not have life (1 John 5:12). They will spend eternity separated from God.

For now and through eternity, we have the possibility of a significant and fulfilling life. This is what God has had in mind for us from the beginning!

Conclusion

The biblical Christian worldview holds that God has revealed himself in two main ways: 1) general revelation, which is the created order; and 2) special revelation, through the incarnate Son of God, Jesus Christ; the Holy Spirit; and the inspired word of God, the Bible. From the Christian perspective, the foundation for everything in life is the opening phrase of the Bible, *In the beginning God created . . .* (Genesis 1:1). Christian theology teaches that God is intelligent, powerful, loving, just, and a holy Being. Moreover, God exists as a trinity: Father, Son, and Holy Spirit. Christianity further proclaims that God took upon himself human form in the person of Jesus Christ and died for our sins.

As Christians, we worship a God who is both Mind and Heart, who with intelligence and power created the world, yet he also loves humankind so much that he sent his Son to die so people can reconnect with him. But this holy and righteous God stands in judgment of our actions as well, most importantly whether we have chosen to accept Jesus' death as payment for our sins. Christian theism declares that God exists, is triune, personal, holy, yet merciful, created the universe, and loved us enough to send his Son for us. And to top it off, God communicates with us—he speaks through the general revelation of creation and the special revelation of Jesus Christ, the Holy Spirit, and the Bible.

Now that you have all this information about God, the question you need to ask yourself is are you listening? When you examine a cell in biology, when you walk through the park, when you study the Bible, when you care for someone in need, are you looking for evidence of God's existence and seeking to glorify him by your actions? Samuel's response to God makes for a great heartfelt prayer: "Speak, LORD, your servant is listening" (1 Samuel 3:9).

ENDNOTES:

1 Darrell L. Bock, *Can I Trust the Bible?: Defending the Bible's Reliability* (Norcross, GA: RZIM, 2001), 52.
2 "2020 Scripture Access Statistics," Wycliffe Global Alliance, October 2020, https://www.wycliffe.net/resources/statistics/.
3 D. A. Carson, *The God Who Is There: Finding Your Place in God's Story* (Grand Rapids: Baker Books, 2010), 20.

Application Story: Shipwrecked

I hate idols. They constantly get my hands dirty when I touch them, and I have to handle them with extreme care. If I don't, I might anger the god the idol represents.

Or, more importantly, I might anger my father.

You see, my father is an idol maker. He's a craftsman from Athens. He travels from town to town selling idols of all shapes and sizes. My two brothers and I go with him, sometimes for months at a time. Most often we travel by cart to local villages. But not this time. This time we took a boat across the Aegean Sea to sell at some of the smaller islands.

That's another reason why I hate idols. They take me away from home. I miss my mother, and, although I'd never admit it, my annoying sisters as well.

Then again, I suppose I should be grateful to the gods. After all, their images provide a steady source of income for my family, and, if I continue to learn the trade from my father, for me as well.

"Kreon, get your head out of the clouds. There's a boat coming! You were supposed to have that crate of Roman gods set up on the table already."

I rolled my eyes at my oldest brother, Titan, which earned me a punch in the arm. "Ow! Alright, already. It only takes me a minute."

"Yeah, well if you don't get it set up by the time father gets back with breakfast, you'll get more than a light smack in the arm."

My mind flashed back to a week ago when my other brother, Sophos, and I were playing a game once Father had left to do some trading. We . . . sort of lost track of time. We hadn't finished our chores by the time Father returned and he . . . well, let's just say I was very sore in a certain tender area for a day.

The memory worked its magic. I grabbed the crate of idols and began setting them out on the table of our portable booth. Each one had to be handled with extreme care. Just a month ago, I accidentally dropped a statue of Zeus himself and broke his head clear off! Although I hid the evidence of my crime, I was plagued with nightmares. In one, ghoulish harpies swooped down on me and let out horrid screeching sounds. In another, I was running for my life as a lightning storm chased me through a darkened forest. I was sure Zeus would punish me.

But the punishment never came. Maybe Zeus wasn't mad at me after all. Or . . . maybe he didn't exist.

I pushed the blasphemy from my mind and focused once again on my task. The light breeze from the Aegean Sea rustled the fabric canopy above and behind me while the morning sun peeked over the eastern hills of the island.

I had just finished setting the last of the statues on the table when I saw Father running down the road toward us. The look of excitement on his face sent my heart beating.

"Here! Eat quickly!" he said as he gave each of us a portion of bread and fruit. "We have to be ready."

"Ready?" Titan asked. "We are ready. See? We just finished."

"No, no, that's not going to work," Father said, glancing at the displays. "Titan, you and I will go back to the tent to get the extra crates of the Poseidon idols. Kreon and Sophos, clear the table. Leave only one of each god over here on the left. We need to make room."

"Yes, Father," I said. "But, why? What's going on?"

"There's been a shipwreck! The boat that's arriving now is bringing what's left of the crew and passengers. Now get to work!" A moment later, he and Titan bolted toward where our tent was perched beneath a large tree, away from the road.

My heart lurched. What's left? That means . . . who knows how many died. "But why . . . why is Father so excited?" I asked Sophos. "People just died!"

Sophos smacked me painfully on the side of my head. "You're such a child sometimes. Don't you get it? A shipwreck means Poseidon's angry. When he's angry, people want to appease him. To appease him, they buy idols and offer incense to him. And where are they going to get the new idol and incense? From us! And the sooner we sell our stock, the sooner we return home."

Although the idea of returning home warmed my heart, I still couldn't banish the image in my mind of people drowning. Was that the way the gods really worked? Were they really so petty as to take their anger out on innocent people? Did the gods even exist?

A memory surfaced from years ago when I was only ten. Father was sculpting an idol I had never seen before.

"Which god is that?" I asked.
"He's a god from the barbarians to the north," Father replied.
"Have you ever met this god?"
"Don't be foolish. Of course not."
"Then, how do you know what he looks like?"

Father turned and stared at me hard as if he was about to reveal a great secret. "I make it up. People don't care what the gods look like. They just want something to worship. I give it to them."

Father and Titan returned with the crates, snapping me back to the present. We quickly set out the figurines of Poseidon even as the boat pulled up to the docks. The moment the gangplank was set, stooped figures wrapped in blankets began to disembark. As Father had predicted, many headed straight for our booth. I moved toward the back of the booth and watched as my father and brothers took coins in exchange for sculpted pieces of clay. Every one of the survivors wore the same haunted expression.

Is this all there is to life? Is there no purpose other than to be the plaything for some spiteful god?

Movement to the left caught my eye. A man and woman with four children around my own age moved among the refugees handing out food and drinks. Their strange clothing set them apart from everyone else in the area.

I leaned closer to Sophos. "Who are they?"

He snickered. "Those are Jews. They're so poor, they can only afford one god, and even he doesn't allow them to make idols. Pathetic losers."

As I watched them go about meeting the needs of strangers, I couldn't help but wonder: Who were the real losers? Is there a greater purpose in life? What is it about those strangers that speaks of hope? What would make them choose to give their own food away to those in need?

I am surrounded by images of gods, yet they seem powerless. I feel a deep sense of emptiness overwhelm me. What is the truth? Are any of these gods real?

Why is it I feel like the one truly shipwrecked?

Getting Started—Santa and God

"I hope Santa brings me the dollhouse I want," Riley said as she helped her cousins decorate the Christmas tree in their grandparents' living room. "I told him exactly which one when I sat on his lap at the mall yesterday."

"Does she still believe in Santa?" Abby whispered to Kara, the oldest of the three.

Kara nodded. "And the Easter Bunny," she whispered back. "And the Tooth Fairy."

"When are her parents going to tell her the truth?" Abby asked.

"I don't know. How old were you when you first learned Santa Claus wasn't real?"

"My parents never told me he was real," Abby replied as she draped a string of lights around the tree. "He was always make-believe, like Rudolph the Reindeer or Jack Frost."

"Believing in Santa doesn't do any harm," Kara said.

"But believing in Santa doesn't make him real either," Abby said quietly. "At some point Riley will realize the truth. Then maybe she'll think God isn't real either."

"God's different," Kara said.

"The two probably sound a lot alike to Riley," Abby suggested. "They both know everything about everyone. They judge who's been good and who's been bad. They can travel to all the homes on Earth in a single night. You ask them to bring you what you want."

"Yeah, that is confusing," Kara admitted.

"Kids believe what the people they trust tell them," Abby said. "They don't have to be told the whole truth, or only the truth; there's lots of room for stories and fairy tales. But they should learn the difference between truth and fiction."

"What is the difference?"

Abby draped more lights and thought about the question. It was a good one. Finally she said, "Truth is what correctly reflects what's real. Something that doesn't accurately match reality is fiction."

"What are you two whispering about?" Riley asked.

"Big girl stuff," Abby replied.

"When will I be a big girl?"

Kara handed Riley a Santa ornament. "You should ask your mom and dad that."

What Is Philosophy?

In the last chapter we learned that everyone's worldview begins with answering some basic theological questions such as: Does God exist? and What is God like? In this chapter, we'll dig into how to think about the answers to these and other important questions by asking another set of key questions:

What is truth?

How do we know?

What is the nature of reality?

The study of these three questions is called *philosophy*. The word comes from two Greek words: *philo*, meaning *love of*, and *sophia*, meaning *wisdom*. As an academic discipline, philosophy is *the study of truth, knowledge, and ultimate reality*.

> **Philosophy**
> The study of truth, knowledge,
> and ultimate reality

Topic 1—Wisdom

The goal of philosophy is wisdom, but what do we mean by that? For many people, wisdom is just the ability to make good decisions. Wise people don't do foolish things. They don't just do what they feel like on the spur of the moment. They think before they act. They do research and gain knowledge before making important decisions. In this sense, anyone can learn to be wise.

But for the Christian, there's more to wisdom than knowledge, self-control, and the ability to think well. Ultimately, it is based on who God is and how he wants his people to live within the world he created. A quick survey of Scripture gives the following highlights concerning wisdom.

In Proverbs, wisdom is personified and calls out, "Listen to me! For I have important things to tell you. Everything I say is right. . . . I love all who love me. Those who search will surely find me. . . . The Lord formed me from the beginning, before he created anything else. . . . I was the architect at his side. I was his constant delight, rejoicing always in his presence. And how happy I was with the world he created; how I rejoiced with the human family! And so, my children, listen to me, for all who follow my ways are joyful. Listen to my instruction and be wise" (Proverbs 8: 6, 17, 22, 30, 33).

Wisdom involves listening and following, learning and growing. It is deeply personal. Wisdom is a chosen way of life: If you are wise and understand God's ways, prove it by living an honorable life, doing good works with the humility that comes from wisdom. . . . But the wisdom from above is first of all pure. It is also peace loving, gentle at all times, and willing to yield to others. It is full of mercy and the fruit of good deeds. It shows no favoritism and is always sincere (James 3:13, 17).

Earlier in his book, James said wisdom is ours for the asking (James 1:5). Truly wise people consciously depend on God to help them grow in wisdom: Fear of the Lord is the foundation of wisdom. Knowledge of the Holy One results in good judgment (Proverbs 9:10).

From a biblical perspective, wisdom is *the ability to make decisions that glorify God in our relationships with him, ourselves, others, and the earth.*

Wisdom appeals to the mind. Wise living grows out of wise thinking. Throughout the Bible, God's people are urged to use their God-given ability to think. For example, through the prophet Isaiah, God pleaded with his people, "Come now, let us reason together . . ." (Isaiah 1:18, ESV). Through his prophets and apostles, God reasoned with those who were not yet his people. When Paul was in Athens, he went to the synagogue to reason with the Jews and the God-fearing Gentiles, and he spoke daily in the public square to all who happened to be there. He also had a debate with some of the Epicurean and Stoic philosophers (Acts 17:17–18).

In John 1, Jesus is called *the logos*, meaning *word*. It can also mean *logic* or *reason*. Indeed, all the treasures of wisdom and knowledge can be found in Jesus (Colossians 2:3). Through his Word made flesh, God reveals himself and calls humanity to believe and accept him (John 1:12). This is a decision of the mind and the heart.

Jesus talked about the importance of the mind. When a religious leader asked him, "Teacher, which is the most important commandment in the law of Moses?" Jesus replied, "'You must love the LORD your God with all your heart, all your soul, and all your mind.' This is the first and greatest commandment" (Matthew 22:36–38). We are commanded to love God with our whole self—heart, soul, and mind.

God made us to think and reason. In 1 Peter 1:13 we are told to prepare our minds for action and to exercise self-control. Some Christians downplay this because of the emphasis often put on personal faith as the key to a relationship with God (Romans 4:5, Ephesians 2:8–9). They think faith and reason are incompatible. They think they have to go against their minds to believe with their hearts. They point to verses that seem to speak against the use of reason, like Colossians 2:8: Don't let anyone capture you with empty philosophies and high-sounding nonsense that come from human thinking and from the spiritual powers of this world, rather than from Christ. But Paul was not telling Christians to avoid philosophy; rather, he is warning about "empty" philosophies that come from corrupt human sources rather than from Christ.

In 1 Corinthians 3:19 Paul also warns, for the wisdom of this world is foolishness to God. As the Scriptures say, "He traps the wise in the snare of their own cleverness." But at issue here is not wisdom but "the wisdom of this world."

As the Scriptures say, "I will destroy the wisdom of the wise and discard the intelligence of the intelligent." So where does this leave the philosophers, the scholars, and the world's brilliant debaters? God has made the wisdom of this world look foolish. Since God in his wisdom saw to it that the world would never know him through human wisdom, he has used our foolish preaching to save those who believe (1 Corinthians 1:19–21).

Once again, Paul wasn't speaking against human thinking. He was declaring that it is foolish for people to think that they can depend only on their own intellectual abilities to understand reality. That is an extremely arrogant attitude. If we look at life realistically, we must admit that we need God. We are not qualified to be our own god.

Topic 2—Faith and Reason

Faith is *a firm trust or confidence in someone or something*. The Bible expands on this in Hebrews 11:1: Faith shows the reality of what we hope for; it is the evidence of things we cannot see.

Notice the words *reality* and *evidence*. Faith is not a blind, irrational leap; neither is it wishful thinking. It involves reasoning about reality. We have to use our minds when relating to God. Many people think that faith and reason are in conflict with one another. Many critics of Christianity try to feed this imaginary conflict and insist that people need to choose between faith and reason. They often suggest that people of faith aren't very good thinkers. They agree with Mark Twain's definition of faith: "believing what you know ain't so."

The faith of the first Christians wasn't based on blind belief in something that didn't exist. It rested on solid evidence: We proclaim to you the one who existed from the beginning, whom we have heard and seen. We saw him with our own eyes and touched him with our own hands (1 John 1:1). John had been with Jesus, but he was writing to disciples who would never see Jesus in the flesh. They had to have confidence in things they could not see, but they had eyewitness evidence and good reasons to believe: The disciples saw Jesus do many other miraculous signs in addition to the ones recorded in this book. But these are written so that you may continue to believe that Jesus is the Messiah, the Son of God, and that by believing in him you will have life by the power of his name (John 20:30–31).

A contemporary Christian thinker puts it this way: "Faith does not overthrow reason but transcends the parameters of reason. . . . Faith is neither a form of conceptual knowledge nor simply an act of the will, but a gift of grace that opens our inward eyes to the truth of what God has done for us in Jesus Christ."[1]

What we believe determines how we live. The Greek word translated "faith" also includes the ideas of loyalty, trust, and faithfulness. Our reason informs our faith, but how can we be certain our reasoning is sound?

In order to think about something, we have to trust our ability to think. In order to make a judgment that something is true, we have to trust our ability to analyze facts. In order to come up with a theory about how something in nature works, we have to trust that nature has an order. Our reasoning about what is true helps us decide where to place our faith: Will this chair hold me? Should I trust this person? Should I buy this item? Can I believe this social-media post? The examples are endless. To know what or whom to trust, we have to know what truth is.

Faith
A firm trust or confidence in
someone or something

Topic 3—What Is Truth?

The question *What is truth?* is often described as the first great question of philosophy because it sets the agenda for everything else. In the simplest sense, truth means *being in accord with fact or reality*. Ideas, thoughts, and beliefs can be said to be true only if they correctly represent reality.

A statement, belief, or thought is true if it correctly reflects reality. "This is a mouse," is a true statement if it describes a real mouse. "Abraham Lincoln was our first president," is not true because it doesn't correspond with the facts of history.

Truth
Being in accord with fact or reality

Part 1—Misunderstanding Truth

Not everything people believe or say about truth is true. Here are two popular but false ideas about what truth is:

1. Sincere Belief: Think back to the opening story of this lesson. A child may sincerely believe in Santa Claus based on what she's seen and heard. Her parents have told her Santa is real. She's seen him at the mall. He

brings her presents. Of course, some of these things actually happened; they just aren't what they appear to be. Mom bought the presents. The mall Santa is a retired bus driver.

People of any age can confuse strong feelings with truth. Or they may sincerely attach false thinking to real things. But their sincere belief may not match the facts.

2. Strong Opinion: *An opinion* is *a broad judgment or value statement about something*. Some opinions are trivial or subjective: "That's the greatest movie ever made." "Chocolate is the best flavor of ice cream." Other opinions, such as "Babies aren't human until they leave the womb" and "Not all races are equal," have serious consequences.

Opinions good and bad are influenced by many external sources—such as family, friends, school, church, and the media. Your experiences also shape your opinions. If your computer constantly crashes, you might decide it's an undependable brand. If you catch a teacher in a lie, you may not believe what he says in class. But as with sincere beliefs, strong opinions don't rise to the level of truth unless they correspond to objective reality. As a US senator put it, "Everyone is entitled to his own opinion, but not to his own facts."[2]

One glaring flaw in both these ideas is that they aren't true for everyone. Sincere beliefs and strong opinions vary from person to person. But what is actually true must be universally true. We may disagree on which road is the best way to our destination, but we can't disagree on which direction is north, not as long as we have a compass to consult. If something is true, it's true whether we like it or not, whether we understand it or not, whether we believe it or not. And true statements can be tested and examined and analyzed.

Part 2—Jesus Is the Truth

If truth is primarily about that which accurately reflects reality, what do you think Jesus meant when he said, "I am the way, the truth, and the life" (John 14:6)? We believe that Jesus tells the truth, but how can Jesus "be" the truth? Later on in that same passage, Jesus gave an explanation: "Anyone who has seen me has seen

the Father! So why are you asking me to show him to you? Don't you believe that I am in the Father and the Father is in me? The words I speak are not my own, but my Father who lives in me does his work through me" (John 14:9–10).

John also linked Jesus with truth earlier in his Gospel: The Word became flesh and dwelt among us, and we have seen his glory, glory as of the only Son from the Father, full of grace and truth. . . . No one has ever seen God; the only God, who is at the Father's side, he has made him known. (John 1:14, 18, ESV).

If we compare these passages with our definition of truth, we can begin to see why Jesus called himself *the Truth*. Just as a true statement accurately reflects the real world, so Jesus accurately reflects the nature of God. The better we know Jesus, the better we know God.

Topic 4—How Do We Know?

To know if something is true, we have to test it using knowledge. Knowledge is information and understanding about a subject. The study of knowledge is called *epistemology*, from the Greek word for *knowledge* and the suffix *logy*, meaning *logical discourse*. It explores the nature, origin, and limits of human knowledge.

There are many ways to acquire knowledge. The ways we choose will depend on the sources we trust, our personal learning habits, our openness to new ways of learning, and many other factors. Here are four familiar ways we gain knowledge:

1. Experience: Experience is getting knowledge or skill from doing, seeing, or feeling things. We learn how to swim through personal time in the water. But we can also learn from the experience of others. We've never been to the moon, but we can learn about its surface from the astronauts who have been there. Firsthand experience—ours or others'—is one of the most useful ways to gain knowledge.

2. Authority: There are many things we can't know through direct experience. When we want to get knowledge about these things, we often look for an authority. School textbooks, reference works, research websites, and how-to videos are just a few examples. If we know people who have direct experience, we can consult them. The authorities we choose matter. Paul was encouraged that his disciple Timothy had trustworthy teachers: *But you must remain faithful to the things you have been taught. You know they are true, for you know you can trust those who taught you* (2 Timothy 3:14).

3. Reason: Mathematics is a great example of this form of knowledge. We use it to make calculations that help us understand aspects of the real world. And we can be sure of our answers even if we haven't actually measured any physical things. We also use our reasoning when we use logic. If we know something is true, logic can point us to something else that is also true. For instance, if A is equal to B, and B is equal to C, then A is equal to C.

4. Intuition: *Intuition is understanding or knowing something without needing to think about it first.* A good example of intuition is conscience. We have an inborn sense of right and wrong. This is true even for people who don't know the Bible or don't go to church. Paul insists that, *even Gentiles, who do not have God's written law, show that they know his law when they instinctively obey it, even without having heard it. They demonstrate that God's law is written in their hearts, for their own conscience and thoughts either accuse them or tell them they are doing right* (Romans 2:14–15).

Topic 5–What Is Reality?

As we've seen, truth and knowledge are based on reality. But what is real? *Real is the state of things as they actually exist.* The branch of philosophy that deals with the fundamental nature of reality is called *metaphysics*.

When we survey what philosophers have said about reality, we can put their ideas into three main categories: materialism, spiritualism, and supernaturalism.

1. Materialism: This is the belief that reality is composed of only physical matter. Supposedly immaterial things—God, angels, demons, minds, ideas, feelings, consciousness—aren't real. The only explanations materialism accepts for things are physical explanations. For example, materialism holds there's no such thing as the human soul. Our thoughts, feelings, intuitions, choices, are simply the result of brain activity. Materialism is connected to naturalism, which holds that all phenomena can be explained in terms of natural causes and laws.

2. Spiritualism: This is the belief that all of reality is spiritual or immaterial. This is the opposite of materialism. According to this view of reality, there are no natural laws; all we have are ideas that we use to organize our perceptions of the world. Spiritualism is often linked to the worldview we call *new spirituality*. According to this worldview, everything we experience is part of a divine consciousness or god. The material world is an illusion; everything is spiritual. There is only one cosmic reality.

3. Supernaturalism: This is the belief that reality is composed of both the physical and the nonphysical. Material reality (what can be perceived by our five senses) is only part of what is real. Reality also has a spiritual realm, which includes angels, human souls, and God himself, who created it all. The major worldviews that identify with supernaturalism are Christianity, Islam, and Judaism. The Bible very clearly teaches supernaturalism. Colossians 1:15–17 declares that through Jesus, God created both material and spiritual reality. Reality owes its existence to Jesus.

Many people have been led to faith in God through studying reality. C. S. Lewis, a brilliant English scholar, thirsty for knowledge, studied philosophy, literature, and many other subjects. But his intelligence wasn't the whole story. He had been through a lot of trauma, including a stressful home life and the horrors of war. He was a dedicated atheist and materialist, and insisted that he didn't need God or religion. However, he began to realize that he was using atheism as a kind of fortress in which to hide from reality. Though he was attracted to the idea of beauty (which is nonphysical), he forced himself to believe only in the material world.

As he reflected on this time in his life, he wrote,

> Nearly all that I loved I believed to be imaginary; nearly all that I believed to be real I thought grim and meaningless. . . . But, of course, what mattered most of all was my deep-seated hatred of authority, my monstrous individualism, my lawlessness. . . . And that was what I wanted; some area, however small, of which I could say to all other beings, this is my business and mine only.[3]

Through long conversations with Christian friends and reading books they recommended, his defenses began to wear down, and he moved from atheism to theism. A few years later, his theism led him to the Christian faith, and he became one the greatest Christian writers of the twentieth century.

Topic 6—Christianity and Science

Scientific knowledge is a specialized kind of knowledge that is very effective when used the way it was designed to be used. Our word *science* comes from the Latin word *scientia*, meaning *knowledge*. Science is *a means of investigating the world through empirical observation, hypothesizing, and experimentation.* The natural sciences are based on what's called *empirical knowledge*, or knowledge gained through our five senses.

The three views of reality we have discussed all have different approaches to science. The main difference is that materialism thinks that physical matter is all there is. Anything that can't be perceived by the five senses or tested in a laboratory doesn't exist. Spiritualism and supernaturalism, on the other hand, believe there is more to reality than the physical.

Materialism faces a real challenge with the natural sciences. If the material world just happened—without purpose or plan—how is any knowledge possible? If the world is a product of random chance, so is the human mind; and if that's true, it's likely that any idea or explanation of natural law is purely imaginary. There would be no difference between a carefully thought-out scientific theory and a fairy tale.

Supernaturalism in the form of Christianity has a clear explanation of why everything exists and is knowable. God made it so. The argument—known as the causal argument—goes something like this: The world is real.

It can be observed, described, tested, and understood. Because the world exists, it must have a cause, and it cannot cause itself. It is caused by something outside it, and that cause must be an ultimate cause. Everything in the world is "contingent" (meaning it didn't have to exist); therefore, there must be one "necessary" cause to account for the existence of the world. That ultimate uncaused cause is God.

Christians believe in a God who is orderly and knowable and who made a world that we can learn about and understand. Creation is a showcase of God's wisdom he meant for us to explore (Jeremiah 10:12, Psalm 104:24). Modern science was founded on this assumption and many of its pioneers were Christians. They understood the connection between what they believed about God and how they thought about the universe.

These scientists included Francis Bacon (developer of the scientific method), Johannes Kepler (discoverer of the laws of planetary motion), Robert Boyle (founder of modern chemistry), and Isaac Newton (coinventor of calculus and discoverer of the law of gravity and the laws of motion). Other notables include Carolus Linnaeus, Francis Collins, Gregor Mendel, Louis Pasteur, Florence Nightingale, Lord Kelvin, and George Washington Carver.

Due to their belief in a Creator, these scientists expected nature to be understandable, orderly, and predictable. Only in the last few centuries has science been seen as incompatible with, and superior to, Christianity. But there's no conflict between the Christian worldview and the study of science. As Francis Collins, who led the Human Genome Project, said, "Science is not threatened by God; it is enhanced. God is most certainly not threatened by science; he made it all possible."[4]

Since this is a lesson on philosophy, we should also note that alongside these Christians who worked in the natural sciences, there have been many outstanding Christian philosophers who have advanced human knowledge throughout history. The list includes Thomas Aquinas, Roger Bacon, Immanuel Kant, Søren Kierkegaard, Francis Shaffer, J. P. Moreland, William Lane Craig, Eleonore Stump, and Alvin Plantinga, to name but a few.

THOMAS AQUINAS

Christians believe that humans have the God-given ability to understand nature and discover its order. Our senses are designed to collect information from our environment. Our minds are designed to analyze this data and develop explanations for what we perceive. The Bible tells us the ultimate explanation is that the creation exists to make known the Creator: *The heavens proclaim the glory of God. The skies display his craftsmanship. Day after day they continue to speak; night after night they make him known. They speak without a sound or word; their voice is never heard. Yet their message has gone throughout the earth, and their words to all the world* (Psalm 19:1–4).

> **Science**
> A means of investigating the world through empirical observation, hypothesizing, and experimentation

Topic 7—Natural Law and Miracles

Scientific knowledge has allowed humans to discover the natural laws by which the universe operates. Materialism insists nothing can happen that isn't according to these laws. But what about miracles?

A miracle is *a supernatural sign or event that is intended to highlight the power and goodness of God.* The word *miracle* comes from the Latin *miraculum*, which means marvel, surprise, and amazement. Miracles are God's supernatural intervention in human affairs.

Many people think it's illogical to believe in miracles because they think natural laws are the only causes in the universe; therefore, believing in supernatural causes is foolish. They insist that if you believe in natural laws, you can't believe in miracles. However, that notion makes no sense. The fact is that natural laws are not causes. They are, "descriptions of those regularities and cause-effect relationships which have been built into the universe by its Creator, and according to which it normally operates. If we did not know them, we should never recognize a miracle if we saw one."[5] God is sovereign over the universe he created. He has the right to get involved whenever and however he wishes.

This truth underlies the miracles described in the Bible. Many miracles have to do with creation, judgment, and deliverance.

DANIEL IN THE LIONS' DEN

Creation: God created the universe and everything in it, including planets, animals, humans, and angels. There were also miracles that showed God's power over the created world, such as healing diseases, calming storms, and feeding thousands of people from one boy's lunch.

Judgment: The great flood, the confusion of languages at the Tower of Babel, the destruction of Sodom and Gomorrah, and the plagues in Egypt are clear examples of judgment miracles.

Deliverance: Sparing Noah from the flood; parting the Red Sea; saving Shadrach, Meshach, and Abednego from the fiery furnace; and rescuing Daniel from the lions are all deliverance miracles. The ultimate act of deliverance and redemption was the crucifixion and resurrection of Jesus.

If we look carefully at the way miracles are described in the Bible, it's hard to write them off as make-believe stories thought up by superstitious, ignorant people. Those who wrote about miracles went out of their way to give specific details that are consistent with careful investigation. This is especially true of the events in the life of Jesus observed by eyewitnesses and recorded in the Gospels.

"We modern people think of miracles as the suspension of the natural order, but Jesus meant them to be the restoration of the natural order," says author Tim Keller. "His miracles are not just proofs that he has power but also wonderful foretastes of what he is going to do with that power. Jesus' miracles are not just a challenge to our minds, but a promise to our hearts, that the world we all want is coming."[6]

> **Miracle**
> A supernatural sign or event that is intended to highlight the power and goodness of God

Conclusion

Everyone—Christian or not—needs to face the three big questions with which we started this lesson: What is truth? How do we know? What is the nature of reality? We have seen that in order to think at all, we need to make some assumptions about human knowledge and reality. Many thinkers refuse to face those assumptions in order to avoid asking questions that their own worldview can't answer.

Christians can face those assumptions head-on. We know that human beings didn't create themselves or the universe we find ourselves in. We know the world around us is understandable and that we have the ability to understand it. God made us in his image and invites us to learn about him through his creation: For ever since the world was created, people have seen the earth and sky. Through everything God made, they can clearly see his invisible qualities—his eternal power and divine nature (Romans 1:20).

Believing in a God who made an orderly universe and put human beings in it to discover and share his glory gives us a foundation for wise living. We are on an exciting adventure that will go on for eternity!

ENDNOTES

1 Scott Larsen, *Indelible Ink: 22 Prominent Christian Leaders Discuss the Books That Shape Their Faith* (Colorado Springs: WaterBrook Press, 2003), 100.
2 Daniel Patrick Moynihan, cited in "An American Original," *Vanity Fair,* October 6, 2010, https://www.vanityfair.com/news/2010/11/moynihan-letters-201011.
3 C. S. Lewis, *Surprised by Joy* (San Francisco: HarperCollins, 1955), p. 267.
4 Francis Collins, *The Language of God: A Scientist Presents Evidence for Belief* (New York: Free Press, 2006), 233.
5 John C. Lennox, *Can Science Explain Everything?* (Denmark: The Good Book Company, 2019), 81.
6 Timothy Keller, *The Reason for God: Belief in an Age of Skepticism* (New York: Dutton, 2008), 95.

Application Story: Follow the Evidence

"They caught him, Inspector! You were right! How did you know the person who kidnapped the woman and started the fire would be her employer? I never would have figured that out."

Of course you wouldn't. You're a simpleton.

I allowed myself to smile at the thought. Aloud I said, "A magician never reveals her secrets. The evidence was all there. You just have to know how to read it."

"Well, thanks to you, the mother is safe. But look at this place! The only thing the fire left standing is the frame of the house. It's a miracle her baby survived."

I frowned. *Why do people always invoke a deity when they don't understand something?* "I'm a woman of science. I don't believe in miracles. I'm sure there is a logical explanation."

Officer Salazar shook his head. "If you say so. Good luck on solving this mystery." He inclined his head toward me in respect, turned, and left me alone in the burned-out shell of a room.

Sunlight streamed in through what was left of the ceiling and illuminated the charred remains of the furniture. Among the rubble was a crib. Salazar's words echoed in my mind. *"It's a miracle her baby survived."* My eyes drifted toward the corner of the room.

Actually, it did defy reason. The fire burned everything except that one corner. Sure, a shelving unit full of toys had fallen diagonally, creating a small protective barrier. But even it had burned in the fire. It certainly wouldn't have been enough to protect an infant.

And how did the child get into that corner in the first place? I imagined the scene in my mind. The fire was set at midnight. The baby would have been sleeping in her crib when the fire alarms awakened her. But at only four months old, how did she get out of the crib? The shelving unit must have fallen after she reached the corner. But how did she get across the room and into the corner?

And that still didn't explain the shape of the unburned area. If it was truly the shelves that protected her from the fire, why was the untouched area circular in shape? And the circle extended onto the walls.

Too many unanswered questions. *Face it. You're stumped!*

No. I can't accept defeat. In my 16 years as an inspector, I only had a handful of cases I couldn't solve. I had a reputation to uphold! *"Marisela García — the most brilliant inspector in all Spain,"* read the headline in the newspapers. Yet despite my scientific and investigative training, I couldn't come up with a plausible scenario to fit the evidence.

"Is everything alright, Inspector García?"

Another officer stepped into the room. With my focus still on the corner, I barely noticed him.

"Yes, yes. Can't you see I'm trying to work?"

The imbecile didn't take the hint. "Is there anything I can do to help?"

His simple question added gasoline to my already simmering anger. I spun to face him. "Do you have degrees in forensics, criminology, criminal justice, or human psychology?"

"No, Inspector," he said. Despite my outburst, he remained surprisingly calm.

"Then no, I don't think you can help me."

"No offense, Inspector, but it doesn't take all those degrees to recognize a miracle."

Frustration roiled within me. *Why was everyone so superstitious?* Almost without conscious effort, I examined the man and created a mental profile.

He was handsome. Strong. Somewhat tall for a Spaniard. His uniform was immaculate. His name badge read, "Guerrero". His eyes . . . something about his eyes were different. I felt a sense of calm I'd rarely felt before.

"Look, Officer Guerrero," I said his name like a curse word, "I'm not paid to consider every fringe theory and pseudoscientific explanation. I work with facts, logic, and science."

"Please, call me Angel," Guerrero said as he crossed the room toward the unburned corner. "It's very commendable to focus on those things. After all, God is the one who created the laws on which science is based. He gives us all minds to use. He wants us to be wise. But science has its limitations."

I could barely contain my irritation. "Really? Please, enlighten me, O Wise One."

Again, he seemed unfazed by my sarcasm. "Science cannot explain the immaterial, like the soul. It can't explain the origin of all matter in the universe, or the laws that govern it. It can't explain love, or the thoughts in our heads."

"But even if I agreed with you, so what? I'm not being paid to philosophize. I'm being paid to solve mysteries and crimes. And for that, science is all I need." What was it about this guy that unnerved me so much? It had to be his eyes. No matter how much venom I threw at him, he didn't even flinch.

"Ah, but there's the problem," he said. "It does make a difference. What if I told you there was no such thing as the number four, then asked you the question: What is two plus two?"

I snickered loudly at the thought. "I'd say that's absurd and you're a fool. It doesn't make sense to rule out a possible answer before asking the question."

"Yet you are doing that exact thing," he shot back. "You say there is no God, then try to solve a mystery in which all the evidence goes against the natural and points clearly to the supernatural. You need to follow the evidence where it leads, even if you don't like the conclusion."

I opened my mouth to respond, but suddenly couldn't form a coherent sentence.

Officer Salazar entered the room again. I turned around to face him, my mind still whirling. "Yes, what is it?" I asked.

"Sorry to disturb you, Inspector. I heard you talking and was wondering who you were talking to."

I looked at him like he was insane before spinning around to point at Officer Guerrero. "Him, of course. I'm talking to—"

He was gone. With only one door leading into the room, there's no way he could have gotten around me. So where did he go?

This time, it was Salazar who was looking at me as if I'd gone insane.

"He was right here! He told me his name was Angel Guerr—" *Angel,* hmmm, could it be?

In the days following that case, I had to wrestle with what I had witnessed. I didn't want to believe it, but I had been trained well. I had to follow the evidence, no matter where it led.

Getting Started—Rules of the Game

As another ball sailed past his outstretched arm, Steve rolled over and stared at the late afternoon sky. He'd only managed to stop two balls in the shooting drill so far. Finally, he got up and moved one of the orange cones that marked the goal area.

"Hey, you can't do that!" Jarod shouted.

"The goal's too big," Steve said.

"That doesn't mean you can just change it," Jarod protested.

"Yes, I can," Steve said smugly. "I'm the goalie."

"No, you can't!" came the booming voice of Coach Briggs. "I don't care if you're Pelé or Beckham. Rules are rules."

Coach Briggs moved the cone back to its original spot. "The rule book says the goal box is 24-feet wide, so that's what it is." He called the players around to make the most of this teachable moment.

"Rules are there for a reason, even the ones you don't like or that make the game harder for you. Without them it would be chaos. Players could do whatever they wanted—throw the ball or run offsides. Refs wouldn't know what was fair and what was foul. You wouldn't even be able to keep score or tell who won without rules. In sports like soccer, the highest score wins, but in sports like golf, the lowest score wins. Which rules apply?"

"Who makes the rules for soccer?" one boy asked.

"The sport is called *football* in most of the world," Coach Briggs said. "The IFAB—International Football Association Board—makes and enforces the rules. Those who play the game of football agree to abide by those rules. It doesn't matter where in the world you live, the rules are the same. Rules aren't there to restrict you in a bad way, rather they help everyone understand and enjoy the game."

He patted Steve on the back and added, "Except for goalies. The rules make being a goalie one of the hardest jobs on the planet, which is why Steve loves it so much. Now back to work!"

What Is Ethics?
Our morality—our personal standard of right and wrong—is based on our worldview. The goal of this lesson is to learn how the biblical Christian worldview should shape our moral decisions. The area of study dealing with our ideas of right and wrong is called *ethics*.

Ethics comes from the Greek word *ethos*, meaning *goodness*. Ethics is *the study of why and how we make moral choices*. It deals with the question "How should we live?" and proposes a way to think through what life is all about.

Ethics has to do with how we define such concepts as good and evil, right and wrong, virtue and vice. Ethics goes beyond personal choices to broader principles that should apply to everyone. Ethics helps us answer such key questions as:

Where do moral values come from?
What's wrong with moral relativism?
How does God's character shape ethics?
Is there a contradiction between law and love?
Is it ever right to do wrong?

> **Ethics**
> The study of why and how we
> make moral choices

Topic 1—Where Do Moral Values Come From?

We make moral decisions every day—lots of them. We rely on many factors to choose a course of action, such as information, standards, desires, and values. And these things must come from reliable sources if we are going to make good decisions. But not all sources of moral standards are reliable. We need to choose carefully.

Many people see themselves as a reliable source of moral guidance. They make their own decisions based on what they think and feel like doing. This approach to decision-making is called *moral relativism*. Moral relativism is *the belief that there are no objective moral norms that apply to everyone.*

Therefore, deciding what's right and wrong is up to each individual or culture. When applied to whole societies, this is called cultural moral relativism, which is *the belief that right and wrong vary from culture to culture.* Moral decisions are shaped by what a community expects and by what its people have been taught.

Here's an example of cultural moral relativism: picture a society that labels certain groups of people as inferior. Members of those groups don't have the same rights as people in the dominant group. Members of the dominant group who mistreat and abuse the subordinate groups aren't even considered bad people. According to cultural moral relativism, no outsiders can come in and judge the people in the dominant group because only their culture determines what's right and wrong for them.

Moral relativism insists that all points of view are valid. What's right and wrong aren't always the same but change according to person, culture, or circumstances. This line of thinking leads to what's called *situation ethics*. This is the belief that right and wrong depend on the situation. One educational expert put it this way: "The morality or immorality of any behavior, including sexual behavior, has been put in the context of 'situation ethics.' In this approach moral behavior may differ from situation to situation. Behavior might be moral for one person and not another or moral at one time and not another."[1]

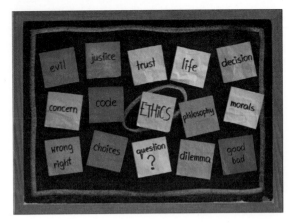

If there's no divine Lawgiver, as the biblical Christian worldview teaches, then humans have to make their own rules. These rules are shaped by evolution, not revelation. Societies learn what works over time or what suits their desires and change the rules whenever they want to. It's all relative!

Every worldview has its own moral codes. You might not know much about some of them, but they influence how billions of people think and act. Here's a brief summary of what four leading worldviews teach about ethics:

Secularism holds that since there is no divine rule giver, it's up to humans to make the rules. "No god wrote the laws of good behavior into the cosmos. Nature has no concern for good or bad, right or wrong."[2] Therefore, we should write our own morality.

Marxism assumes that anything that advances the goals of communism is ethical, including socialism and violent revolution. Rules are simply tools for achieving a communist utopia. As one writer put it: "Ethics, in short, is good only as anything else is good, for what it can accomplish, for the direction in which it takes men."[3]

Postmodernism embraces the idea that truth and morality are whatever a culture wants them to be. No one can second-guess his or her choices. As a postmodern psychiatrist wrote: "No adult can know what's best for another adult; and, by the same token, no group or society can know what's best for another group or society."[4]

New spirituality claims that the basis for morality is found within each of us, not outside us in some divine code. Old ideas and rules don't apply; as divine beings we set our own standards. One popular new spiritualist teacher insists, "The Truth is inseparable from who you are. Yes, you *are* the Truth. If you look for it elsewhere, you will be deceived every time."[5]

These worldviews might make sense if we ignore what God has revealed about how we are to behave. But even then, moral relativism has some problems.

> **Moral Relativism**
> The belief that there are no objective moral norms that apply to everyone

> **Cultural Moral Relativism**
> The belief that right and wrong vary from culture to culture

Topic 2—What's Wrong with Moral Relativism?

Many people believe moral relativism is the kindest way to decide moral issues. We don't have to argue or fight with those we disagree with. We don't have to insist everyone accept the same standards of right and wrong. It's more peaceful to just "live and let live." That may sound good at first, but it doesn't work for at least two reasons.

© Ⓢ Walking in Truth Grade 8

First, when it comes to moral decisions, we can't trust our motives. Jeremiah 17:9 tells us the human heart is deceitfully wicked. This means our sinful nature distorts our thinking. Our feelings, desires, and self-interest deceive us into a warped view of reality. We explain away or excuse selfish behavior. For example, a person might think it's wrong to hit others, but he might also have trouble controlling his temper. One day someone makes him mad and he punches that person. As he's walking away, he says to himself, "I shouldn't have done that, but he made me mad. He deserved it. I didn't do anything wrong." Because we are sinful, we can't trust our thoughts and feelings to provide fair standards of right and wrong. We need external guidelines that are not dependent on us.

Second, moral relativism can't help a community or culture make moral choices because some people will believe a certain behavior is wrong while others think it's perfectly acceptable. It could be as minor as traffic laws. One driver slows down in a school zone while another speeds through because he's in a hurry. Or it could be something major, such as abortion. Many citizens might believe a child in the womb is a person with rights, but the government may say that it's not a child until it's born or decide that a life can be ended if it's inconvenient to the mother.

When different value systems are in conflict, the result is not consensus but chaos. No one wants to yield to those they disagree with and there's no outside standard to which both parties can appeal. It's like every batter getting to call his own balls and strikes because there's no umpire, and each base runner deciding if he's safe or out.

Such personal freedom doesn't lead to harmony but to confusion and disorder. What happens then is that those with the most power take control. They set the standards and enforce the rules that best serve their interests. People may be forced to do things they don't accept and be forbidden to criticize their leaders.

There was a time in Israel's history when all the people did whatever seemed right in their own eyes (Judges 17:6). You only have to read the book of Judges to see that this didn't turn out well for the people or the nation.

Topic 3—How Does God's Character Shape Ethics?

Moral relativism doesn't have a good basis for deciding what's right and wrong, but the biblical Christian worldview does because it believes in moral absolutes. Moral absolutes are *universal moral standards that are true for all people, at all times, in all situations.*

These absolutes are based on God's righteous and holy character. God's purpose is for us to be holy as he is holy. The Hebrew word for holy is *qodesh*, which means *apartness, sacredness,* or *separateness.* There is a distinction between what is holy and what isn't that is determined by God. The philosopher Francis Schaeffer explains:

> One of the distinctions of the Judeo-Christian God is that not all things are the same to Him. That at first may sound rather trivial, but in reality it is one of the most profound things one can say about the Judeo-Christian God. He exists; He has a character; and not all things are the same to Him. Some things conform to His character, and some are opposed to His character.[6]

Christian ethics is all about conforming to God's character: But now you must be holy in everything you do, just as God who chose you is holy. For the Scriptures say, "You must be holy because I am holy" (1 Peter 1:15–16). As we learned in the theology lesson, God's existence is clearly revealed through general revelation and his character is revealed through the special revelation of Scripture.

While the Bible doesn't address every specific ethical situation we might face, we are given enough principles, guidelines, and commands to know the difference between what is holy and what isn't—in other words, between right and wrong. We not only get specific guidance from laws such as the Ten Commandments (Exodus 20) and teachings like the Sermon on the Mount (Matthew 5–7), we also see God's character reflected in historical narratives, poetry, prophecy, parables, and other types of writing.

The Christian theory of ethics is built upon Matthew 22:36–40. When asked about the greatest commandment, Jesus said Christians should love God and love their neighbor. Not only is God holy, but 1 John 4:16 tells us, "God is love." The word *love* used in this context is a translation of the Greek word *agape*. This kind of love looks to the needs of others rather than to its own needs. Earlier in that same chapter, John described God's love as the standard to guide all relationships: This is real love—not that we loved God, but that he loved us and sent his Son as a sacrifice to take away our sins. Dear friends, since God loved us that much, we surely ought to love each other. No one has ever seen God. But if we love each other, God lives in us, and his love is brought to full expression in us (1 John 4:10–12).

Since God's character doesn't change, his moral standards don't change either. These absolute standards are not subjective or relative.

> **Moral Absolutes**
> Universal moral standards that are true
> for all people, at all times, in all situations

Part 1—Written in Our Hearts

Because God's standards are absolute and apply everywhere, does that mean everybody knows them? In a way, yes. In Romans 1:20, Paul said that by looking at the world God has made, people can clearly see his invisible qualities—his eternal power and divine nature. God's divine nature includes his character, which is the foundation for moral absolutes.

Paul went on to say that everyone has an inborn sense of right and wrong: Even Gentiles, who do not have God's written law, show that they know his law when they instinctively obey it, even without having heard it. They demonstrate that God's law is written in their hearts, for their own conscience and thoughts either accuse them or tell them they are doing right (Romans 2:14–15).

We can see this truth in action in our own experience. Have you ever done something and then immediately realized it was wrong? Or have you had two choices and known ahead of time which was the right thing to do? That's your conscience at work. The conscience is that inner sense of what is right or wrong in one's motives or conduct. It's based on the laws God has written in every human heart.

If everyone has the same external evidence of creation and the same internal witness of a conscience, why do different cultures have different ideas about right and wrong? Their standards aren't all that different when you come down to it, as C. S. Lewis shows with this illustration:

> Think of a country where people were admired for running away from battle, or where a man felt proud of double-crossing all the people who had been kindest to him. You might just as well try to imagine a country where two and two make five. . . . Men have differed as to whether you should have one wife or four. But they have always agreed that you must not simply have any woman you liked.[7]

At the end of his book *The Abolition of Man*, Lewis provides an appendix more than 20 pages long describing many universal moral standards. His examples come from various cultures across the globe and over the centuries. From ancient times to today, people agree on a core group of moral absolutes, including: being kind rather than cruel, telling the truth rather than lying, sharing with others rather than stealing, being loyal rather than betraying a friend, and pursuing justice rather than injustice, to name just a few.

A professor at George Washington University made the same case based on his own extensive research. He concluded: "There is a basic pattern of similarity among [ethical codes]. Such things as murder, lying, adultery, [and] cowardice are, for example, almost always condemned. The universality of the ethical sense itself (the "oughtness" of conduct), and the similarities within the codes of diverse cultures indicate a common moral heritage for all mankind which materialism or naturalism cannot explain."[8]

Christians see these common ethical systems among different cultures as evidence of a universal law and thus a universal Lawgiver.

Part 2—Moral Absolutes Point to the Existence of God

In each lesson, we have presented an argument for the existence of God based on the subject of the lesson. The topic of ethics sets us up for what's often called the moral argument for God's existence. It reasons that *if objective moral values exists, then there must be a moral Lawgiver.* This moral Lawgiver is God. Dr. Jeff Myers puts the argument in this logical form:[9]

- If objective moral values and duties exist, then God exists.
- Objective moral values and duties exist.
- Therefore, God exists.

We've already learned some good reasons for agreeing with these statements. There are many moral standards that are universally held across a great diversity of cultures, locations, and historical eras. Some people have suggested that evolution can account for the development of common standards. The famous skeptic Michael Shermer says moral behavior evolved naturally because we are a social primate species. We learn there are consequences for our behavior, and we have to work together and get along to survive. Shermer believes that evolution, not God, gave us morality. He uses marriage to illustrate this claim. We know adultery is wrong, even if there is no God. It's part of our social contract. Society would fall apart without morals regarding marriage fidelity.

Evolutionists emphasize differences when trying to explain diversity among people groups, so it's difficult to see how those same differences can explain moral standards that are common to all groups. But even if evolution had an influence, it could only explain *what* people do; it can't explain *why* people think they *should* do some things. That moral awareness points beyond human nature to a code people didn't just make up—a universal sense that some things are right, and some are wrong, regardless of people's feelings or situations.

> **Moral Argument**
> The belief that since moral law exists, there must be a moral Lawgiver

Topic 4—Is There a Contradiction between Law and Love?

The fact that objective moral laws exist, and that they are based on God's love, can produce confusion for those who see a contradiction between law and love. But these two are actually compatible and dependent on one another. God created a universal moral order because of his love for us. Think of the Ten Commandments. Living according to these laws is a way of showing love to God and other people. Not obeying them results in harm to ourselves and others.

When Jesus was asked about God's law, he emphasized its connection to God's love:

One of the teachers of religious law was standing there listening to the debate. He realized that Jesus had answered well, so he asked, "Of all the commandments, which is the most important?" Jesus replied, "The most important commandment is this: 'Listen, O Israel! The LORD our God is the one and only LORD. And you must love the LORD your God with all your heart, all your soul, all your mind, and all your strength.' The second is equally important: 'Love your neighbor as yourself.' No other commandment is greater than these.   Mark 12:28–31

Jesus wasn't teaching anything new. Both these commandments come from the Old Testament (Deuteronomy 6:5, Leviticus 19:18). His followers would go on to preach the same message: Owe nothing to anyone—except for your obligation to love one another. If you love your neighbor, you will fulfill the requirements of God's law. For the commandments say, "You must not commit adultery. You must not murder. You must not steal. You must not covet.' These—and other such commandments—are summed up in this one commandment: 'Love your neighbor as yourself." Love does no wrong to others, so love fulfills the requirements of God's law" (Romans 13:8–10).

Because the moral law is based on God's love, there is no conflict between law and love. When our conscience reminds us to obey God's moral standards, we are also being reminded to be more loving. It's our responsibility, which is more than simply our duty. Duty implies that only our outward behavior matters. But as Jesus emphasized in the Sermon on the Mount (Matthew 5–7), true ethics has to do with our hearts and not just our outward actions. That's why he could equate hatred with murder and lust to adultery.

Obeying God's law from the heart will result in loving our neighbor. Jesus made the point in the parable of the good Samaritan that anyone in need is our neighbor. His message was very clear. We have a responsibility toward other people. Our faith is not to be a private affair. We are a part of human society where we are to be salt and light (Matthew 5:13–16, Ephesians 5:8). And we have a special relationship with other

members of God's family—the Church. There are a multitude of verses that call on us to love one another as God loves us, including John 13:34, 1 Peter 3:8, and 1 John 4:7.

It may seem that rules are simply a way for someone else to control us or force us to live a certain way. While some humans have made and enforced laws to dominate others—think dictators and abusive parents—this isn't how God operates. As he is our Creator and Designer, he knows what's best for us. His commandments, rules, and principles for living reflect his loving wisdom. His intent is to protect us and help us flourish (John 10:10, Romans 8:28–29).

God is often referred to as *a father* in Scripture. A good father puts rules in place to protect and teach his children: Look both ways before you cross the street. Don't touch a hot stove. Obey your mom. Be nice to your sister. Don't talk to strangers. The list could go on and on, but such rules have one thing in common; they are for the good of the child, even if the child doesn't think so at the time.

Obviously, rules can have something else in common. They can feel restrictive. We want to do what we want to do when we want to do it. We think we are wise enough to make our own rules. This stubbornness goes all the way back to the garden of Eden (Genesis 3). Our first parents disobeyed the only rule God gave them because they wanted to be in charge of their own lives. The serpent said they could get away with disobeying God, and they believed it!

We have the same sinful nature, so it's not surprising that sometimes we resist rules, even when we know they are for our good. Of course, we have the freedom to rebel and resist, but that won't turn out well in the end. The Bible and life experience teach us that. Sometimes, in the short term, we can ignore God's laws and appear to get away with it. We can ignore the physical law of gravity and jump off a roof. If we survive, we could say, "I almost killed myself, but at least I did what I wanted." But that choice will have consequences.

Topic 5—Is It Ever Right to Do Wrong?

Christians believe in absolute right and wrong based on God's character, but what do we do when ethical absolutes come into conflict? This kind of dilemma doesn't happen often, but it does arise from time to time. For instance, we are commanded to tell the truth and not lie. But we are also told to protect the innocent and preserve human life whenever possible. If you lived in 1940s Poland and were hiding Jews in your home, which of these two moral standards would guide you, telling the truth or protecting the innocent?

Or say your village in Afghanistan was overrun by the Taliban searching for Christians to behead. When they asked about the missionary who was just there, would you lie and say he's gone or tell them he's hiding in a nearby field?

Lying to protect Jews from the Nazis or Christians from the Taliban is exactly what Rahab did when she hid the Hebrew spies and lied to the authorities in Jericho (Joshua 2). She wound up in the Faith Hall of Fame for her actions (Hebrews 11:31).

Here's another example from the pages of Scripture where doing right involved disobeying a direct command. Paul tells us that: Everyone must submit to governing authorities. For all authority comes from God, and those in positions of authority have been placed there by God. So anyone who rebels against authority is rebelling against what God has instituted, and they will be punished (Romans 13:1–2). But the Hebrew midwives in ancient Egypt lied and disobeyed Pharaoh's orders to drown the Hebrew baby boys, and God rewarded them for it (Exodus 1:15–21). The apostles themselves disobeyed the authorities who forbade them to talk about Jesus (Acts 4:19). From their time down to today, missionaries who preach the gospel in closed countries disobey the laws of the land in order to obey a higher law.

These instances may seem like situation ethics, and in a way they are. A choice has to be made based on the situation, but that choice is still directed by God's laws. Our ethical choices have to be workable in a sinful world where the right is not always obvious and not always easy to carry out. Not everything legal is right, and unjust laws have no meaning if they defy the law of God. When his commands appear to come into conflict, the law of love should always prevail.

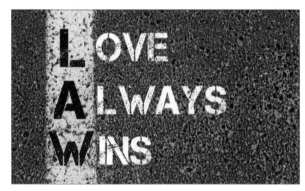

Jesus said the greatest commandment was to love God with all our heart, soul, mind, and strength, and the second greatest was to love our neighbor as ourselves (Luke 10:27). The application of this ethic is simple and straightforward: Do to others whatever you would like them to do to you. This is the essence of all that is taught in the law and the prophets (Matthew 7:12).

Conclusion

The Christian worldview believes that ethics are grounded in the character of a holy and loving God who is absolute and unchanging. This God has made himself known through creation, conscience, and the Bible. The ultimate revelation of his character is seen in Jesus Christ, God in the flesh. He is the role model of how we should think and act (1 John 1:6).

All the laws and principles that guide our ethics can be summed up in two simple commandments: Love God and love our neighbor. When we are faced with a moral dilemma or hard choice, just ask, "What's the loving thing to do?" Then ask God for his help to do it. And remember, Don't just pretend to love others. Really love them. Hate what is wrong. Hold tightly to what is good. Love each other with genuine affection, and take delight in honoring each other (Romans 12:9–10).

ENDNOTES:

1 Arthur E. Gravatt, quoted in William H. Genne, "Our Moral Responsibility," *Journal of the American College Health Association* 15 (May 1967): 63.

2 Simon Blackburn, *Ethics: A Very Short Introduction* (Oxford: Oxford University Press, 2001), 114.

3 Howard Selsam, *Socialism and Ethics* (New York: International Publishers, 1943), 98.

4 Quoted in Algis Valiunas, "Mental Health," *Weekly Standard* 11, no. 9 (November 14, 2005): 41.

5 Eckhart Tolle, *A New Earth* (New York: Plume, 2005), 71.

6 Francis Schaeffer, "Christian Faith and Human Rights," *Simon Greenleaf Law Review*, 2 (1982–3): 5.

7 C. S. Lewis, *The Abolition of Man* (New York, NY: Macmillan, 1973), 78.

8 Carl F. H. Henry, ed., *Baker Dictionary of Christian Ethics* (Grand Rapids: Baker, 1973), 620.

9 Jeff Myers, *Understanding the Faith* (Manitou Springs, CO: Summit Ministries, 2016), 255.

Application Story: The Dragon

Where am I?

A cold mist surrounds me and fogs my vision. I appear to be in a large room built from stone. I can make out vague shadows that appear to be chairs, tables, and other types of furniture. The only light source comes from a brazier a few feet away. Blue flames dance in its depths and lick upward to form a burning spire.

My body feels heavy. It always feels heavy when I wear my armor, as I am now. But this is different. Something . . . some presence . . . is weighing me down. The air is filled with a pungent odor. I grip my sword tighter. My heartbeat is heavy and pounds in my ears as fear claws at my mind.

Then I see them. Two yellow orbs appear out of the mist. Each is split down the middle with a thin, black iris. These are not the eyes of a human.

These are the eyes of a reptile. And a particularly large one.

"Welcome, Paladin. What is your name?"

"Sir Alcott the Just."

"Well, Sir Alcott, what brings a Knight of the Cross to my domain?" A dragon emerges out of the mist and takes a step toward me. Its scales appear midnight blue in the shifting flames of the cauldron.

My mouth has gone dry and I fumble for the right words. "I . . . I seek no quarrel with you. I . . . must have . . . lost my way."

"Indeed you have," the dragon hisses. "But then, all who foolishly submit themselves to that archaic set of rules and demands you call the Creed are always lost."

My sense of honor burns at the challenge. "The Creed gives meaning and direction to life! It offers everyone a path to encounter the Creator and know his ways. It is those who deny the Creed who are lost!"

The great dragon lets out a mirthless chortle. "Foolish man. Your blind devotion has clouded your mind. The Creed was written by evil men as a tool to control and manipulate the weak-minded. It's a list of rules and regulations that forges shackles within the mind, making slaves out of those who follow it."

"No," I say, conviction adding strength to my voice. "It offers freedom."

"Ha! Spoken like a true brainwashed puppet. Don't be so closed-minded. Allow me to show you the truth of the matter." The dragon's massive head draws closer until one if its reptilian eyes is right in front of my own. I'm unable to turn away; its hypnotic gaze pulls me in. His breath flows into my body, causing my head to swim.

"The Creed would have you believe there is a God who created everything," the dragon says, its voice soothing. "But that is an evil told by simpletons. They repeat this lie generation after generation because they find comfort in it. They do not have the mental fortitude to grapple with the harsh realities of life, and so make up stories of a loving God who will take them to paradise when they die. Those of us who are more highly evolved need no such myths.

"Freed from these superstitions, we recognize that truth is what we make it. We must look inward for guidance. We must be true to ourselves to reach our maximum potential! What may be right for one may be wrong for another. 'Right' and 'wrong' are simply labels we use for our own preferences."

The dragon's words infiltrate my thoughts. Have I been deceived all my life? How could I have been so wrong? His reasoning sounds so convincing. Yet at the same time, something doesn't feel right. Pull yourself together. Think! Is what he is saying true?

Truth.

Like a strong wind chasing away a thick fog, my mind clears. "Is what you are saying 'true'?"

The dragon backs away slightly, as if caught off guard by my question. "Yes. Of course it is. I wouldn't lie to you."

"Right. Because lying would be 'wrong'. Your words contradict themselves. In one breath, you imply lying is 'wrong', and yet you say 'right' and 'wrong' are mere preferences."

This time there is no mistake. The dragon recognizes the trap but cannot avoid it. "The only absolute truth is that there are no absolutes!"

This time, it is my turn to laugh. "Ha! Truth is not some ship on the ocean, blown and tossed by the waves. It is a rock upon which we build our lives. Truth is that which matches reality. By definition, it is true for all people, in all places, in all times. If not, then it isn't true at all, but a matter of opinion."

As I speak, I feel my strength returning. I draw my sword, causing the dragon to retreat toward the burning brazier. "You lying snake! It is not the wise who look inward for truth, but the foolish who do so! For the human heart is deceitful and full of wickedness. Morals are not what we make them. They are laws imprinted on our hearts. And in order for there to be laws, there must be a Lawgiver. Our maximum potential is discovered only when we empty ourselves and submit to the one who created us!"

The dragon howls in pain as if wounded. Then, to my amazement, it begins to dissolve. In its place is a man dressed in flowing robes. The instant my eyes lock onto his, he falls to his knees and cowers at the base of the brazier.

I sprint forward, grab the metal brazier lid that rests on a nearby table, and slam it into place, snuffing out the flame. With my other hand, I place the tip of my sword against the man's chest.

"Mercy! Mercy!" he cries out. "I plead for mercy!"

Shouts echo in the hallway. A moment later, two other knights enter the room. "Sir Alcott! We heard a cry and came at once."

"Inform the king I have captured the so-called 'sorcerer'. His tricks and deceitful words will no longer ensnare our people."

The knights nod, then depart. I reach down, grab the front of my prisoner's robes, and haul him to his feet. "You should be grateful the king does not share your view of morality. Perhaps your time in the castle dungeon will help you find the Maker of all truth. Only then will you find freedom from the dragon that ensnares you."

Biology

Getting Started—3D Printer

"Hi, Mrs. Grable," Gwen said politely. "I'm in a real bind, and Mia thought you might be able to help me."

"What is it?" Mrs. Grable asked as she sat across the kitchen table from her daughter, Mia, and Mia's best friend, Gwen.

"I need a part for my robotics project, and I can't find it anywhere in town," Gwen said. "And it will take too long to order it online. So, could you print it for me? Mia says your new 3D printer is amazing."

It should be, considering what it cost, Mrs. Grable thought. Out loud she said, "I'll see what I can do. Do you have an STL file for the part?"

Gwen frowned. "What's that?"

"STL files are created by a CAD program," Mrs. Grable explained. "It's like a blueprint that shows the printer what to make. And since it's metal, you'll need the right powdered-materials cartridge as well."

"All I have is this," Gwen said, showing Mrs. Grable a photo on her phone.

Mrs. Grable shook her head. "Having an idea or a picture isn't enough to make something. You need a program and a way to execute it."

"Unless you're making a universe," Mia said with a smile. "Our biology teacher says the whole universe, including us, just made itself by chance over billions of years. There's no blueprint, no program to run it."

"I don't know about billions of years ago," Mrs. Grable said, "but if you want to make anything real these days, even as small as this," she tapped Gwen's phone, "you must have a detailed plan, the right materials, and someone who knows what she's doing."

"Or you could just wait a few billion years for the part to make itself," Mia suggested.

"No, thanks," Gwen said. "I need it by Tuesday. Mrs. Grable, will you help me?"

Does It Really Matter?

Biology is *the study of living things and their origins.* Our ideas of biology are influenced by our beliefs about God, the nature of reality, and how we gain knowledge, which we have studied in previous lessons.

Biology is an essential part of our worldview. Our understanding of who we are and where we come from shapes our values. Seeing humans as made in God's image leads to a different worldview than seeing humans as advanced primates struggling for survival.

Compare these two accounts of human origin, one from the Bible and the other from an evolutionary biologist:

So God created human beings in his own image. In the image of God he created them; male and female he created them (Genesis 1:27).

Man is the result of a purposeless and natural process that did not have him in mind. He was not planned. He is a state of matter, a form of life, a sort of animal, and a species of the Order Primates, akin nearly or remotely to all of life and indeed to all that is material.[1]

What we believe about the origin of life affects how we think and act today. We refer to ourselves as *homo sapiens*, which is Latin for "wise man." But are we just a "higher" species of bipedal primates (according to evolution) or a little "lower" than the angels (according to the Psalm 8:5)?

This lesson takes us into the creation versus evolution debate. We will deal with these key questions:
What are the main differences between the theory of evolution and the theory of intelligent design?
Can the principles of evolution account for the origin of life and the complexity we see in nature?
Is a belief in intelligent design a matter of blind faith or evidence-based faith?

Topic 1—Darwinism or Design?

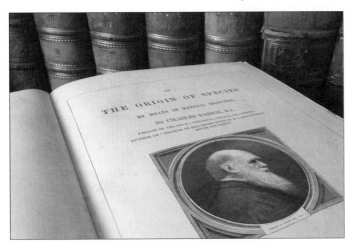

In 1859, Charles Darwin published *On the Origin of Species*. It laid out his theory about how life arose and developed on Earth. Since then, his theory has been hotly debated, from science labs to biology classrooms and the courts. How are we to sort through the conflicting viewpoints, especially as Christians?

Some Christians want to argue every time evolution is brought up in conversation. Others accept the idea of evolution and, consequently, may doubt the biblical account of creation. Still others try to reconcile evolution with the Bible. And then there are those who just back away from the subject altogether. In this lesson we will take a closer look at the teachings of Darwin and also the case for intelligent design.

The theory of evolution states that billions of years ago life on this planet began from nonliving chemicals acted upon by random, natural processes. The theory is based on naturalism and atheism. It does not require a divine Creator to bring about life. Many who hold to evolution assume the idea of God is something primitive humans thought up to explain the mysteries of life. God did not make humans in his image; we made God in our image. We invented him to cover the gaps in our knowledge. Now that we know more about physics and biology, we no longer need a God—or his rules.

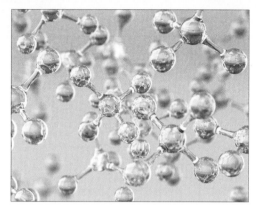

In terms of the choices we make (ethics), evolution implies our ideas about right and wrong are just what cultures have developed over time. These rules can change as we evolve. Morals are therefore relative. As the highest form of life on the food chain, we are basically good and getting better all the time. There is no sin problem and no holy God to hold us accountable for our actions.

Part 1—Neo-Darwinism

Darwin's original theory has been impacted by genetics and expanded into what is now called *neo-Darwinism*. Neo-Darwinism is *the theory that new species arise from natural selection acting over vast periods of time on chance mutations in DNA.* Given enough time, species will evolve into entirely new species.

Neo-Darwinism claims that life began as a single-celled organism. It then evolved over time into all the different plants and animals that have ever existed. The word *evolve* simply means *change*. A mutation occurs when there is a change in the genetic code of an organism. Natural selection is when genetically changed offspring are "selected" because they are better at surviving and reproducing. In this way, nature selects the fittest animals and eliminates the unfit.

Neo-Darwinism teaches that the diversity and wonder of life are the results of purely natural laws. Life may look like it has been designed, but that's an illusion. As the well-known atheist Richard Dawkins said: "Biology is the study of complicated things that give the appearance of having been designed for a purpose."[2] He admits that life looks as if it were designed, but then quickly dismisses this conclusion:

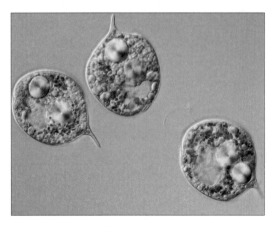

SINGLE-CELLED ORGANISMS

It seems so obvious that if you've got a garden there must be a gardener who created it and all that goes with that. What Darwin did was to show the staggeringly counterintuitive fact that this can be explained by an undirected process. . . . He showed not only a garden but everything in the living world . . . has an explanation which can be derived from simple beginnings by comprehensible rational means.[3]

But evolution can't explain the "simple beginnings" part of the equation. It doesn't have a good explanation for the beginning of life, nor for the fine-tuning of the universe needed for it to exist and grow. Although it tries, evolution can't explain how life started in the first place. The theory of intelligent design can.

> **Neo-Darwinism**
> The theory that new species arise from natural selection acting over vast periods of time on chance mutations in DNA

Part 2—Intelligent Design

The theory of intelligent design says *the universe did not come into existence by chance but was the creation of an intelligent mind*.

The idea of an intelligent Designer is a key part of a biblical worldview. The Bible teaches that life is the handiwork of a personal Creator. The first chapters of Genesis summarize the creation of the universe and of life on Earth. Since this is an introductory-level chapter on biology, we won't get into the details of the creation account or the age of the earth. We will focus on the major issues separating the biblical and secular views of biology.

The Bible teaches that all living things were designed with a purpose. Human beings were created to glorify God through an intimate relationship with him (Romans 11:36, Revelation 5:13).

What the Bible does not explain in detail is how organisms are made. To find this out, we have to study the world around us. What do we see in nature? Are natural laws and random processes a better explanation for the origin and diversity of life? Or do the facts point to intelligent design?

> **Intelligent Design**
> The theory that the universe did not come into existence by chance but was the creation of an intelligent mind

Topic 2—Abiogenesis or Biogenesis?

Most biology textbooks teach that life arose from some kind of chemical "soup." They may include an experiment by Stanley Miller and Harold Urey showing how the building blocks of life could have formed by themselves. This experiment is sometimes used to support a theory for the origin of life called *abiogenesis*. *Abios* is the Greek word for *lifeless* and *genesis* is Greek for *origin, source, or beginning*. Abiogenesis is *the theory that life originally came from nonliving matter more than 3.5 billion years ago*.

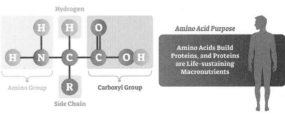

But have scientists actually been able to grow life in a laboratory? Not so far. In actuality, the Miller-Urey experiment produced amino acids—the building blocks of life—not life. Even if they did create life by combining the right chemicals with the right electrical stimulus and the right amount of atmosphere, that wouldn't prove that life came about all by itself in nature. After all, it took intelligent designers perfect conditions to create just amino acids in a laboratory. How much less likely is it to have happened in the early chaotic days of Earth without an intelligence guiding the process?

Biologists must start with pure ingredients to get the results they want. In a natural setting, there would be all sorts of impurities affecting the chemical reactions. There are additional laws of chemistry that would keep evolving molecules from becoming living organisms. Even Richard Dawkins admits that the origin of life from natural processes was an "initial stroke of luck."

Along with this lucky break, Dawkins also assumes "a very large number of planetary opportunities."[4] As it turns out, proposing multiple earthlike planets throughout the universe is another unfounded assumption on his part.

In their book, *The Privileged Planet*, Guillermo González and Jay Richards describe research into how the earth is uniquely designed to favor complex life. These are the perfect conditions the planet must have:
- an optimal distance from the right kind of star
- a perfectly sized moon to stabilize the planet's axis
- the right amount of oxygen and water
- an intricate system of plate tectonics[5]

Mathematically speaking, González and Richards estimate that the probability of a planet having all of the necessary conditions to support complex life is ten to the negative fifteenth power (10^{-15}). That's 1 in 1,000,000,000,000,000!

A renowned physicist agreed, "For me, the idea of a creation is not conceivable without invoking the necessity of design. One cannot be exposed to the law and order of the universe without concluding that there must be design and purpose behind it all."[6]

Dawkins believes that, given unlimited opportunities and a whole universe full of luck, anything can happen. Well, only if the "anything" is in the realm of possibility. Some things will never happen no matter how many times you try or how much luck you have. That is because some things are simply impossible.

Some impossibilities are based on well-established science, like the fact that it's impossible for an unaided living organism to survive in the vacuum of space. It is this kind of impossibility that Dawkins fails to appreciate. His origin-of-life theory turns a blind eye to the theory of biogenesis. Biogenesis is *the theory that life only comes from preexisting life; it cannot generate itself.*

Abiogenesis
The theory that life originally came from nonliving matter more than 3.5 billion years ago

Biogenesis
The theory that life only comes from preexisting life; it cannot generate itself

Part 1—Francesco Redi and Louis Pasteur

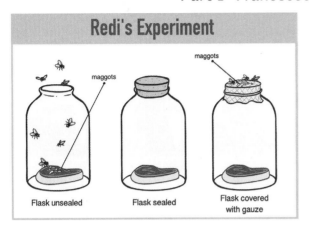

Redi's Experiment

maggots

maggots

Flask unsealed   Flask sealed   Flask covered
with gauze

For most of human history, people believed in abiogenesis, which is sometimes called *spontaneous generation*. They thought living organisms emerged directly from nonliving things like mud and rotting food. For example, it was believed that food left outside would spontaneously produce maggots and flies. Then, in 1668, Francesco Redi did an experiment. He covered some rotting meat with a screen and discovered that swarming flies laid eggs on the screen. The maggots didn't come from the rotting meat; they came from eggs put there by flies.

French scientist Louis Pasteur followed this with his own novel experiments in 1860. Pasteur showed that even microscopic organisms like bacteria do not arise suddenly on their own. He noted that some bacterial spores floated in the air, landed in various mixtures, and then grew into life-forms. When these mixtures were properly cleaned and protected from the airborne spores, no bacteria grew in them.

LOUIS PASTEUR

Experiments like these have disproved abiogenesis and proved biogenesis. So why do evolutionists still ignore this fact? Perhaps because their belief in atheism forces them to hold onto their theory despite the evidence. As one Nobel Prize winner admitted, it is the only alternative to believing "in a single, primary act of supernatural creation."[7]

In contrast to neo-Darwinism, the Christian worldview is in line with what science has proven—life only comes from life: In the beginning the Word already existed. The Word was with God, and the Word was God. He existed in the beginning with God. God created everything through him, and nothing was created except through him. The Word gave life to everything that was created, and his life brought light to everyone (John 1:1–4).

Paul affirmed this in Colossians 1:16: For through him God created everything in the heavenly realms and on earth. He made the things we can see and the things we can't see. . . . Everything was created through him and for him.

Part 2—Macroevolution and Microevolution

So much for the beginning of life. How does it develop and change and grow? Neo-Darwinism teaches that natural selection and random genetic mutations produce new species. Darwin assumed that complex life comes from simpler forms of life. Some call it the "amoeba to man" theory, or macroevolution. Macroevolution refers to *the belief that small, adaptive changes are capable of accumulating over time to produce entirely new species.*

In 1835, Darwin made his now famous voyage that included a visit to the Galapagos Islands off the coast of Ecuador. There he studied finches with different beak sizes and thought he had discovered evolution in action. But this turned out not to be the case. The birds began as finches with beaks and ended up as finches with beaks, just of slightly different sizes.

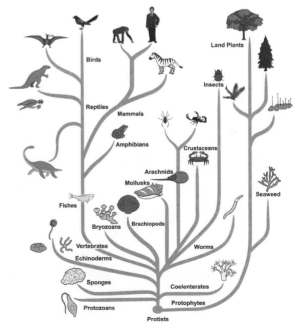

Birds

Land Plants

Insects

Reptiles

Mammals

Amphibians

Crustaceans

Arachnids

Mollusks

Seaweed

Fishes

Bryozoans   Brachiopods

Vertebrates   Worms

Echinoderms

Sponges   Coelenterates

Protozoans   Protophytes

Protists

What Darwin called *natural selection* is actually just *adaptation.* This is when certain organisms become better suited to survive in their environment. We find an example of adaptation when bacteria develop resistance to certain chemicals. When a population of millions of bacteria are exposed to an antibiotic that kills most of them, there will be a few bacteria that mutate slightly in just the right way so they aren't affected by that chemical. These survivors live and reproduce. Their offspring inherit that same resistance.

But here's the catch. These small changes within a species' gene pool have never been shown to produce whole new species. Macroevolution has never been observed. Instead, it is inferred from instances of microevolution that are observed. Microevolution refers to *small adaptive changes over a relatively short time within a species' gene pool that do not lead to wholly different organisms.*

"That natural selection can produce changes within a type is disputed by no one, not even the staunchest creationist," writes Robert Sawyer in his book *Calculating God.* "But that it can transform one species into another—that, in fact, has never been observed."[8]

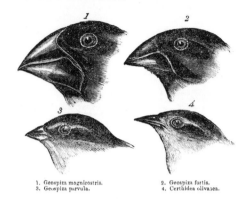

1. *Geospiza magnirostris.*
2. *Geospiza fortis.*
3. *Geospiza parvula.*
4. *Certhidea olivacea.*

THE BEAKS IN THESE
FINCHES ARE AN EXAMPLE
OF MICROEVOLUTION.

Macroevolution
The belief that small, adaptive changes are capable of accumulating over time to produce entirely new species

Microevolution
The belief that small, adaptive changes are capable of producing variations within the gene pool of a species

Topic 3—Natural Selection or Divine Creation?

If the theory of evolution does not provide a credible answer to the questions of how life began or developed, then we need to consider the alternative. Genesis 1 tells us that God created plants and animals to reproduce "of the same kind" (Genesis 1:12, 21, 25).

The phrase "of the same kind" suggests a boundary between kinds set by reproduction. A "kind" is an interbreeding group. For example, the entire cat family—from domestic cats to leopards and tigers—forms a breeding group; a single kind. So does the dog family, from friendly beagles to wolves and jackals. Even though there is variety within a kind, these animals are considered an interbreeding group.

In the fossil records we find the remains of fully developed creatures. What we don't see is fossil evidence for the gradual progression of one species to another. In other words, there isn't a clear line of small changes over time as the theory of evolution suggests. Instead what we find in the earth's layers seems to confirm the theory of biogenesis and the statements in Genesis: Life only comes from life and living things reproduce after their own kind.

Science and the Bible are in agreement on this. Life can't create itself or change from one thing to another. That's why the Christian worldview insists there is a divine Craftsman at work: The heavens proclaim the glory of God. The skies display his craftsmanship (Psalm 19:1). For ever since the world was created, people have seen the earth and sky. Through everything God made, they can clearly see his invisible qualities—his eternal power and divine nature (Romans 1:20).

But revelation isn't the only thing Christians have to go on, as one biologist explains:

> The conclusion of intelligent design flows naturally from the data itself—not from sacred books or sectarian beliefs. Inferring that biochemical systems were designed by an intelligent agent is a humdrum process that requires no new principles of logic or science. It comes simply from the hard work that biochemistry has done over the past forty years, combined with consideration of the way in which we reach conclusions of design every day.[9]

Part 1—Coded Messages

Think for a moment of this example. Say you are walking on the beach and see ripples in the sand. You naturally assume the waves or wind made them. But if you see the words, "John loves Mary" written in the sand, you would think someone with intelligence had written the message. A pattern is one thing; a message is something else. It implies a plan and a purpose.

Science is constantly searching for messages in creation. The entire SETI Project (Search for Extra-Terrestrial Intelligence) is looking for coded messages from space.[10] Science also seeks to find coded messages in life on Earth. This approach is called *information theory*.

The clearest example of coded messages in biology is DNA; the genetic code found in all living things. This genetic code is like a language. The chemical bases (represented by the letters *A*, *T*, *G*, and *C*) combine with two other types of molecules in human DNA to make "words" (nucleotides), that are strung together in "sentences" (genes), that provide a meaningful sentence structure for life.

The DNA instruction book for a human being—our genome—has about 3 billion base pairs (a combination of the chemical bases mentioned above). These pairs are the coding for about 20,000 genes that are organized in 23 pairs of chromosomes.

Structure of DNA

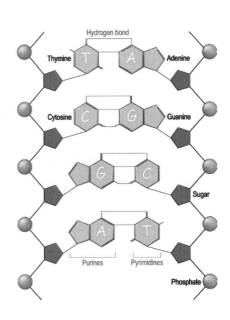

To quantify just how much data is contained within this code—both in the parts we all share, and how we differ—physics engineer Derek Muller applied information theory to the complex nature of DNA . . . to discover the entire code equates to just 1.5GB. . . . Expanding this further, Muller continued that each cell in the human body contains this 1.5GB of data, and there are 40 trillion cells. This works out at 60 zettabytes of information, or 60 followed by 21 zeros.[11]

Microsoft™ founder Bill Gates said, "DNA is like a computer program but far, far more advanced than any software ever created."[12] And he should know!

Gates wasn't the only one impressed by the coding in DNA. Antony Flew was one of the most influential philosophers and atheists of the 20th century. He wrote many essays and books promoting atheism. He shocked the world in 2007 when he coauthored the book, *There Is a God: How the World's Most Notorious Atheist Changed His Mind*. So why the switch?

Flew told an interviewer: "The findings of more than fifty years of DNA research have provided materials for a new and enormously powerful argument to design."[13] In the book he writes:

ANTONY FLEW

[T]he most impressive arguments for God's existence are those that are supported by recent scientific discoveries. . . . The argument for Intelligent Design is enormously stronger than it was when I first met it. . . . The philosophical question that has not been answered in origin-of-life studies is this: How can a universe of mindless matter produce beings with intrinsic ends, self-replication capabilities, and "coded chemistry?" Here we are not dealing with biology, but an entirely different category of problem.[14]

Before his death in 2009, Flew went so far as to encourage the British government to teach intelligent design in state schools.[15]

Part 2—Blind Faith or Evidence-Based Faith

Let's zoom in from the entire human body to just the eye for a moment. Charles Darwin used the eye to illustrate how complex organs could have evolved. But instead of providing actual evidence, he told a story about how several intermediate stages could have led from "simple" light-sensitive spots to "complex" eyes. It was a good story, but it wasn't good science.

An absurdly complicated arrangement of molecules makes up the eye. Just the retina, the thin tissue lining the back of the eye, has:
- 7 million cone cells for color assessment
- 125 million rod cells for adaptation to the dark
- 1.2 million nerve cells that collect billions of bits of information[16]

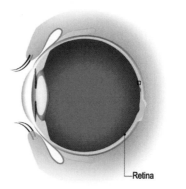

But what good would 125 million rod cells be if there weren't also 1.2 million nerve cells to make the connections? The entire arrangement needs each part, or it doesn't work!

ANATOMY OF A HUMAN EYE WITH
ROD AND CONE CELLS

Darwin's explanation was totally inadequate to explain the complexity of the eye. Even after 150 years of research, evolutionary scientists have not come up with a better explanation. While we observe various kinds of eyes througout the animal kingdom today, there is no clear fossil evidence of any kind to support Darwin's step-by-step evolution from simple to complex chemical pathways needed for light.

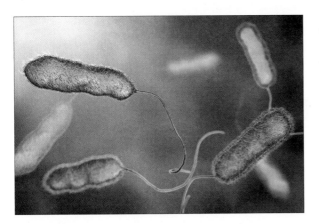

Another example of complex design is found in the molecular machinery in every living cell. It's like an engine with all kinds of parts that combine to produce motion. One such biological engine is found in bacteria that have a flagellum. This is a long tail-like structure that acts like a propeller. Bacteria swim by rotating this flagellum. It takes over 40 different proteins to make this engine go. Each of these proteins must be combined in exacting detail or the engine won't work, and the bacteria can't move in its watery environment.

These are just two examples of the organs and processes in living things that are far too complex to have come about through a random, unguided process. There are no known biological, chemical, or mechanical processes that can produce the specific instructions and machinery every organism needs to survive and reproduce.

This level of complexity seems to require intelligent design. Think about it; if you were climbing into a jumbo jet to fly across the country, would you wonder at how many millions of years it took for all six million of its parts to evolve from buried minerals and eventually assemble themselves into a flying machine? Or would you marvel at the aeronautical engineers and skilled craftsmen who built it?

In their popular debate, Dr. Richard Dawkins and Dr. John Lennox, both professors at Oxford University, argued whether evolution offered a better explanation for the complexities of creation than Christianity. Dr. Lennox pointed out that science requires a rational universe, but irrational, or nonthinking, processes can't produce one. Only an intelligent designer can.

This belief is not based on blind faith, but on evidence-based faith, which the Christian finds in science, history, and personal experience. The difference between science and religion is more a matter of worldview than of evidence.

DR. JOHN LENNOX, 2015

Conclusion

The arguments we've considered in this lesson all point toward a divine Creator. The universe is designed in just the right way to allow for human life. There are irreducibly complex systems necessary for life that can't have evolved from simpler systems through any known process. They appear to have been engineered on purpose. This includes the almost 3 billion base pairs in human DNA. Someone had to write this book of life! An intelligent mind seems far more likely than random chance.

If the evidence suggests that creation was designed in a specific way to support life, then someone must have designed it. This is known as the design argument—*if something exists that is designed, then it must have a designer.*

Many people believe intelligent design makes the most sense of the world. As one interviewee told Dr. Sean McDowell:

As I started to look into the biological evidences I was awestruck at how obvious it was to make a design inference based on the inner workings of the cell. The molecular machines that are working inside each of our bodies at this moment scream of a designer. If more Christians understood the beautiful structure of how the different processes within our bodies function, I know it would not only strengthen their faith but would give them a much greater sense of just how amazing God's creation really is. And this is certainly true for students who are often not exposed to the evidence for ID (Intelligent Design) since our schools only teach Darwinian evolution.[17]

The Christian worldview maintains that the only adequate explanation for the origin and great diversity of life is an all-wise, all-powerful Designer: *Long ago you laid the foundation of the earth and made the heavens with your hands* (Psalm 102:25). *He holds in his hands the depths of the earth and the mightiest mountains. The sea belongs to him, for he made it. His hands formed the dry land, too* (Psalm 95:4–5).

"Gravity explains the motions of the planets," Isaac Newton said, "but it cannot explain who sets the planets in motion." That's where the Bible steps in: *"To whom will you compare me? Who is my equal?" asks the Holy One. Look up into the heavens. Who created all the stars? He brings them out like an army, one after another, calling each by its name. Because of his great power and incomparable strength, not a single one is missing* (Isaiah 40:25–26).

The evidence for a supernatural Creator is visible across the universe and around this planet. At the pinnacle of it all are human beings, made in his image and given dominion over his creation (Genesis 1:26–31). We are not the product of endless time and random chance. We were created on purpose and for a purpose. The Westminster Shorter Catechism puts it this way: "Man's chief end is to glorify God, and to enjoy him forever."

> **Design Argument**
> If something exists that is designed,
> then it must have a designer

ENDNOTES

1 George Gaylord Simpson, *The Meaning of Evolution* (New Haven, CT: Yale University Press, 1971), 345.

2 Richard Dawkins, *The Blind Watchmaker* (New York, NY: Norton, 1986), 1.

3 Richard Dawkins and John Lennox, "The God Delusion Debate," filmed October 3, 2007 at the University of Alabama-Birmingham's Alys Stephens Center, video, 1:46:39, https://www.youtube.com/watch?v=zF5bPI92-5o&t=6s.

4 Richard Dawkins, *The God Delusion* (Boston, MA: Houghton Mifflin, 2006), 140.

5 Guillermo González and Jay Richards, *The Privileged Planet: How Our Place in the Cosmos is Designed for Discovery* (Washington DC: Regnery Publishing, Inc., 2004), 195–220.

6 Wernher von Braun, letter to California State Board of Education, 14 Sep 1972, https://www.sandiegoreader.com/news/2012/jul/18/excerpt-letter-california-state-board-education/

7 George Wald, "The Origin of Life," *Scientific American* 190 (August 1954), 46, from *In the Beginning* by Walt Brown, p. 7.

8 Robert Sawyer, *Calculating God* (New York, NY: Tor Books, 2009), 102.

9 Michael Behe, *Darwin's Black Box: The Biochemical Challenge to Evolution* (New York: Free Press, 2006), 193.

10 William Dembski, *Intelligent Design: The Bridge Between Science and Theology* (Downers Grove, IL: InterVarsity Press, 1999), 90–91.

11 Victoria Woollaston, "How many gigabytes does it take to make a HUMAN?," Daily Mail.com, updated July 4, 2014, https://www.dailymail.co.uk/sciencetech/article-2680849/How-gigabytes-does-make-HUMAN-Physicians-works-genetic-code-just-1-5GB-data.html.

12 Bill Gates, *The Road Ahead* (London: Penguin: 1996), 228.

13 Anthony Flew and Gary Habermas, "My Pilgrimage from Atheism to Theism: A Discussion between Antony Flew and Gary Habermas," *Philosophia Christi* 6, no. 2, (2004): 201.

14 Antony Flew, *There Is a God: How the World's Most Notorious Atheist Changed His Mind"* (New York: Harper One, 2007), 124.

15 Ragnar Oborn, "Antony Flew Considered Intelligent Design," *Consider the Gospel* (blog), January 31, 2012, https://considerthegospel.org/2012/01/31/antony-flew-considered-design/

16 Geoffrey Simmons, *What Darwin Didn't Know* (Eugene, OR: Harvest House, 2004), 114.

17 Sean McDowell, "What is the Best Evidence for Intelligent Design? Interview with Brian Johnson," *Josh McDowell Ministry* (blog), February 6, 2017, https://www.josh.org/what-is-the-best-evidence-for-intelligent-design-interview-with-brian-johnson/

Application Story: The Designer

"Hurry! That fighter's coming around for another pass! Head toward that small waterfall!"

Rigo Acuna's two companions heeded his warning and bolted toward the rocky outcropping near the edge of the cascade. Rigo followed at a slower pace. He kept his laser rifle cradled in his arms and continued to glance over his shoulder at the rapidly approaching enemy spacecraft.

Heavy laser blasts rent the sky and struck the ground a hundred feet from his current location. With each second, the deadly hailstorm of energy drew ever closer. Rigo fired several futile shots toward the ship, then turned and sprinted toward the others. To his horror, the two scientists seemed frozen in place. He reached them and suddenly understood why.

The rocky area on which they stood was like an island. They had run into a dead end surrounded by sheer cliff walls.

"We need to hide in the water!" Tung-Mei said, her voice trembling with fear.

"But I can't swim!" Levi shouted in panic.

Rigo prepared to shove him into the pool of frothing water when the approaching laser blasts from the fighter shook the ground beneath his feet. The soil shifted and heaved, causing him to lose his footing. A second later, he was falling.

When he regained consciousness, he found himself blanketed in darkness with only a sliver of light coming from somewhere above. The air was thick with mist and his soldier's uniform was already becoming heavy with moisture. He flicked on the small headlamp attached to his helmet. The beam of light was diffused by the water in the air, yet he could see enough to confirm his suspicions.

He was in a cave. Levi and Tung-Mei lay nearby. They began to stir as Rigo examined their surroundings.

"What happened?" Levi asked, sitting up.

"We fell into a cave. That last attack must have collapsed a portion of the ceiling, dropping us inside. It looks like it caused part of the nearby cliff to crack and cover our entrance. We're lucky we didn't get crushed by any of the debris."

Tung-Mei stood and brushed dirt off her clothes. "How do we get out?"

Rigo shined his light down the passage to his left. "We can try this way, or," he turned and pointed his flashlight down the passage on the right but never finished his sentence.

Tung-Mei let out a blood-curdling scream at the sight of the gruesome visage staring back at her. Rigo's instincts kicked in and he withdrew his pistol from its holster in a flash. His finger was just about to pull the trigger when his mind finally realized the truth.

He took several deep breaths to dispel the adrenaline that coursed through him. "It's okay. It's just a skull embedded in the wall. Some kind of domesticated beast of burden from the looks of it. The tunnel collapse probably caused it to be exposed."

"It's more than that!" Levi announced in sudden excitement. "It's not just the skull. Most of the body is here as well. This is an astounding find!" He traced the protruding structures with a loving finger as he spoke. "Based on what we know of the creatures on this planet, I'd say this was likely the evolutionary ancestor of the wild visoc. See this bony ridge on its back? It likely evolved into the large spinal plates. The leg bones are highly similar. And here! See these bony protrusions on the tail? That probably became the defensive spikes on modern visocs."

Rigo could tell by the frown on Tung-Mei's face she wasn't buying his explanation. "Let's not jump to conclusions. Just because it has similarities doesn't mean it is a common ancestor, but it could have had a common designer."

Levi gave her a lopsided grin. "Really? You want to resurrect that debate now?"

"I'm just saying you should consider other viewpoints," Tung-Mei responded. "Don't impose your bias on the evidence."

Levi scoffed. "It's a wonder you religious types ever go into science. What's the point of doing science if you can explain everything by saying, 'God did it?'"

"But we don't say that unless the evidence points that way. Look here," she said, crossing over to the fossil. "See how these bones fit perfectly together along the spine? And the ribs are curved at the precise angle to provide maximum support. If you saw these features in any nonliving thing, you'd immediately say it had to have been designed. All I'm saying is, don't rule out a possible answer before asking the question."

Having grown bored with the conversation, Rigo started examining the passage leading away from the waterfall and pool beneath it. A hint of color drew his attention to an object lying at the base of the wall. He reached down and picked up a long, cylindrical object. "Hey, you two brainiacs. Here's more fuel for your debate."

Intrigued by his statement, the two scientists rushed over to join him. Levi took the object from his hands with the care of a mother cradling her newborn. "It's a flute made of bone! This craftsmanship is exquisite. Look at the designs around the finger holes. And although the paint has faded, the blue and gold trim along the outer edges would have once been beautiful."

"Careful," Tung-Mei said with a grin. "Don't jump to conclusions. This could have come from a creature that evolved these holes in its bones. Just because it appears designed doesn't mean it was designed."

Levi scowled at her. "This is totally different."

"I don't think so," she said. "Let's ask a neutral party. Mr. Acuna, what do you think?"

Rigo threw up his hands. "I don't want any part of your squabble."

"Fine, I'll keep it generic. Does evidence speak for itself? Does this flute have any labels telling us where it came from?"

"No."

"And if two scientists with the same PhDs draw opposite conclusions using the same evidence, should both views be considered valid?"

"Makes sense to me."

Tung-Mei turned to face Levi. "See? The average person recognizes the logic of it. When you see evidence of design, the most logical, scientific conclusion is that it was designed, just like this flute was designed by . . . " Her expression became one of shock. "That's it! Don't you see? This is proof!"

Rigo stared at her as if she had gone mad. "Proof of what?"

"The markings! This is Shingarian writing," she said excitedly. "It proves their people colonized this planet before the Antarians. This evidence could end the war!"

Rigo smiled. "You're right. The flute and the cave paintings should be more than enough proof."

"Cave paintings?"

Rigo pointed at the wall near him. Both scientists practically jumped with excitement. He gave them 15 minutes to examine the paintings before urging them down the tunnel. Every minute could mean another death for one of his people. Now, he held the end of the war in his hand. And it was all thanks to some scratches on a bone and paint on a wall that pointed to a designer.

Getting Started—Body and Soul

"He was a great actor," Greg said as the movie came to an end. "I don't understand why he committed suicide. The guy was at the top of his game. Handsome, rich, married to a model."

"We can never know what's going on inside someone else's head," Shaun said.

Greg muted the TV as the credits rolled. "His self-talk was more powerful than what the world was telling him. And a lot more negative, too, since it drove him to end it all."

"But did he really end it all?" Shaun said thoughtfully. "What about his soul? Is he happier now or is he in trouble with God for killing himself?"

"I read somewhere he was an atheist," Greg said. "He probably didn't think about his soul."

"That doesn't mean he didn't have one."

Greg shrugged. "How do we even know we have souls?"

"Because we're more than just machines, or animals," Shaun replied. "We can think and feel and make choices."

"That could just be stuff our brain does. It doesn't mean we have souls."

Just then, Shaun got an idea. "Give me the remote."

Greg handed it over.

"Let's say the TV is your body and the movie is your soul. They work together. They need each other." He turned off the TV. "What happened to the movie? Does it still exist?"

"Sure," Greg said.

Shaun pointed to the blank screen. "Where is it, then?"

"It's on the airwaves, I guess," Greg said, waving his arms.

"How do you know?"

"Give me the remote, and I'll show you," Greg said.

"What if I broke your TV so you could never watch the movie again?"

"Then you'd have to buy me a new one," Greg said. "But I get your point. Destroying my TV doesn't destroy the movie. The TV is just the vehicle for watching the movie, and our bodies are just the vehicles for interacting with our souls. They are separate things."

Shaun turned on the TV and started flipping channels. "Okay, now let's see if there's anything interesting going on in that soul of yours."

How to Live with Yourself and Like It

Your attitude often determines how much you enjoy life. Are you happy and satisfied? It's likely because you think that way. Are you sad or depressed? Sometimes those feelings stem from the way you think about yourself.

So what is the source of your thoughts and ideas? In order to answer this question, it is crucial to first answer another: Who are you? The root of both questions is the definition of human nature. When you ask what human nature is, you are entering into the study of psychology—knowledge of the "psyche" or soul. Psychology seeks to understand what you are like on the inside, the place where you do all of your real living.

Therefore, to enjoy life to its full potential, you need to clear your mind of certain ideas that are wrong. Then you need to build a new set of ideas from a proper understanding of biblical Christian psychology! As you're about to find out, God has a lot to say about who you really are.

In this lesson, you will explore the answers to these key questions:

What is human nature?
What are human beings?
Do human beings have value?

Topic 1—What Are Human Beings?

A TV is a physical object. The shows it displays are digital signals, patterns of information. But the two are designed to work together. The same is true of computer programs. A computer is just a machine. What makes it so amazing and versatile is software, the invisible code that tells the computer what to do and monitors its behavior.

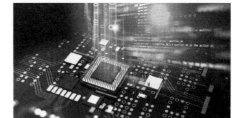

Human beings are another example of the material and the immaterial combined in a well-designed partnership. The story of our creation in Genesis accounts for both our physical bodies, which were made from the dust of the earth, and our souls, or spirits, which were breathed into us by God: Then the LORD God formed a man from the dust of the ground and breathed into his nostrils the breath of life, and the man became a living being (Genesis 2:7).

Naturalistic evolution teaches that humans are merely mammals because we share the same physical features as other animals in this class. More specifically, we are in the subgroup of mammals called *primates*, and the subgroup of primates called *great apes*. This subgroup includes gorillas, orangutans, chimpanzees, and bonobos. Humans, chimpanzees, and bonobos share about 98 percent of the same DNA.

We have many things in common with animals because we're made of the same physical stuff. But we all know there's more to being human than DNA. We have something that no other animal has—a soul. Regardless of what it is called—consciousness, mind, soul, spirit—this immaterial part of us makes us unique. God's breath carried with it God's image: So God created human beings in his own image. In the image of God he created them; male and female he created them (Genesis 1:27).

Since God doesn't have a physical body, being made in his image refers to our nonphysical, spiritual nature. Theologians call this concept the *imago Dei*. It includes the ability to think, feel, create, choose, love, and so many more attributes of what we might call *personality*. We express these soul traits through our physical bodies. This combination, like everything else God made originally, was pronounced "very good" (Genesis 1:31).

Even secular thinkers and writers acknowledge the existence of the soul. One popular, non-Christian writer famously said:

The other more important part of the consciousness is the soul. Now, I don't ask you to believe in God or not believe in God. I'm a writer, not a missionary. That is not my department. But I do ask you to believe that you have a soul. There is some piece of your consciousness that has no shape, size, weight, or color. This is the piece of you that is of infinite value and dignity. The dignity of this piece doesn't increase or decrease with age; it doesn't get bigger or smaller depending on your size and strength. Rich and successful people don't have more or less of it than poorer or less successful people.[1]

Topic 2—What Is Psychology?

To understand human beings, we have to study the body *and* the soul. Biology, medicine, and other disciplines focus on the body. The soul is the focus of psychology. Psychology is *the study of the human mind and the behavior it produces*. How people approach this study will depend on how they see the world.

You probably remember from the philosophy lesson that naturalists reduce the world to matter while new spiritualists claim that reality is primarily spiritual. But we made the case that reality is actually two-dimensional, consisting of both the material and the immaterial. It's not either/or when it comes to the natural and supernatural, it's both.

The same is true of human beings. We have physical bodies of flesh and blood, but we also have the breath of God in us. If we ignore either aspect of who we are, we cannot hope to understand how we should behave.

A person's theological and philosophical perspective will determine his or her view of human nature. If someone believes in naturalism, then she will logically conclude that our self-consciousness and other mental actions are just chemical activities in the brain. Everything we think and do can be explained naturally. We are nothing more than physical organisms that respond to physical stimuli either inside or outside our bodies. Mental functions are reduced to mere brain functions. Mind is nothing more than gray matter.

New spiritualists believe that only the spiritual realm exists. It is the "life force" within all things that is real; everything else is an illusion we must learn to see through if we want to become enlightened and understand the true nature of reality. The physical is just the manifestation of the spiritual; the ultimate reality is consciousness.

The biblical Christian worldview acknowledges both the physical and spiritual dimensions of human beings. It takes into account the natural and the supernatural. It looks outside of ourselves to God for wisdom and direction as to how we should live.

> **Psychology**
> The study of the human mind
> and the behavior it produces

Part 1—Materialism, Spiritualism, and Supernaturalism

The worldview a person holds will influence his or her approach to psychology. This will be reflected in three basic views of reality known as *materialism*, *spiritualism*, and *supernaturalism*.

- Materialism, or naturalism, is physical. It teaches that reality consists of only physical matter. Materialists have a naturalistic worldview and believe that humans do not have spiritual attributes, only physical ones. The thoughts in our heads are nothing more than chemical reactions in our brains. Psychological materialism is *the belief that humans are purely material beings without immaterial minds.*
- Spiritualism is nonphysical. It teaches that reality consists of only the spiritual or immaterial. Spiritualists have a nonmaterialistic worldview and maintain the exact opposite of materialism. Spiritualists believe nothing is physical; everything is spiritual, including human beings. Psychological spiritualism is *the belief that humans are purely spiritual beings whose minds are part of a divine consciousness.*
- Supernaturalism teaches that reality is made of both the physical (material) and nonphysical (spiritual). Supernaturalists have a dualistic worldview. They insist that reality is composed of both the physical (material) and the nonphysical (spiritual). Psychological supernaturalism is *the belief that humans are both physical and spiritual beings with material bodies and immaterial minds.*

Mind means something different to each of these views:

To the materialist, the mind refers to some of the functions of the physical brain. If you look inside someone's head, you could see a brain but not a mind.

To the spiritualist, the mind is just the way people experience the divine consciousness. The physical brain, like the body, is an illusion. Everything is spiritual and connected to the cosmic reality—which they call *god.*

To the supernaturalist, the mind is the nonphysical mental activities we experience—thoughts, feelings, intuitions, choice, conscience, and so on. The brain is necessary for the mind, but it is not sufficient to explain it entirely.

Christianity's view of psychology is psychological supernaturalism because it accepts the biblical teaching that humans are both physical and spiritual beings. Adam's body came alive when God breathed into it (Genesis 2:7), and when the soul leaves the body, the body dies. (James 2:26). We are not purely physical, as naturalists believe, nor are we simply spiritual, as the new spiritualists claim.

In his book *God's Crime Scene: A Homicide Detective Examines the Evidence for a Divinely Created Universe*, J. Warner Wallace writes, "If atheism is true, our natural universe is nothing more than space, time, matter and the laws of physics and chemistry that govern such things. In this material, physical environment, it's easy to account for brains, but difficult to explain our experience of 'mind.'"[2]

Psychological Materialism
The belief that humans are purely material beings without immaterial minds

Psychological Spiritualism
The belief that humans are purely spiritual beings whose minds are part of a divine consciousness

Psychological Supernaturalism
The belief that humans are both physical and spiritual beings with material bodies and immaterial minds

Part 2—The Mind Argument

C. S. Lewis is famous for pointing toward the existence of God. "Suppose that there is no intelligence behind the universe," he said. "In that case, nobody designed our brain for the purpose of thinking. Thought is merely the random by-product of atoms within our skull. But if so, how can I trust my own thinking to be true?"[3]

To better grasp his point, think about what would happen if a monkey typed away on a keyboard in an effort to write a computer program. The program would never work because the monkey would be hitting random keys. It doesn't have a thought-out goal and a logical plan to reach it. In the same way, a thoughtlessly random process of molecules bumping into each other could never produce a mind capable of thinking and discerning truth from error. But what if an intelligent, trained computer scientist wrote a program? It would work, and it would

tell us something about the programmer by the skill and beauty reflected in the program. So it is with the human mind. The fact that we have a mind is the result of being made in the image of our Creator. The mind argument states that because we have a mind to think, feel, reason, imagine and create, there must be a Creator who has these attributes as well.

God created human beings as embodied spirits. From Genesis on, the Bible talks about the body and the soul. Jesus's statement about fearing the one who could put "both soul and body" in hell in Matthew 10:28, and the apostle Paul's prayer for the spirit, soul, and body, in 1 Thessalonians 5:23, are just two examples.

Our future hope is not that we will be spirits in heaven, but that, like the Lord Jesus, we will be reunited with God in our resurrected, glorified bodies (1 Corinthians 15:35–44). For time and eternity, we are spirit and body together.

> **Mind Argument**
> Since human beings have have a mind to think, feel, reason, imagine, and create, there must be a Creator who has theses attributes as well

Part 3—Supporting Evidence

Besides what the Bible teaches, are there other reasons to believe humans are more than just physical beings? Is it possible to demonstrate that the mind is more than just a physical brain? Here are three reasons to think so.

Reason #1: Mental Events
We can measure the weight and size of our brains. We can study the electrical firings between its synapses. But mental events—thoughts, emotions, ideas, choices—can't be seen, weighed, or measured. They have no color, taste, texture, or other physical properties; nevertheless, they exist. The brain is physical. The mind is nonphysical. They are not the same thing. The brain is necessary to experience the mind, but the brain is not sufficient to explain the mind.

To see the difference, try this experiment. Pick up a rock and decide if it is true or false. Then hold a leaf in your hand and determine if it is good or evil. What makes this so silly is that purely physical objects don't have nonphysical or moral qualities. To mix these categories is what's known as *a category mistake*.

A rock cannot be false or morally wrong, but our thoughts about it can be false or morally wrong. For example, we might think a rock is granite when it is actually sandstone. Or, we might hit someone with a rock because we don't like him, and then blame the rock. But the rock is not at fault for having been thrown; it cannot think or act. A physical object like a rock is in the category of things that have mass but no moral standing. A nonphysical idea like truth or blame has no mass, but it has moral properties. Mental events exist, but they are not physical objects.

Reason #2: Unity of Identity
A second reason that supernaturalism makes more sense than materialism or spiritualism is that supernaturalism is a better explanation for our self-consciousness. We have what could be called *a unity of identity*. Even though the 37 trillion cells in our bodies and the 100 billion cells in our brains are constantly changing, our personal identity does not change. We are the same people we were as toddlers, just bigger and more experienced. No

matter how much we grow or experience, our personal identity remains the same throughout life.

This is significant because it shows that our identity is not tied to our physical bodies but rather resides in our nonphysical, spiritual selves. In a similar way, our memories remain even though the cells in our brains die and are replaced many times over the years: "What research has shown us thus far, is that there is no precise one-to-one relationship between any fragment of memory and the nerve cells in which it is supposed to be encoded."[4] Our memories, and the personalities they shape, cannot simply be located in our physical brains; nonetheless, they are real.

Reason #3: Freedom to Choose

Finally, without allowing for the mind to be supernatural, there is no explanation for our freedom of choice. If our thoughts are just physical reactions in our brains, then free will is an illusion. Our thoughts, ideas, beliefs, and actions are like balls on a billiard table. One ball hits another, and it moves according to the laws of physics. We have no choice. We can only say, "My synapses made me do it."

Ironically, this means if naturalism is true, we have no good reason to choose to believe it. Our belief is not really a choice; it is just a response to our environment. But this doesn't match reality as we know it. We think, talk, and act as if we actually have free choice. We make decisions every day; to sit here or stand there, to talk or remain silent, to read a book or watch a movie. The exercise of personal choice assumes we have a mind

that is separate from our brain and not enslaved to the physical chain of cause and effect.

Animals have brains, but they are controlled by instinct. They don't have minds that can think and reason and choose like humans do. That's why we don't hold them morally accountable for what they do. A lion never goes on trial for murder. It takes a mind to be able to choose. And with choice comes accountability and responsibility. Every civilization throughout history, even naturalistic ones, have treated people as free moral agents, not machines or animals. This reality is just too obvious to ignore.

Topic 3—Sin and Responsibility

The biblical Christian worldview not only affirms the dualism of body and soul, it teaches the truth that both have been affected by sin. Physically and spiritually, all human beings have been affected by Adam and Eve's disobedience (Genesis 3:1–6:5). Our bodies die, and our souls are bent toward selfishness and sin, referred to as *a sin nature.*

This sinful nature is the ultimate source of most psychological problems. Human beings have an innate tendency to revolt against God and his laws. This is the essence of sin—the willful rebellion against God. This fracture in our relationship with God leads to a fracture in all of our relationships. Sin negatively affects who we are and how we relate to others and the world around us.

If humans are simply physical machines, as materialism teaches, then sin would just be mechanical failure. Without the ability to choose, we would not be responsible for our actions. Nor would we experience guilt. If a machine stops working, it isn't held responsible and punished. But if the machine operator—a human being—stops working, he or she is held accountable and reprimanded, or fired. There is responsibility because, "If [the human being] is something more than merely a mechanism, then his failure must be judged as something worse than the breakdown of a machine."[5]

We hold people accountable because they have choices. The actions of wicked people—like the oppression of the innocent or the abuse of women and children—cannot be excused simply as programmed behavior. We have laws, courts, and police precisely because we believe people are responsible and accountable for their actions. We also know deep down that we are responsible for our own sinful behavior.

Acknowledging the reality of human responsibility leads to the reality of personal sin: "The great benefit of the doctrine of sin is that it reintroduces responsibility for our own behavior, responsibility for changing as well as giving meaning to our condition."[6]

Topic 4—Christian Psychology

If psychology is the study of the human mind and the behavior it produces, *Christian psychology* is *the study of the human mind and the behavior it produces through the lens of biblical truth*. It begins with the understanding that personhood grows out of our being made in the image of God. This gives every human intrinsic value. But

we also have deep problems because of how sin has affected our souls and bodies. Although we were created in God's image, we cannot live up to his moral standards. Romans 3:23 reminds us that we all fail to live up to God's glorious standards. This means that we often respond to situations in life in selfish, sinful ways. This can lead to feelings of guilt, discouragement, or even depression, since sin breaks our fellowship with God.

But our story doesn't end there. There is good news! The gospel message is that our sins have been forgiven through Jesus' death on our behalf. When we accept that forgiveness and give him control of our life, we gain a restored relationship with God and new life, joy, and peace.

Christian psychology takes these three truths into account: 1) we are made in God's image and have infinite value, 2) we have been damaged by sin and the problems it causes, and 3) we can be redeemed and made new through faith in Jesus Christ. When we trust in Jesus, we are accepted by God and he breathes his Holy Spirit into us anew (Romans 8:11, 2 Timothy 1:14).

Our greatest psychological need is not self-esteem; rather, it is the realization of who we are, how sin has affected us, and where we can find forgiveness and redemption. Only after being made right with God through Jesus Christ can we begin to understand our value as creatures made in God's image. Only then can we truly live triumphant and rewarding lives.

Part 1—Human Nature and the Problem of Sin

Much of what psychology deals with is the effect of sin on our thoughts and behaviors. When the Bible states that we are all sinners, it is not saying that we always act out the worst that is in us. We are capable of doing good, and often do. But we rarely act out the very best that is in us either. We often choose to act selfishly and do what we want, whether it is in accordance with God's moral law or not.

Not only does our sin nature affect what we do, we are also influenced by the culture and the people around us. The world itself is opposed to God: Do not love this world nor the things it offers you, for when you love the world, you do not have the love of the Father in you. For the world offers only a craving for physical pleasure, a craving for everything we see, and pride in our achievements and possessions. These are not from the Father, but are from this world (1 John 2:15–16).

Our personal friendships, entertainment choices, and social settings can either be sources of temptation to do wrong or sources of encouragement to do right. The apostle Paul warns, Don't be fooled by those who say such things, for "bad company corrupts good character" (1 Corinthians 15:33).

Despite these external pressures, we are responsible for what we say and do. Everything that comes out of our mouths or makes us act a certain way originates from deep inside us. Even though we have many influences around us, we are responsible for how we react to these influences. Therefore, we must guard our hearts (Philippians 4:7) and renew our minds, so that we will learn to know God's will . . . which is good and pleasing and perfect (Romans 12:2).

So how do we do this? James teaches us to examine ourselves when we are tempted, because the root of that temptation may be our own hearts: And remember, when you are being tempted, do not say, "God is tempting me." God is never tempted to do wrong, and he never tempts anyone else. Temptation comes from our own desires, which entice us and drag us away. These desires give birth to sinful actions. And when sin is allowed to grow, it gives birth to death (James 1:13–15).

We cannot blame others for our evil thoughts and deeds. In fact, God promises us that he will not allow us to be overwhelmed by temptations: The temptations in your life are no different from what others experience. And God is faithful. He will not allow the temptation to be more than you can stand. When you are tempted, he will show you a way out so that you can endure (1 Corinthians 10:13).

This means that we can never legitimately say, "I couldn't help myself," or "He made me do it." The responsibility for our thoughts and deeds rests squarely on us. Remember these words from the apostle Paul: And now, dear brothers and sisters, one final thing. Fix your thoughts on what is true, and honorable, and right, and pure, and lovely, and admirable. Think about things that are excellent and worthy of praise (Philippians 4:8).

Our only hope in addressing and overcoming our sinful nature is the redeeming work of Jesus and the indwelling transformation of the Holy Spirit. Paul explains this transforming work in Romans 8:1–4:

> So now there is no condemnation for those who belong to Christ Jesus. And because you belong to him, the power of the life-giving Spirit has freed you from the power of sin that leads to death. The law of Moses was unable to save us because of the weakness of our sinful nature. So God did what the law could not do. He sent his own Son in a body like the bodies we sinners have. And in that body God declared an end to sin's control over us by giving his Son as a sacrifice for our sins. He did this so that the just requirement of the law would be fully satisfied for us, who no longer follow our sinful nature but instead follow the Spirit.

There is a new way of life now open to the believer because of what Christ has accomplished on our behalf.

The old has passed away, all things are new (2 Corinthians 5:17). The human mind, the concern of psychology, now has a choice. It can stay rooted in the sinful flesh or yield to the Holy Spirit. According to Romans 8:5–9, this choice impacts every aspect of life and makes all the difference in the world:

> Those who are dominated by the sinful nature think about sinful things, but those who are controlled by the Holy Spirit think about things that please the Spirit. So letting your sinful nature control your mind leads to death. But letting the Spirit control your mind leads to life and peace. For the sinful nature is always hostile to God. It never did obey God's laws, and it never will. That's why those who are still under the control of their sinful nature can never please God. But you are not controlled by your sinful nature. You are controlled by the Spirit if you have the Spirit of God living in you. (And remember that those who do not have the Spirit of Christ living in them do not belong to him at all.)

ENDNOTES

1 David Brooks, *The Second Mountain: The Quest for a Moral Life* (New York: Random House, 2019), 46.
2 J. Warner Wallace, "Are Atheists Correct When They Claim Mental States Are Merely Brain States?," *Cold Case Christianity* (blog), August 17, 2015, https://coldcasechristianity.com/writings/are-atheists-correct-when-they-claim-mental-states-are-merely-brain-states/.
3 C. S. Lewis, *Broadcast Talks* (London: B. Bles, 1944), 37–38.
4 Arthur C. Custance, *Man in Adam and in Christ* (Grand Rapids, MI: Zondervan, 1975), 256.
5 Ibid, 268.
6 Paul Vitz, *Psychology as Religion: The Cult of Self-Worship* (Grand Rapids, MI: Eerdmans, 1985), 43.

Application Story: The Coach

Life is *so* unfair! I mean, I wasn't even looking at anything bad and Mom just freaked! Ugh. She needs to just respect my privacy and realize I'm not a kid anymore. I'm already fourteen. I'm old enough to make my own choices. I can't wait to graduate and get out on my own. Instead, I'm forced to do some 'volunteer' work by visiting a nursing home. Mom says I have a 'choice', but if I don't spend at least half an hour here, I don't get my phone back for a week! Ewww. I hate this place! It reeks of old people.

I follow my mom through the main doors and try to keep from puking. Everywhere I look I see wheelchairs, breathing tubes, and people who are half asleep. Or maybe they *are* asleep. I can't tell the difference.

Mom guides me to a table in the living area. "Have a seat here, Abigail. I'll be right back."

Why do adults do that? Why do they switch to your full name when they're mad at you?

I wait for what seems like twenty minutes. I'm bored out of my skull. Some stupid game show that was popular thirty years ago is playing on a TV. I reach in my pocket out of habit. My fingers twitch and I look around for something—anything—to distract me. Unfortunately, everything is either super old or . . . yeah, I'm not touching that.

Mom *finally* returned. "Abigail, this is Mrs. Laney. She's an old friend of mine. I want you to keep her company for a little bit, okay?"

'Old' is right! It takes Mrs. Laney like a whole minute to sit down. Her hair, what's left of it, is curly and white. She's wearing a pair of huge glasses with thick lenses, and she's a bit overweight, at least in my opinion. Her clothes? I won't even go there. I've seen poodles dressed better than her.

Once the old lady was seated, mom turned to me. "Be polite," she whispered. "Give her a chance. You may actually learn something."

Yeah right. Like *that's* gonna happen. But, to make Mom happy, I put on my best smile. "Okay, Mom."

Once she's gone, I slouch down in the chair. Only twenty-nine minutes and fifty-five more seconds to go . . .

"So, Abigail, your mom tells me you're on the basketball team at school."

"Yeah," I mumble.

"It takes a lot of discipline to play a sport."

My eyes are already starting to glaze over.

"I was a gymnast in my time. In fact, I was once the best in the state."

Really? This lady could barely move. It was surprising to think of her as a state champion in gymnastics. "That's cool. But, why gymnastics? Why not play a sport?"

Mrs. Laney shrugged. "I guess it was because I loved the grace and elegance of it."

I snorted. "If you say so."

"So, how good are you at basketball?"

I play it cool. I don't want to sound prideful. "Pretty good. I'm not the best, but I'm not the worst either."

"Do you go to all the practices and games?"

"Most of them. My coach gets pretty mad if we miss any. Lindsay missed a practice last week and got chewed out for it."

"Is Lindsay a good player?"

"Not really. She skips out and doesn't practice enough."

"Who would win a shooting match, you or her?"

"Me, of course," I say confidently.

"Why?"

"Because I practice more." I give her a look like, duh, isn't that obvious?

"Do you think the coach was right to get upset at Lindsay for skipping practice?"

"Yeah. She lets the whole team down. It's frustrating. Last game, she only made two shots."

"Abigail, your mom told me why she brought you here."

I roll my eyes. We were having such a good conversation. Here comes the lecture.

"I'm guessing you think she overreacted?"

I snicker. "Of course. I was just watching this video on YouTube™. I mean, it had some stuff in it that wasn't great, but it was really funny. She acted like I just got caught shoplifting or something."

"What kind of stuff was in it that wasn't so great?"

Ugh. I don't want to tell her. "Well, there was some foul language in it, and . . . other stuff."

"Was it something you would show to your younger sister?"

"No! I mean, she's only eleven."

"So, you wouldn't show it to her, but you feel it's okay for you to watch?"

"Well, yeah. I'm older. I can handle it."

"I see. Let me ask you something: do you understand the difference between the body and the spirit?"

Oh, boy. Here we go. Better to play dumb. "I'm not sure. What do you mean?"

"I know you've probably been taught differently in school, but we are much more than just evolved animals. We have a spirit. Have you ever been to a funeral? I certainly have. I can tell you, the body in the coffin may be the same, but something is definitely missing. That's our spirit."

"Yeah, okay."

"But the problem with us humans is that our bodies—that is, our physical wants—often fight against our spiritual needs. They are like two players shooting hoops. Guess which one is going to win?"

I can tell she is expecting me to know the answer, but I still don't know what she's trying to . . . Oh. Now I get it. "The one that practices, right?"

"I knew you were a smart one! You see, Abigail, while you may be 'old enough to handle' some bad content, your mom is worried that you aren't 'practicing' good habits. If you only feed your mind with junk and starve the good within you, eventually the bad will win. Think about it: What would happen if you only ate fast food all the time?"

"I'd blow up like a blimp and get super fat."

Mrs. Laney pushed her glasses back up on her nose. "Right. So not only do you need to feed your spirit, but you need to feed it the right things. Some entertainment is good for us. It makes us laugh, stirs our emotions, and helps us relax. But other types feed the darker parts of our spirits, or even our physical desires. If you practice bad habits, and don't practice the good ones, it will change who you are."

To my surprise, the time passed quickly. Mrs. Laney didn't preach to me but treated me like an adult and simply asked me really great questions. The next thing I knew, Mom was standing at the table.

"Well, Mrs. Laney, what do you think?"

The old lady gave me a broad smile. "She is a fine young lady. She just needs a little 'coaching' now and again."

Mrs. Laney smiled at me, and, to my own surprise, I smiled back. I stood and said goodbye. When I got near the door, I turned back toward Mrs. Laney. "Thanks, Coach!"

Getting Started—Dumb Idea?

"That's a dumb idea," Emma said in response to the youth pastor's suggestion.

"What would our friends think?" Sarah asked.

Other kids chimed in, but no one in the group of 20 or so teens seemed in favor of the experiment. Going off social media for a week would be social suicide!

"I'm not saying abandon your friends," the youth pastor clarified. "All I'm saying is talk to them in person for a week. Spend more time with your families instead of staring at a screen." He waved his hand around the room. "Hang out with each other. Go to the mall or a movie. Use your eyes when you talk with someone, not your thumbs."

"It's quicker to do things online," Emma said.

"And easier," Sarah added.

The pastor nodded. "Relationships can be messy. They take work. They can't be reduced to 140 characters or six-second videos. Besides, it's too easy to hide behind screens and not share your true selves. You can have a thousand friends 'following' you and still be lonely."

No one spoke, as the words hit close to home.

"God made us for relationships," the pastor went on. "From the beginning he said it wasn't good for humans to be alone. That's why we're born into families. That's why we need to be involved in a church family. That's why you're part of this youth group."

"I'm here because my parents make me come," Bruce said.

Everyone laughed.

"We're glad they do," the pastor said. "You're a lot of fun. We would miss you if you stopped coming." He looked around the group. "We need each other. I need you. All I'm asking is that we concentrate more on being present for seven days."

A few of the kids were nodding now.

"There's a place for social media," the pastor said. "But it shouldn't take the place of face-to-face interaction."

"Can I quote that?" Bruce asked.

The pastor smiled. "That depends on what the group decides to do. Are you ready to vote?"

People in Community

In the last lesson, we looked at psychology, the study of how individuals think and behave. Here we will look at sociology, which is *the study of human societies and institutions*. Society is people coming together in community. It is what humans have always done.

Most people naturally want to be around other people. That's why we get together for almost any reason: holidays and special occasions, concerts and sporting events, family reunions and parties; the list is endless. When we're not together, we're constantly reaching out to others through calls, texts, emails, chat rooms, and the like.

We're made for human relationships. It's how God designed us from the beginning. One of the first things he said after creating Adam was, "It is not good for the man to be alone. I will make a helper who is just right for him" (Genesis 2:18). Then God told the couple, "Be fruitful and multiply. Fill the earth and govern it" (Genesis 1:28). And looking ahead to when this would happen, he told them to start new families from existing ones, "This explains why a man leaves his father and mother and is joined to his wife, and the two are united into one" (Genesis 2:24).

Couples expand into families. Families join into tribes. Tribes merge into societies. At each level we have to learn how to get along. We have to maximize the benefits of being together and minimize the dangers. That's what sociology is all about—how individuals behave in society.

Scripture talks about three key building blocks of society—the family, the church, and the state, or government. Each has a different role to play in how we get along.

1. Family: Where we all start out. It is meant to be a place of love and learning how to get along with others.

2. Church: The family of God united through faith. It is the physical body of Christ carrying on his ministry in the world.

3. State: God-ordained protector of God-given rights, such as life and liberty.

We will explore the first two of these social institutions—family and church. We will touch on the third by looking briefly at a Christian's dual citizenship. In this lesson, these key questions will be addressed:

What makes for a healthy society?
Are the traditional institutions of marriage and family outdated?
What role should the church play in society?

> **Sociology**
> The study of human societies
> and institutions

Topic 1—A Healthy Society

"What makes for a healthy society?" This is a question every worldview must address.

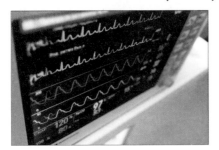

A physician can check certain vital signs to determine if a patient is healthy. She will measure bodily functions like temperature, pulse, blood pressure, and oxygen level. If any of these are outside the normal range, there is cause for concern.

As with individuals, societies have certain vital signs that show how healthy they are. Cultural vital signs include: crime rates, divorce rates, substance abuse, sexual promiscuity, babies born out of wedlock, homelessness, suicides, education, civil rights, racism, voter turnout, and the influence of charities, among others.

Part 1—Atheistic Worldviews

If we don't score very well as a society, whose fault is it? And whose responsibility is it to improve our health? Different worldviews have different ideas about the source of our problems and their cure.

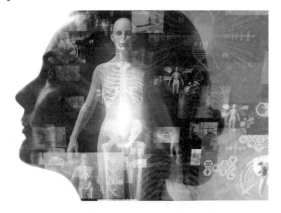

Atheistic worldviews are materialistic (only matter exists) and naturalistic (all that happens is the result of natural causes). These worldviews reject the idea that human beings are made in God's image. They don't have a solid basis on which to say that every human has inherent worth, or certain rights and responsibilities. Instead, they purport that our value comes from what we can do. Moreover, they teach our thoughts and actions are determined by our genetic makeup and our cultural environment.

Because there is no God, there are no absolute standards. Humans have no ultimate purpose. Here's a glimpse at what the three leading atheistic worldviews mentioned in other lessons teach about sociology.

Secularism professes that there is no universal, absolute standard for human behavior. Concepts such as right, wrong, normal, good, and bad refer to things that people have decided to agree on. What seems right is not the result of the image of God within us  but is simply what we have picked up from society as being right or what we think will make us happy. When it comes to personal and public problems, human reason has the solutions, not God. Secularism isn't opposed to religion; it just doesn't believe that religion should have a say in how society is run. People should have the freedom to practice religion privately, but religion shouldn't be used to shape public standards and policies.

Marxism is firmly rooted in Darwinism. It sees humanity as evolving biologically and socially. Society needs to move beyond socialism and then eventually to a "communist" utopia. Marxists believe that once communism is achieved, religion will disappear, socioeconomic classes will melt away, government will no longer be necessary, and everyone will own everything in common. Our meaning and purpose don't come from God but from our collective struggle to bring about this communist utopia. One of the founding fathers of communism, Karl Marx, said, "It is not the consciousness of men that determines their existence, but their social existence that determines their consciousness."[1] In other words, society makes us who we are; it shapes our morals and desires.

Postmodernism denies the existence of absolute truth, teaching that when worldviews claim to know the truth, death and destruction inevitably follow. Postmodernists cite the thousands of Christians and Muslims who died in the Crusades fighting for their version of the truth, and, in the last 100 years, the tens of millions who died because of Marxists trying to bring about communism. Postmodernism teaches tolerance of all personal beliefs and sees religion, especially Christianity, as intolerant. In a postmodern world, everything possible becomes permissible, everything permissible becomes desirable, and everything desirable becomes normal.

Part 2—The Christian Worldview

In stark contrast to these worldviews, Christianity says sin is the problem with people and societies. The answer to this problem is the grace of God and the power of Jesus Christ. It is in him that we find the only real hope for health and wholeness.

The Christian worldview teaches that humans are made in God's image and that he gave us free will. This was evident in the freedom to disobey him that was present from the beginning (Genesis 3). If we have free will, then we are responsible for our actions. We must face the consequences of our ideas and actions. We can't blame society. As one author put it:

> If man's behavior were somehow conditioned by genetic code or social externals, then no just judge could blame him for the evil he commits. But Scripture teaches unequivocally that God blamed Adam and Eve for succumbing to the temptation to disobedience and punished them accordingly.[2]

The "fall" of Adam and Eve brought discord into the world. Harmony with God, ourselves, others, and nature was knocked out of sync. The result is that instead of reflecting God's love, we consistently break his two greatest commandments: to love God with all our heart, soul, mind, and strength; and to love others as ourselves (Luke 10:27).

Our relationships with God and others are broken and in need of healing. This is also true of the societies we form. But this doesn't mean Christians should have a negative view of society. In fact, Christians have the most cause to be hopeful because of the redemptive work of Jesus Christ. His power is greater than the power of sin.

"For I am not ashamed of this Good News about Christ," declared the apostle Paul. "It is the power of God at work, saving everyone who believes—the Jew first and also the Gentile" (Romans 1:16). The Bible declares that through God's grace we are made new: "This means that anyone who belongs to Christ has become a new person. The old life is gone; a new life has begun" (2 Corinthians 5:17).

Those who have been made new should not only be able to live better lives; we should help create better societies. We are not to hide our light under a basket but, "instead, a lamp is placed on a stand, where it gives light to everyone in the house. In the same way, let your good deeds shine out for all to see, so that everyone will praise your heavenly Father" (Matthew 5:15–16).

Worldviews that fail to understand the image of God in humankind, or our sinfulness, aren't able to identify and address the true causes of social problems. This is why they end up with the wrong solutions. There is a definite connection between how a worldview sees who we are (psychology) and how it sees society (sociology).

Part 3—Two Approaches

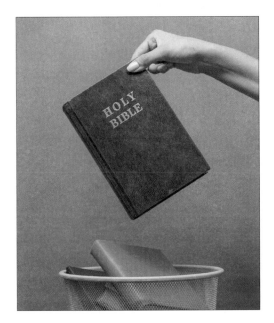

We will examine two basic approaches to understanding society. The first approach, the one taken by atheistic worldviews, holds that social institutions are more important than individuals. This approach is championed by secularism. Secularism is an atheistic and materialistic worldview that advocates for a public society free from the influence of religion. It assumes that humans can be ethical and moral without God. It is based on human reason alone. Anything to do with God or the supernatural is rejected.

Secularism insists that since God does not exist, our ethics should be based on human experience and not based on supposedly divine revelation. We must rely on science and human reason to solve societal problems. While people only live for 70 or 80 years, societies last for centuries. Therefore, secularists reason that societies are more important than individuals.

A second approach to understanding society comes from monotheistic worldviews like Christianity. Based on the Bible, Christianity says that every human being has inherent worth as an individual, not just as part of a larger society. Each person has an eternal soul and is created in God's image. In God's view, societies are here just for a moment, whereas individuals are eternal. Moreover, it is the individual who has been granted authority and responsibility for shaping the larger society. However, this does not downplay the importance of sociology. We were created to be social beings. Just as God has perfect relationships within the Trinity, humans as his image-bearers were also created for relationships. We enter into the first, and most important, of those relationships at birth.

> **Secularism**
> An atheistic and materialistic worldview that advocates for a public society free from the influence of religion

Topic 2—The Family

The family is one of the basic institutions of society. However, not all worldviews see the traditional family in the same way. Atheistic worldviews have very different attitudes about family than the biblical Christian worldview.

Part 1—Atheistic View of the Family

What do the atheistic worldviews say about the traditional family?

Secularism denies that there is a universal, absolute model for the family. What people call a normal family is simply a matter of individual choice or social agreement. Secularism sees the traditional notions of marriage and family as relics of outdated religious beliefs. They don't really care if people practice their religion privately; they just don't want religion dictating how others should live. Limiting marriage to just two adults of the opposite gender is too restrictive for a modern secular society. Adults should have the freedom to pursue alternatives like cohabitation, open marriage, polygamous marriage, same-sex marriage, and the like. Adults should be allowed, even encouraged, to form whatever type of relationship they believe works best for them. And they should have the freedom to raise children within those alternative families however they see fit. One leading

psychology professor even goes so far as to say, "Marriage and family life have been largely responsible . . . for today's prevailing neurotic climate . . . and it is precisely this climate that makes so difficult the acceptance of a different, healthier way of life."[3]

Marxism doesn't only want to abolish private property; the nuclear family must go as well. Marxists believe that the traditional family is an unnecessary holdover from capitalism. *The Communist Manifesto* says, "The bourgeois family will vanish as a matter of course when its complement vanishes, and both will vanish with the vanishing of capital."[4] Traditionally, having and raising children has been one of the primary purposes of marriage. Under Marxism, the government assumes the burden of educating children. So, marriage is no longer a necessary condition for children. And once communism is reached, the collective is ultimately responsible for child-rearing. Adults are free to copulate with whomever they wish. Without the burden of children, marriage is no longer vital.

Postmodernism denies the existence of truth and is very suspicious of any worldview that claims to know how the world really is. Since Christianity claims to be true, postmodernism is opposed to it and its teachings that limit marriage and family. The Christian worldview claims that God created the world and designed traditional marriage as the optimal institution for raising healthy children. Postmodernism rejects this. There is no God, and there is no design for the family or optimal family for raising children. Anyone who claims that the best marriage is one man and one woman devalues all other marriage and family formations. Traditional marriages and families aren't better or worse than any other. There is no right way to view love, sex, marriage, and family in a postmodern world. As one postmodernist psychiatrist says, "The only sane foregone conclusion about any relationship is that it is an experiment."[5] In other words, every marriage and family structure is just as good as the next.

Part 2—Christian View of the Family

The Christian worldview teaches that the family is the initial, and most vital, building block of society. When a man and a woman are joined together, they become "one flesh" (Genesis 2:24). This union is meant to last a lifetime, as Jesus affirmed: But 'God made them male and female' from the beginning of creation. 'This explains why a man leaves his father and mother and is joined to his wife, and the two are united into one.' Since they are no longer two but one, let no one split apart what God has joined together (Mark 10:6–9).

Christianity holds that the covenant of marriage and the institution of the family were ordained by God (Genesis 1:28, 2:23–25). They are designed to provide a loving environment that encourages mental, emotional, and spiritual growth. The basic unit has always been a husband, a wife, and their children. Although this structure may be altered through death, divorce, or infertility, these don't change the original family structure.

Scientific studies show that this family makeup is best for individuals and society. After surveying more than 130 studies, a leading professor of medicine concluded: "Married people live longer and generally are more emotionally and physically healthy than the unmarried."[6]

Traditional marriages have been the backbone of civilization. As one family researcher noted: "It can be demonstrated from history that no society has ever survived after its family life deteriorated."[7] The traditional man-and-woman marriage is good for society. According to extensive research done by United Families International, traditional marriage leads to:

- Better health and greater longevity
- Less crime, less violence
- Safer homes
- Safer communities
- Less poverty, more wealth
- Better intimate relations
- Less substance abuse and addiction
- Less hardship and better outcomes for children
- Less government, lower taxes
- More happiness[8]

Part 3—Christian Values under Attack

Despite these and other positive benefits, the traditional view of marriage and family has been under attack for decades in our society. There are social and legal pressures to change the definition of marriage and family. This push comes from the people who see the traditional family as outdated, believing that it inhibits sexual freedom. Atheists say we are only animals after all, and sex is just a natural physical drive we should express any way we want.

Today, children in sex-education classes are taught that homosexuality is a perfectly natural lifestyle. Students are given condoms and advised to use them. Teenage girls are instructed on how to get abortions without parental knowledge or consent. Two prominent evangelicals once described such sex-ed programs as "a crash course in relativism, in immorality, and in anti-Christian philosophy."[9]

What is being taught in public schools reflects the messages in popular culture that promote sexual immorality. Movies, TV shows, music, and social media encourage every form of sexual activity and having children out of wedlock. It's not surprising that attempts to redefine marriage and family are pushed by supporters of moral relativism (the belief that there are no objective moral norms that apply to everyone).

Besides attacking the traditional definition of family, atheistic worldviews also oppose its role in educating children. In the Bible, we see God giving parents the job of passing on a spiritual heritage to their offspring: And you must commit yourselves wholeheartedly to these commands that I am giving you today. Repeat them again and again to your children. Talk about them when you are at home and when you are on the road, when you are going to bed and when you are getting up (Deuteronomy 6:6–7).

Parents still have the ultimate responsibility for their children's education. But in a society that is deeply influenced by atheism, the state often claims greater authority over children than parents have. The state, not the family, controls what is taught in public schools. As a prominent American cleric writes,

> Any time you try to argue that someone, or some "institution," owns the family, you will end up viewing the family as just a human creation, a mere contract. If that's all it is, then there's no reason for the State not to violate it, just as it violates all sorts of private contracts. What principle is to prevent the State from taking a family's children, re-educating them, or breaking it up whenever it seems socially and politically expedient?[10]

The US educational system has long been a target of atheists. They see it as the primary way to influence young people with their naturalistic belief system. As far back as 1930, humanist Charles Francis Potter wrote, "Education is the most powerful ally of Humanism, and every American public school is a school of Humanism. What can the theistic Sunday-schools, meeting for an hour once a week, and teaching only a fraction of the children, do to stem the tide of a five-day program of humanistic teaching?"[11]

Because of this atheistic influence, many Christian parents choose to teach their children at home or enroll them in private Christian schools. It is their way of seeking to pass on a godly heritage to the next generation:

> We will not hide these truths from our children; we will tell the next generation about the glorious deeds of the LORD, about his power and his mighty wonders. For he issued his laws to Jacob; he gave his instructions to Israel. He commanded our ancestors to teach them to their children, so the next generation might know them—even the children not yet born—and they in turn will teach their own children. So each generation should set its hope anew on God, not forgetting his glorious miracles and obeying his commands.
>
> (Psalm 78:4–7)

Topic 3—The Church

Our word *church* comes from the Greek word *ekklesia*, which means *a called-out assembly or congregation*. From this original idea of church, the word went on to mean

- a local congregation of Christians
- a Christian denomination
- the building where believers meet

The church is the body of Christ on Earth (1 Corinthians 12:12–13). It is the primary channel God uses to share the good news and to make disciples (Matthew 28:19–20). We gather together as the church to learn more about our relationship with God and to become equipped to show his love to others. As Peter wrote, . . . *for you are a chosen people. You are royal priests, a holy nation, God's very own possession. As a result, you can show others the goodness of God, for he called you out of the darkness into his wonderful light* (1 Peter 2:9).

When it is healthy, the church

- teaches people about their ultimate need for fellowship with God (Romans 10:14–15),

- helps Christians grow as disciples and come to know God more fully (1 Peter 4:10–11),

- gives believers a context in which to worship God and enjoy fellowship together (Hebrews 10:24–25), and

- provides an example of what true community is (1 Peter 4:8–11).

Part 1—Salt and Light

Jesus calls his followers to be salt and light in our earthly societies (Matthew 5:13–16). This is something the church has done with varying degrees of success throughout history.

When the church was born, Roman civilization had brought peace to much of the world. But within 400 years, Rome fell to northern barbarians. During the next few centuries, chaos reigned in Europe. Cities and cultural centers disappeared. Literacy and law crumbled. But one force kept barbarism from completely taking over—the church.

The medieval church kept the spark of civilization alive. Monks preserved not only the Bible but classical literature as well. For example, during the seventh century in France, the clergy were the best-educated and reportedly the least immoral group in Europe. French monks ran schools and sheltered orphans, widows, and paupers. They built aqueducts, opened hospitals, and gained the respect of a population staggering under greedy and dishonest political leaders.[12]

The same was true in other European countries. Because Christians got involved in society, the Dark Ages gave way to the light of Christian culture. As one sociologist points out:

> It was during the so-called Dark Ages that Christian monks, throwing off the stultifying grip of Roman repression and mistaken Greek idealism, developed or improved innovations like the three-field system of agriculture, eyeglasses, the water wheel, and clocks. All of these remarkable developments can be traced to the unique Christian conviction that progress was a God-given obligation, entailed in the gift of reason.[13]

Social evils were addressed and changed by Christians such as missionary William Carey and William Wilberforce, a British statesman. He worked through church and government to end the slave trade in much of the world.[14]

Many other Christians made a difference in their spheres of influence, such as Abraham Kuyper (1837–1920). This Dutch theologian and pastor worked diligently to influence public life in the Netherlands. He founded a Christian university, published a newspaper, and was even elected prime minister. His social, political, and educational reforms benefit the Netherlands to this day.[15] Other examples could be given for many countries around the globe.

WILLIAM WILBERFORCE
1759–1833

Part 2—Dual Citizenship

A *citizen* is *a member of a state or nation*. Citizens owe allegiance to their government and are entitled to its protection.

The duties of citizenship include: obeying the laws of the country, respecting the rights of others, paying taxes, and defending the country when necessary. In return, citizens are granted certain rights. In the US, these include the rights to freedom of speech and worship; to vote in elections; to a fair trial by jury; and to life, liberty, and the pursuit of happiness.

Christians have dual citizenship. We are citizens of heaven (Philippians 3:20), but we also have a civic responsibility to be good citizens in our culture. Pastor Tony Evans says the church is made up of people who have been, "called out from the general population to serve in the parliament, congress, or counsel of the community in order to establish the governance, guidelines, rules, and regulations for the broader citizenry. To be a part of the church of Jesus Christ, as Jesus defined it, is to be a part of a spiritual legislative body tasked to enact heaven's viewpoint in hell's society."[16]

Christians are told to obey government leaders as being ordained by God: Everyone must submit to governing authorities. For all authority comes from God, and those in positions of authority have been placed there by God (Romans 13:1).

Paul tells us to pray for our civil rulers so that we may live at peace: I urge you, first of all, to pray for all people. Ask God to help them; intercede on their behalf, and give thanks for them. Pray this way for kings and all who are in authority so that we can live peaceful and quiet lives marked by godliness and dignity (1 Timothy 2:1–2).

Yet if our leaders ask us to do anything that conflicts with God's Word, we must obey God rather than any human authority (Acts 5:29). In every ocassion we should do things in such a way that everyone can see you are honorable. Do all that you can to live in peace with everyone (Romans 12:17–18).

Conclusion

Sociology is the study of how human beings live with each other. The premise of Christian sociology is that society functions best when it is organized around the family (father, mother, and children) and supported by the church.

Christian sociology recognizes the value of every person as God's image-bearer. It strives to maintain the balance in society among the God-ordained institutions of family, church, and state. Atheistic worldviews want to dismantle and reorganize these institutions. They see religion and the traditional family as holdovers from a prescientific age that hinder human growth. They view the biblical teachings about the sinfulness of humans and the need for a broken world to be redeemed as destructive. Humans are inherently good, they insist, and society has to evolve to allow us to reach our full potential.

The Christian worldview, on the other hand, teaches that we are sinful and selfish. Evil in our societies is rooted in the human heart. When human hearts are changed through the saving power of God's grace, our societies will change. The vehicles through which this can happen are the family and the church.

Christian author and professor Andy Crouch challenges us to take an active role in making society better:

I wonder what we Christians are known for in the world outside our churches. Are we known as critics, consumers, copiers, condemners of culture? I'm afraid so. Why aren't we known as cultivators—people who tend and nourish what is best in human culture, who do the hard and painstaking work to preserve the best of what people before us have done? Why aren't we known as creators—people who dare to think and do something that has never been thought or done before, something that makes the world more welcoming and thrilling and beautiful?[17]

What would taking this challenge to heart mean in your life?

ENDNOTES

1 Karl Marx and Frederick Engels, *The Individual and Society* (Moscow: Progress Publishers, 1984), 162.
2 William A. Stanmeyer, *Clear and Present Danger* (Ann Arbor, MI: Servant Books, 1983), 42.
3 Robert Rimmer, "An Interview with Robert Rimmer on Premarital Communes and Group Marriages," *The Humanist* (March/April 1974): 14.
4 Karl Marx and Friedrich Engels, *The Communist Manifesto* (New York: Penguin Books, 2002), 240.
5 Algis Valiunas, "Mental Health," *The Weekly Standard* 11, no. 9 (November 14, 2005): 41.

6 "Several Studies Link Good Health With Religious Belief, Prayer," AP Wire Service, *Statesville Record & Landmark* (February 13, 1996): 8–A.

7 Paul Popenoe, quoted in "Behavior: The American Family: Future Uncertain," *Time* (December 28, 1970): 34.

8 Marcia Barlow, *A Guide to Family Issues: The Marriage Advantage*, (Gilbert, AZ: United Families International, 2008), 33–77, https://www.unitedfamilies.org/wp-content/uploads/2015/09/Marriage-Guide.pdf.

9 James C. Dobson and Gary L. Bauer, *Children at Risk: The Battle for the Hearts and Minds of Our Kids* (Dallas, TX: Word, 1990), 112.

10 Ray Sutton, *Who Owns the Family? God or the State?* (Nashville, TN: Dominion Press, 1986), 3.

11 Charles Francis Potter, *Humanism: A New Religion* (New York, NY: Simon and Schuster, 1930), 128.

12 William Grimes, review of *The Victory of Reason: How Christianity Led to Freedom, Capitalism and Western Success*, by Rodney Stark, *New York Times*, Jan. 22, 2006, https://www.nytimes.com/2006/01/22/arts/the-victory-of-reason-how-christianity-led-to-freedom-capitalism-and.html.

13 Ibid.

14 Hugh Thomas, *The Slave Trade: The Story of the Atlantic Slave Trade: 1440–1870* (New York: Simon and Schuster, 1999), 550.

15 Charles Colson, *Against the Night* (Ann Arbor, MI: Servant Books, 1989), 133–4.

16 Tony Evans, *Oneness Embraced* (Chicago: Moody, 2011), 251.

17 Andy Crouch, *Culture Making: Recovering Our Creative Calling*, (Downers Grove, IL: IVP Books, 2013), 97.

Application Story: The Dog Park

I can't wait! We're almost there! I can smell it!

The feel of the wind on my face is so refreshing. I open my mouth and let my tongue hang out. After being cooped up in the house day after day . . . this is pure bliss.

And, it's a rare treat. My master isn't cruel, he's just rarely around. He leaves early in the morning most days, and comes home long enough to feed me and let me out to relieve myself before leaving again. When he finally comes home for the night, he stumbles into the house and collapses onto his bed . . . if he makes it that far. Sometimes he sleeps on the couch, or even the floor.

But today—oh glorious day!—he's taking me to the dog park! I'll have to figure out what I did to earn his favor so I can—ahhhh! A squirrel! C'mon, Master! Get this car parked so I can go chase it.

Bark! Bark! Bark!

"Shut up, Thor!"

I stop immediately, although I really, REALLY, want to go after that squirrel. It's so close . . . but Master will be angry with me, and I definitely don't want to upset him. He might take us back home.

The car finally stops and Master opens the door. I wait for him to attach the leash, then I leap out of the car. A minute later, we're past the pair of gates and inside dog heaven! A pair of retrievers and a large poodle greet me with a round of sniffing. Master pushes them aside and removes my leash. And with that, I'm gone!

I'm still making my way around the perimeter and marking my territory when a brown English bulldog makes her way over to me. "Hey, there big guy. Do you remember me?"

I cock my head to the side. She smells familiar. "Helga, right? We met last time I was here."

"That's right. Not bad for a Rottie. And here I thought your breed was all muscle and no brains."

"Ha. That's funny coming from a bulldog," I tease in return. My gaze is drawn toward a group of young German Shepherds tearing off after a ball thrown by one of the humans. "Don't they ever get tired of that?"

"Obviously not," Helga said. She turned to look at them and I can see one of her long canine teeth sticking out from her jowls. "Then again, that's what their human alpha expects from their pack."

"Speaking of that, where's your human?"

"Over there," Helga points with her snout toward a middle-aged blonde woman dressed in a T-shirt and jeans. Two preteen girls stand nearby petting a couple of other dogs.

"Are those her cubs?" I ask.

"Yep. They're part of my pack. Whenever they're home, we spend all our time together."

I try to imagine what that would be like. I think back to those rare moments when Master pets me. What would it be like to have that all the time from multiple humans? "You're lucky to have them."

Helga snorts. "Yeah, but it wasn't always that way."

"What do you mean?"

"My human and her mate would fight constantly, and sometimes he would take out his anger on me. I spent many long nights recovering from his abuse. It was even worse when I would see Master or her cubs crying. I did what I could to comfort them.

"But one day, he left. After that, a strange thing happened to Master. Once a week, she would get herself and the girls all dressed up and leave the house in the morning. It was different from their normal routine. And when they returned, they carried with them a different set of smells. Their scents changed. They no longer gave off the musky odor of sadness. They smelled joyful. They go to the same place at least once every week."

Speaking of smells, something in the grass catches my attention. I flop onto my back and roll in it. The sunlight warms my belly. "Did she ever say the name of the place?"

"Yes. Its name is kind of like the sound you make when you sneeze. CHERCH!"

I roll back to my paws. "This cherch sounds like a great place. And it's a good thing her mate is no longer around to hurt you."

Helga looks down at me. "That's the weirdest thing. He came back a few months ago, but he had the same smells on him that Master and the cubs get when they go to cherch. And even more, he acts differently. He doesn't fight with Master nearly as much as he used to. When they do fight, he doesn't hurt us anymore. He's changed. He—look out!"

Helga's warning sends me leaping to my feet—my senses on high alert. Rapid movement to my left causes me to turn just in time to see a snarling Labrador barreling toward me. The attacker hits me full force and knocks me backward. His teeth are dangerously close to my neck, but I'm able to twist out from under his weight. Now that I'm back on my feet, I square off with him.

"What's your problem?" I growl.

"This is my territory! I marked it before you arrived. Now get out of here!"

"I don't think so." I'm a Rottweiler. I don't get bullied easily. I lunge at him, and he dodges. I hit him on the side of his head with one of my heavy paws. He retaliates with a snap of his teeth. A human leg pushes me to the side while another pushes the Lab in the opposite direction. Soon, strong hands grab my collar and pull me back.

"You need to control your dog!" Master shouts at the other human.

"What are you talking about? Your dog started it!"

The two humans begin to yell at each other until Helga's Master and several other humans intervene. While Master is distracted, Helga comes up next to me.

"Are you okay?"

"Yeah. What's with that Lab?"

Helga glances over at the dog, who was now being held down by his Master. "I've seen him a few times. He's wild. His human alpha has the same scent as my Master's mate used to have. I think it has to do with training. You know how they train us to obey? I think some humans need that as well. I think that's what happened to my Master and her mate. I think they go to cherch once a week for training. When they learn to control themselves, the pack is happier. Unfortunately, that Lab and his Master lack training, and the world is a more dangerous place because of it."

I stand motionless, stunned by her words.

"C'mon, Thor. We're leaving."

Master begins walking toward the exit and I have no choice but to follow. I glance back at Helga, her words still echoing in my mind. I never thought about the fact that human alphas might need training also. I guess even they have wild natures and instincts that need correction. I can only hope someone convinces my Master to go to cherch to get the training he needs.

Getting Started—Superman or Jesus?

Five-year-old Jessie whirled the Superman™ action figure through the air in front of his older brother. Dean was sitting on the bed reading his Bible, something he did a lot these days.

"Who's stronger, Superman or Jesus?" Jessie asked. His brother was 10 years older and knew everything.

Dean looked up and returned his brother's earnest stare. "They're not the same. Jesus is a real person. Superman is pretend."

"Superman is real," Jessie protested. "I've seen him in movies and comic books."

"That's an actor pretending to be Superman. And comic books are fiction. This, on the other hand, is history." Dean tapped the Bible.

Jessie looked puzzled. "What's history?"

"History means something that really happened," Dean said. "It's a record of past events that can be studied and checked. It's not made up."

"Is that a history book?" Jessie pointed at the Bible.

"Not exactly, but it has a lot of history in it, including facts about Jesus, like where he was born and how he died."

"Superman was born in Kryptonopolis," Jessie said.

Dean sighed. "There's no such place. But you can visit where Jesus was born; it's a town called Bethlehem. You can walk where he walked and hear what he said because some of his friends wrote it down."

"Did Jesus fly?" Jessie asked.

"Probably not," Dean admitted. "There is no evidence in the Bible that he did."

"Did he stop bullets?"

"Well, they didn't have guns back then, so probably not."

"What was his superpower then?"

Dean thought for a moment, and then said, "Love."

Jessie frowned. "That's not a superpower."

"It is the way Jesus did it," Dean said. "His love changed the world. We can see it at work throughout history from his day to ours."

Dean took the action figure from Jessie. He held it in one hand and the Bible in the other. He raised the figure. "Superman is a story—fiction." Then he lifted the Bible. "Jesus is history—fact."

Jessie nodded. "So they're both superheroes, right?"

Dean smiled. "Most definitely."

The Power of Story

Stories are how we make sense of the world. They guide us through life just as the stars and constellations guided ancient explorers across uncharted seas. Stories are told in various forms—fables and fairytales, poems and songs, epics and comics, plays and movies.

During prehistoric times—the time before written history—stories were shared orally. Storytellers didn't report like journalists do today. They used myths and stories to give a memorable structure to the truth they wanted to pass along. Their stories were rooted in reality but the details were crafted to make a point. And that point usually had to do with a big idea. Think of it like a spear, with the point being the idea and the story being the weighty shaft that drives it home.

Humanity went from prehistoric (oral) to historic (written) times around 3400–3100 BC when writing developed in Mesopotamia, Egypt, and, later, in China and in Peru. Written records solved the problem of details being changed by the storyteller. And writing provided something more—accurate records of past events, or history. History is *the study of the past, with a view to how it affects the present.*

Certain people and events show us ideas worth pursuing and errors worth avoiding. As a famous philosopher once said, "Those who cannot remember the past are condemned to repeat it."[1]

> **History**
> The study of the past, with a view to how it affects the present

Topic 1—What's the Big Idea?

History tends to focus on the big ideas that humans have always thought about: How did everything get here?—creation stories. Who controls what happens to us?—God stories. How do we relate to the world around us?—nature stories. What makes for a meaningful life?—moral stories.

Big ideas exert a pull that shapes our thoughts in the same way a magnet pulls iron filings into a pattern. Take the big idea of personal freedom. *Freedom* is *the ability to live as one chooses without undue interference.* The Bible records one of the first quests for freedom in the book of Exodus. The Hebrews had been in captivity and forced into slavery in Egypt for hundreds of years. Over three thousand years ago, they rebelled against Pharaoh, and with God's grace Moses led the Hebrews out of Egypt to freedom.

The idea of freedom spurred the gladiator Spartacus in 73–71 BC to lead his fellow slaves in a rebellion against their Roman masters.

A thousand years later, the desire for freedom motivated Christians from Europe to march into the Middle East to free fellow Christians who were under the thumb of Islam in what became known as *the Crusades*.

Around AD 1297, it led a Scottish peasant named *William Wallace* to defy the king of Britain. As interpreted by the film *Braveheart*, Wallace's last word as he was being tortured to death was the cry of "Freedom!"

RECONSTRUCTION OF THE PLYMOUTH COLONY ESTABLISHED IN THE 17TH CENTURY

Desire for freedom led the Puritan pilgrims to sail to the shores of America in 1620. That same spirit gave our founding fathers the courage to put their lives on the line for a world-changing Declaration of Independence. "Four score and seven years" later, the country fought a civil war to free the slaves. More than a century after that, the Civil Rights Movement sought to make that freedom real for African Americans who were still excluded from mainstream society.

Different continents. Different centuries. Different people. A common idea. Freedom was, and is, an idea worth fighting for!

As we said in the first lesson of this book, "Ideas have consequences, both good and bad. Ideas form our beliefs, shape our convictions, and solidify into habits of behavior." Once we grasp the main ideas that have shaped the past, history becomes relevant to the present.

Why? Because the big issues in life don't change. The names change—who did what. The technology becomes more sophisticated— from gramophones to smartphones. But the basic ideas remain the same.

There are important lessons to learn from the past. Even the Bible tells us so. In referring to events recorded in the Old Testament, Paul said, These things happened to them as examples for us. They were written down to warn us who live at the end of the age (1 Corinthians 10:11). In fact, the Bible gives far more space to historical events than to theological ideas, perhaps because human experience is such a great teacher.

The ancient Hebrews did an excellent job of recording history. According to a professor of ancient Middle Eastern history: "In terms of general reliability . . . the Old Testament comes out remarkably well."[2]

Whether it's secular history or biblical history, the same overarching story is being told, just from different angles. It's the story of humanity. Our focus in this chapter will be on the Christian approach to history and its main events. We will look at these questions:
   What's unique about the biblical view of history?
   Did all the events in the Bible really happen?
   Are the Gospels historically reliable?
   Did Jesus really rise from the dead?

Part 1—A Linear Progression

The Bible takes a unique approach to history for its time. It treats history as following a chronological pattern of cause and effect. It tells a story with a beginning, a middle, and an end. History isn't a repetition of endless cycles as was commonly believed in the ancient world. Still today, some worldviews like Hinduism see history as going in circles. Events endlessly repeat without ever reaching a final goal. The concept of reincarnation is an example of this cyclical process.

The biblical worldview sees history as linear. The linear view of history says our story is progressing in a straight line toward a specific end. It has a predetermined flow and focus.

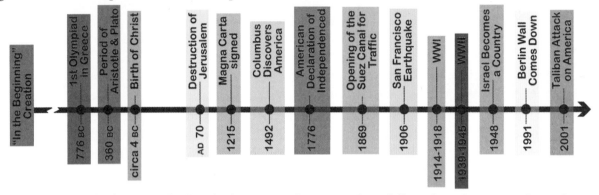

The Bible opens with these words, "In the beginning." Its story line follows key characters through time and peaks at the resurrection of Jesus. It looks ahead to the climax of history at his return (John 5:28, 29; Titus 2:11–13). He will bring about new heavens and a new earth (Revelation 21–22).

Jesus Christ was an actual person who lived at a certain time, in a certain place, and was written about by certain eyewitnesses. One of those eyewitnesses was the apostle John, who was one of the first disciples Jesus chose to follow him. He wrote stating, we proclaim to you the one who existed from the beginning, whom we have heard and seen. We saw him with our own eyes and touched him with our own hands. He is the Word of life. This one who is life itself was revealed to us, and we have seen him. And now we testify and proclaim to you that he is the one who is eternal life. He was with the Father, and then he was revealed to us (1 John 1:1–2).

Before we dig into the Christian worldview, let's look briefly at how the four worldviews we've been considering approach history.

Part 2—Nonbiblical Worldviews

Our view of the past is influenced by our worldviews and their assumptions. Sometimes people use history to advance their own agendas rather than to search for truth. They tend to look for what supports the story they believe and to ignore what contradicts it. Sometimes they do this unconsciously based upon their preconceptions. A preconception is *an idea or opinion formed before enough information is available to make a valid conclusion.*

Here are the main preconceptions behind these leading worldviews.

Secularism assumes history is all about social progress. It holds that society will continually improve through human effort. Progress is inevitable because it is built into the laws of nature. Most secularists see a future paradise on Earth brought about through science, human intellect, and technology.

Marxism understands history through the lenses of atheism, and something called *historical materialism*. This is the idea that history is driven by the class struggle between the haves and have-nots. Societies will move from capitalism, through socialism, to a classless, stateless utopia of communism.

Postmodernism doesn't believe in objective facts. It sees all historical accounts as fiction made up by biased historians to support the positions of those in power. Because some radical postmodernists don't see any purpose to the study of history, they hold to something called *nihilism—the belief that the world and human existence are without meaning, purpose, or value.*

New Spirituality claims history is the record of our spiritual evolution toward godhood. The focus is on the future when we will all realize our divinity. The only reason to look back is to realize the dogmas we have outgrown. As popular new spiritualist Joseph Campbell writes, "The old-time religion belongs to another age, another people, another set of human values, another universe. By going back you throw yourself out of sync with history."[3]

> **Preconception**
> An idea or opinion formed before enough
> information is available to make a valid conclusion

Part 3—The Biblical Metanarrative

From the Christian perspective, history is a beautiful unfolding of God's ultimate plan for humanity. The Bible tells a cosmic metanarrative that begins at the creation of the universe. A *metanarrative*, as you'll recall, is *an overarching story of events that provides a structure for people's beliefs and gives meaning to their experiences.* The biblical metanarrative has four parts—creation, fall, redemption, and restoration.

Creation: The story begins with God creating all things (Genesis 1, 2). He made man and woman in his image and gave them authority over the world (Genesis 1:26–28). He set boundaries for the first human pair by forbidding them to eat of one particular tree (Genesis 2:16–17).

Fall: Adam and Eve chose to disobey God and ate from the Tree of the Knowledge of Good and Evil (Genesis 3:6). This resulted in: separation from God (Genesis 3:8, 23), a curse upon the earth (Genesis 3:17), and the passing on of a sinful nature to all humans (Romans 3:23).

Redemption: God promised a Messiah who will restore his people to wholeness (Isaiah 53:4–6). Then, at just the right time, he sent Jesus to pay for our sins (Galatians 4:4–7). Jesus not only saves us from God's wrath to come (1 Thessalonians 1:9–10), he frees us from bondage to sin even now (Romans 6:6, 17–18).

Restoration: At an appointed time in the future (Acts 17:31), God will bring all humanity before Jesus for reward or punishment (Matthew 25:31-46; Romans 2:12–16). Redemption will be complete with the resurrection of our bodies (Romans 8:22–23), the renewal of all creation (Revelation 21:1–7), and the lifting of the curse of sin (Revelation 22:3).

The parts of this metanarrative that took place during recorded history—during the kingdom of Israel in the Old Testament and the life of Jesus in the New Testament—are based on facts. The biblical authors wrote about what actually happened as God worked in the lives of real men and women, and recorded the promises he made about what is yet to come.

Topic 2—Did All That Stuff Really Happen?

Christianity makes specific claims about past events, especially those written about in the Bible. These claims are open to scrutiny by friends and foes alike. Central to the Bible's message is the person of Jesus Christ. Either he is a historical figure who lived, died, and rose from the dead or the Christian faith is bankrupt: And if Christ has not been raised, then all our preaching is useless, and your faith is useless. And we apostles would all be lying about God—for we have said that God raised Christ from the grave. But that can't be true if there is no resurrection of the dead (1 Corinthians 15:14-15).

We can't look at all the Bible in this chapter, so we'll focus on the Gospels—Matthew, Mark, Luke, and John. These are just legends written by zealous Christians who didn't know any better—right?

Wrong!

Popular preacher and author Tim Keller summarizes why this isn't so:

> The Gospels' form precludes their being legends. The biblical Gospels are not legends but historically reliable accounts about Jesus' life. Why? 1) Their timing is far too early for them to be legends. The Gospels were written 30–60 years after Jesus' death—and Paul's letters, which support all the accounts, came just 20 years after the events. 2) Their content is far too counterproductive to be legends. The accounts of Jesus crying out that God had abandoned him, or the resurrection where all the witnesses were women—did not help Christianity in the eyes of first-century readers. The only historically plausible reason that these incidents are recorded is that they happened.[4]

There are at least three lines of evidence supporting the assertion that the Gospels are historically true. The first two relate to material inside the New Testament itself and are referred to as *internal evidence*. Internal evidence is *evidence from Scripture that supports the claims of the Bible*. The third line is external evidence, which we will consider in a few pages.

> **Internal Evidence**
> Evidence from Scripture that supports
> the claims of the Bible

Part 1—Internal Evidence

Internal Evidence #1: The gospel authors wrote about actual events.
The gospel authors were interested in researching and preserving what actually happened:

Many people have set out to write accounts about the events that have been fulfilled among us. They used the eyewitness reports circulating among us from the early disciples. Having carefully investigated everything from the beginning, I also have decided to write an accurate account for you, most honorable Theophilus, so you can be certain of the truth of everything you were taught (Luke 1:1–4).

The early Christians valued eyewitness testimony so much that the apostles were required to be men who had actually seen Jesus (Acts 1:21–22). Their preaching and writing were based on what they had personally experienced (2 Peter 1:16, 1 John 1:1–3). They also appealed to the eyewitness knowledge of countless others, as one biblical scholar points out:

> [O]ne of the strong points in the original apostolic preaching is the confident appeal to the knowledge of the hearers; they not only said, "We are witnesses of these things," but also, "As you yourselves also know" (Acts 2:22). Had there been any tendency to depart from the facts in any material respect, the possible presence of hostile witnesses in the audience would have served as a further corrective.[5]

Even the apostle Paul, who did not see Jesus during his earthly ministry, was granted a vision of the Lord so he could testify as an eyewitness (1 Corinthians 15:3–8).

Internal Evidence #2: The Gospels were written within the lifetime of eyewitnesses.
This second line of evidence expands on the eyewitness aspect of the Gospels. They were written during a time when they could be corroborated or contradicted by people who were still alive. Interestingly, the authors of the Gospels supported one another unintentionally with obscure details between the accounts.

Both the gospel of Luke and the book of Acts were written by Luke—a physician and companion of Paul's. The book of Acts ends while Paul is still in Rome. It never mentions his death, which probably took place between AD 61–64.[6] Given Luke's attention to the deaths of other important church leaders (Acts 7:54–8:1), Paul's death would surely have been mentioned. Therefore, Acts must have been written before AD 64.

Luke wrote his gospel before writing Acts (Luke 1:1–4, Acts 1:1–3). This means it was also written before AD 64. And since Luke consulted other accounts of Jesus' life (Luke 1:1–4), it's possible he made use of Mark's gospel. Most scholars believe Mark is the earliest gospel. If so, we can date Mark even earlier than Luke and Acts.

There are several other factors supporting a date earlier than AD 70 for the Gospels. One of the most significant is the destruction of Jerusalem and its temple in AD 70. The event shook Judaism and Christianity to the core, but the Gospels never mention it.

Based on this evidence in the Gospels themselves, they were probably written within 30–40 years of the events they record. This is well within the life span of eyewitnesses, who could have corrected any exaggerations or mistakes.

J. Warner Wallace also offers the following summary of the internal evidence:

The Gospels were written as eyewitness accounts within the long and rich evidential tradition of the early Christian community. The early Church placed a high value on the evidence provided by Jesus and the authority of the apostles as eyewitnesses. The Gospels were accepted and affirmed due largely to their status as eyewitness accounts. This authority was inherent to the Gospels, commissioned by Jesus, affirmed by the Gospel authors, confirmed by the first believers, foundational to the growth of the [c]hurch and used to validate the New Testament canon.[7]

Part 2—External Evidence

The internal evidence for the historical reliability of the Gospels is also supported by external evidence, which is *evidence outside the Bible that confirms the historical reliability of Scripture.* That evidence includes:

- Archaeology corroborates many people, locations, and events described in the Gospels.
- Ancient Jewish, Greek, and pagan accounts corroborate the outline of Jesus' identity, life, death, and resurrection.
- The gospel authors correctly identified minor, local geographic features, and cities in the region of the accounts.
- The gospel authors correctly cited the ancient proper names used by people in the region of the accounts.
- Much of the Gospels (and all the critical features of Jesus' life) can be confirmed in the writings of the [c]hurch [f]athers.
- The vast number of ancient copies of the Gospels can be compared with one another to identify and eliminate late additions and copyist variants within the text.
- The earliest caretakers of the text considered it to be a precise, divinely inspired document worthy of careful preservation.[8]

One of the most valuable sources of external evidence is archaeology. *Archaeology* has to do with *the physical evidences of past societies recovered through excavation.* We can't detail all the archaeological discoveries made in relation to the New Testament, but we will mention two important finds.

1. Peter's house (Mark 1:29, Luke 7:44), has been discovered in ancient Capernaum:

Considerable material has been brought to light at Capernaum, some of which bears on the location of Peter's house and his association with the mission among his fellow Jews. The house was built about the first century BC. It became a center of religious activity, a house church or meeting house, already in the second half of the first century AD. *Minim* (as the Jewish Christians were later called) were numerous and lived continuously in Capernaum and kept alive this tradition; their graffiti on the plastered wall of the place of worship testify to their faith in Jesus, the Christ, the Lord, the Most High and God, and to their veneration for Peter, the local saint.[9]

THE ARCHAEOLOGICAL SITE OF PETER'S HOUSE IN CAPERNAUM. JESUS PROBABLY STAYED WITH PETER AND HIS FAMILY WHILE IN CAPERNAUM. THE PILGRIMAGE CHURCH OF SAINT PETER WAS BUILT OVER THE ANCIENT REMAINS.

2. Pontius Pilate was the governor of Judea who ordered the execution of Jesus (Matthew 27:2, 11–26; John 18:28–19:16). In 1961, physical evidence was first uncovered about Pilate's rule:

THE PILATE STONE IN CAESAREA MARITIMA
INSCRIPTION READS:
THIS BUILDING - TIBERIUM
BY PONTIUS PILATUS
PREFECT OF JUDEA
HAS BEEN BUILT

> In 1961, a team of Italian archaeologists was digging in Caesarea, on the shore of the beautiful Mediterranean Sea in Israel. While clearing away the sand and overgrowth from the jumbled ruins of a Roman theater, these archaeologists made an astonishing find. They uncovered a limestone block that bore an inscription in Latin dating to the early part of the first century that mentioned "Pontius Pilate, Prefect of Judea."[10]

External Evidence
Evidence outside the Bible that confirms the historical reliability of Scripture

Part 3—Following the Evidence

Whether we look at the internal evidence in the New Testament or look outside its pages to the archeological finds, there's abundant proof that the events recorded therein are historically accurate. In the words of a Yale University archaeologist, "Archeological work has unquestionably strengthened confidence in the reliability of the scriptural record. More than one archeologist has found respect for the Bible increased by the experience of excavation in Palestine."[11]

Sir William Ramsay was one such archaeologist and historian. We can see how the evidence changed Ramsay's worldview as recorded in the online book, *Archeological Evidence*:

> Ramsay was very skeptical of the accuracy of the New Testament, and he ventured to Asia Minor over a century ago to refute its historicity. He especially took interest in Luke's accounts in the Gospel of Luke and the Book of Acts, which contained numerous geographical and historic references. Dig after dig the evidence without fail supported Luke's accounts. . . . Ramsay became so overwhelmed with the evidence he eventually converted to Christianity. Ramsay finally had this to say: "I began with a mind unfavorable to it . . . but more recently I found myself brought into contact with the Book of Acts as an authority for the topography, antiquities, and society of Asia Minor. It was gradually borne upon me that in various details the narrative showed marvelous truth."[12]

The evidence has converted not just archaeologists but a number of skeptics as well. Some, like author Josh McDowell, have gone on to promote the faith they once tried to disprove.

> As a young scholar I asked this question: How can I prove that Christianity is false? I traveled to many libraries in the US and Europe in my search to find the answer. After trying to shatter the historicity, validity, and authenticity of the Scriptures, I came to the conclusion that the Bible is historically trustworthy. I also discovered that if one discards the Bible as being unreliable, then one must discard almost immediately all literature of antiquity. . . . One must apply the same test, whether the literature under investigation is secular or religious. Having done this, I believe we can hold the New Testament in our hands and say, "It is trustworthy and historically reliable."[13]

Topic 3—The Resurrection of Jesus

Christianity stands or falls on one thing—the resurrection of Jesus. It's what sets Christianity apart from every other religion. Every other religious leader in history has left a body in a tomb somewhere. But Jesus' tomb is empty, proving he is who he said he is. Of course, atheists and naturalists deny the resurrection because of its supernatural nature. They might admit Jesus was a great moral teacher but they won't accept his deity or bodily resurrection.

What kind of historical evidence do Christians have to support the resurrection of Jesus? The internal evidence from the Gospels includes these details:

- Jesus' death was predicted (John 2:19–21, 10:10–11; Isaiah 53:5–10).
- He died on the cross in front of many eyewitnesses (Mark 15:37, 44–45; John 19:34).
- His body was sealed in the tomb of a well-known Jewish leader (Matthew 27:57–61, Mark 15:42–47).
- Over 36 hours later, when the tomb was visited, Jesus' body was no longer there (Matthew 28:1–8, Luke 24:1–10).
- The apostles and many other disciples met the resurrected Jesus (John 20:16–18, Luke 24:13–49, Acts 1:3–4).
- The attitude of the disciples was transformed from cowardice and despair to great hope and boldness (Acts 2:42–47).
- All the apostles except John died martyrs' deaths because they believed in a risen Christ.

Only the resurrection of Jesus can explain the abrupt turnaround of the apostles from betrayers and cowards to missionaries and martyrs. Even James, the brother of Jesus, had a radical change of heart after the resurrection and became a leader in the Jerusalem church.

The resurrection also explains the dramatic conversion of opponents of Christianity like Saul, who became the apostle Paul (Acts 21:39–22:21). From that time until now, millions of people from around the world have followed these apostles, disciples, and early opponents in experiencing the power of the resurrection.

If the story of Jesus' resurrection were not true, it would be rather difficult to imagine so many eyewitnesses dying for a story they made up. If they were mistaken, then we could believe they gave their lives for something they thought was true. But if they were lying about Jesus' resurrection . . . if they invented the story . . . it's difficult to believe they would have all given their lives for a story they fabricated.

The resurrection truly changes everything. It's more than a factual event that happened two thousand years ago. It's a present reality: All praise to God, the Father of our Lord Jesus Christ. It is by his great mercy that we have been born again, because God raised Jesus Christ from the dead. Now we live with great expectation (1 Peter 1:3). "The point of the resurrection," as Bishop N. T. Wright says:

Is that the present bodily life is not valueless just because it will die . . . What you do with your body in the present matters because God has a great future in store for it . . . What you do in the present—by painting, preaching, singing, sewing, praying, teaching, building hospitals, digging wells, campaigning for justice, writing poems, caring for the needy, loving your neighbor as yourself—will last into God's future. These activities are not simply ways of making the present life a little less beastly, a little more bearable . . . They are part of what we may call building for God's kingdom.[14]

Conclusion

Based on the Bible, which is a historically reliable source of information, the Christian believes God has a plan and a purpose that can be traced throughout history. In Acts 17:26–28 we read that: From one man he created all the nations throughout the whole earth. He decided beforehand when they should rise and fall, and he determined their boundaries. His purpose was for the nations to seek after God and perhaps feel their way toward him and find him—though he is not far from any one of us. For in him we live and move and exist.

Not only does God's plan affect all of humanity; it affects all of us as individuals. We are living in the flow of what God is doing. He is active in us, as Paul told the believers in Ephesus, For we are God's masterpiece. He has created us anew in Christ Jesus, so we can do the good things he planned for us long ago (Ephesians 2:10).

This truth gives great meaning to every moment of our lives. We have a part to play in history. God is the author of the story and we are the actors who are to study and follow his script:

Indeed, the curtain on the stage of history has already fallen, and we believers know how the story ends. We know that Christ is coming back and time as we know it will one day be over. But that does not absolve us of the responsibility to faithfully carry out our God-given daily tasks. Some of us are called to feed the animals on a farm and others are called to plan some great campaign that may benefit history a hundred years from now. Deep in our hearts we know Christ is coming back, time will come to an end, and our plans for tomorrow may never come to fruition. But it doesn't matter. The important thing is this: that we were at our post when the inspection comes.[15]

ENDNOTES

1 George Santayana, *The Life of Reason* (Middlesex: Echo Library, 2006), 131.

2 K. A. Kitchen, *On the Reliability of the Old Testament* (Grand Rapids: Eerdmans, 2003), 500.

3 Joseph Campbell, *The Power of Myth* (New York: Doubleday, 1988), 18.

4 Tim Keller, "Can We Trust the Bible?," *Daily Keller—Wisdom from Tim Keller 365 Days a Year* (blog), March 24, 2015, https://dailykeller.com/can-we-trust-the-bible/.

5 F. F. Bruce, *The New Testament Documents: Are They Reliable?* (Downers Grove, IL: InterVarsity Press, 1960), 46.

6 E. P. Sanders, "St. Paul the Apostle," Britannica.com, accessed August 12, 2020, https://www.britannica.com/biography/Saint-Paul-the-Apostle.

7 J. Warner Wallace, "Is the Bible True? The Cumulative Case for the Reliability of the Gospels," February 15, 2019, https://coldcasechristianity.com/writings/is-the-bible-true-the-cumulative-case-for-the-reliability-of-the-gospels-free-bible-insert/.

8 J. Warner Wallace, "The Case for the Eyewitness Status of the Gospel Authors," June 1, 2018, https://coldcasechristianity.com/writings/the-case-for-the-eyewitness-status-of-the-gospel-authors/.

9 Gaalyah Cornfeld and David Noel Freedman, *Archaeology and the Bible: Book by Book* (New York: Harper and Row, 1976), 280.

10 Charles Campbell, "Can We Trust the Bible?," accessed August 10, 2020, https://alwaysbeready.com/can-we-trust-the-bible/#archaeology.

11 Millar Burrows, *What Mean These Stones* (Living Age Books: 1957), 1.

12 Fred Williams, *Evidences of the Bible*, "Archeological Evidence," https://bibleevidences.com/archaeological-evidence/.

13 Sheri Bell, "Archeology Helps to Confirm the Historicity of the Bible," January 31, 2018, https://www.josh.org/archeology-validates-bible/?mwm_id=241874010215&mot=J79GNF&gclid=EAIaIQobChMI_MOstuHo6AIVXPzjBx0ErgPKEAMYASAAEgJSwfD_BwE.

14 N. T. Wright, *Surprised by Hope: Rethinking Heaven, the Resurrection, and the Mission of the Church*, (Grand Rapids, MI, Zondervan, 2010), 193.

15 Alex McFarland in a lecture for Summit Ministries (paraphrasing C. S. Lewis' essay "The World's Last Night"). Cited in Jeff Myers, "We Know How the Story Ends," https://www.summit.org/resources/articles/we-know-how-the-story-ends/, November 5, 2015.

Application Story: Hidden Treasure

"There you are. I've been looking all over for you."

Uri looked up from the scroll he had been studying to see his younger brother had entered the tent. "Greetings, Joel. I'm glad you came to visit me! I finished copying the book of Daniel just today. Look, it's—"

"There's no time for that," Joel said before his brother could finish the thought. The urgency in Joel's voice drove all playful banter from Uri's mind. "Father sent me to find you. A Roman legion is advancing in this direction! They'll be here within an hour or so. We've got to get out of here!"

Uri felt his insides twist in shock. The leaders of his sect of Jewish scribes had been worried about this possibility since they had settled in this region. Fortunately, they had also developed a plan for what to do in this situation.

Uri stood and began gathering the scrolls that cluttered his work station. He noticed Joel watching him in agitation.

"Didn't you hear what I said? We've got to go now!"

"Yes, I heard you," Uri replied as he began placing the scrolls into a carry bag. "Do the others know?"

"Yes! Several of the men I came with are spreading the word around the camp. Now forget the scrolls and grab your stuff. If we leave now, we can get out of the area before they arrive."

Uri paused and stared at his brother with intensity. "Forget the scrolls? I'd sooner die! They are my life's work!"

Joel growled in frustration. "And they're going to be the death of you if we don't get moving!"

Uri turned back to his work of gathering the scrolls. "Then you go on ahead. I have to get these to safety."

Loud voices and shouts came from outside the tent, accompanied by the sounds of hurried activity as those in the camp scrambled to collect their things. Uri put the last of the scrolls into the bag and exited the tent, his brother hot on his heels.

"Fine. I'll help you," Joel said. "Where are we going?"

Uri walked rapidly toward the edge of camp. "We're taking these to the caves we've prepared. They should be safe there."

Joel caught up to his brother and matched his pace. "I never understood why you are so devoted to rolls of parchment. They're definitely not worth risking your life over. There are so many other more important things in life."

Uri shook his head. "Like what? What could be more important than God's Word? Oral transmission is subject to corruption. But the words written on these scrolls will remain for hundreds, maybe even thousands, of years.

"Think about it, Joel," Uri said with passion. "We can read the very words written by Moses over two thousand years ago! Everything we know about the patriarchs—Adam, Noah, Abraham, Isaac, Jacob—all of it was written and preserved for us! The history of God's plan for the redemption of people is found in the Scriptures. How else could we know our place in the history of the universe?"

Joel remained silent as they continued their trek across the barren terrain. When they reached the limestone mounds, Uri led them up the path that wound its way to the cliffs.

"How much further?" Joel asked as he continued to cast worried glances over his shoulder.

"We're almost there." Uri hefted the bag of precious scrolls up the steep incline. Several minutes later, they reached the dark opening in the cliff face.

Uri ducked his head as he passed through the small opening and entered the cave. He set the bag of scrolls down gently on the floor. Then, he grabbed a nearby candle and lit it with the tinderbox positioned next to it.

Joel's surprise was audible. "Wow. Are there scrolls in each of these clay jars?"

"Yes," Uri said. As he spoke, he began placing the scrolls from his bag into empty jars near the back of the small cave. "We are doing our part to preserve God's Word for future generations. We're not like the Greeks or Romans, Joel. Our faith isn't made up of fanciful stories told to frighten children. Our faith is grounded in real history. It tells of how God has worked in the lives of men and women since the beginning of creation."

"I get it," Joel said. He had positioned himself at the mouth of the cave, his gaze fixed on the camp. "But is it worth sacrificing your life? Because that's what's going to happen if we don't leave soon."

Uri placed the lid on one jar and started on the next. "This is a sacred calling, Joel. Our lives are but part of the great story! We are one link in the chain of history. If future generations do not know the account of creation, or the fall of Adam and Eve, or the founding of the nation of Israel, and especially the promise of the coming Redeemer, how will they understand what role they are called to play? These scrolls do more than instruct; they provide evidence of the truth of the histories they contain. They must be saved at all costs."

"Oh no! I can see them! They're coming down the road toward the camp!"

"I'm almost finished," Uri said. He placed the last scroll into a jar and put the lid on it. He hurried toward the entrance and turned around. He gazed longingly at the precious treasure trove and prayed one last time that his life's work would be preserved. At last he blew out the candle, set it aside, and followed his brother down the hill.

"It's too late for us to go back to the camp to get your belongings," Joel said.

Uri turned his face toward the southeast. "Then we'll have to escape another way. C'mon. I know a path that will lead us along the shore of the Dead Sea."

Getting Started—Too Christian

"Are you kidding!" Meghan practically yelled. "You got Tim Tebow for our eighth-grade graduation! How did you manage that?"

"My uncle was an assistant coach at the University of Florida when he was there," Zoe said. "They became good friends and stayed in touch. I called my uncle—I'm his favorite niece, you know—and he called Mr. Tebow. He not only agreed to come but waived his speaking fee because he likes my uncle so much."

That set the whole student council to talking all at once. It was their job to select the graduation speaker, and Zoe Duncan, student body president, had come through big time.

"That's amazing!" Juan said.

"Not yet, it isn't," Zoe replied. "The principal says he can't be our speaker."

"What!" Juan cried. "The guy won the Heisman Trophy. He played professional football and baseball. He's helped thousands of kids through his foundation. He's . . ."

"He's too Christian," Zoe interrupted. "The principal told me the school board thinks Tebow is too public about his faith. They might get complaints from some parents, so we can't invite him."

Meghan's jaw dropped. "What about freedom of religion?"

"I guess it's free so long as it isn't too Christian," Zoe said.

"That's not fair," Juan said. "It shouldn't matter if Mr. Tebow's an outspoken Christian. His faith is a big part of why he's such a great role model."

"What can we do?" Meghan asked.

"We're going to fight this," Zoe said. "We'll tell our parents. Then we'll go to the next PTO meeting and tell even more parents. It's our graduation, and we should be able to have the speaker we want."

A seventh-grader asked, "What if most of the parents agree with the board?"

"Then we'll start a student protest," Zoe said. "This is religious persecution. I, for one, won't accept it."

"Careful," Meghan warned. "You could get in trouble for being too Christian yourself."

Clash of Worldviews

Being a Christian in America today is not easy. Secularism continues to push hard to get religion out of society in general and schools in particular. In the 1930s a group of atheist and agnostic professors published *The Humanist Manifesto*, a document outlining their agenda. They wanted to get rid of what they considered outdated religions, especially Christianity. Recall that *secularism* is *an atheistic and materialistic worldview that advocates for a public society free from the influence of religion.*

Secularists insist personal belief doesn't belong in government, education, or the media. They are motivated by their worldviews—mental maps that tell us how to recognize the rules and patterns that exist, so we can navigate life successfully. As we've seen throughout this book, worldviews are powerful!

Everyone thinks his or her worldview is reasonable and accurately describes how the world works. But is there an objective way to judge among worldviews? What should a worldview get right in order to be a trustworthy map of reality?

The authors of *Making Sense of Your World* suggest four tests for evaluating worldviews.

1. **Test of reason:** The test of reason evaluates the reasonableness of a worldview. Can it be logically stated and defended?

2. **Test of evidence:** If a worldview is true, there should be external corroborating evidence to support it. Does the worldview affirm ideas that are directly contradicted by evidence?

3. **Test of life experiences:** A valid worldview must adequately address the victories, disappointments, blessings, crises, and relationships of our everyday world. The challenge of this test is not to allow mere feelings to shape our interpretations of the dilemmas of life. If we tend to be reactive to our life experiences, we may settle for a worldview that cannot satisfy our deepest longings

4. **Test of real-world application:** A worldview may look compelling, but when the assumptions of that worldview are actually applied in a particular cultural setting, its shortcomings are revealed. Do the ideas of the worldview result in good or bad consequences? When that worldview is lived out, does it make the world better or worse?[1]

So far, we have shown how the Christian worldview passes these tests. It is the worldview that most accurately explains the world we live in. It also gives the best direction for living a meaningful life.

Topic 1—Worldviews and Worldview Questions

In this book, we have looked at five leading worldviews—secularism, Marxism, postmodernism, new spirituality, and Christianity—and the big worldview questions in seven major areas of study:

The Big Questions

Theology	*What about God?*
Philosophy	*What is true and how do we know?*
Ethics	*How should we behave?*
Biology	*What is the origin of life?*
Psychology	*What does it mean to be human?*
Sociology	*What makes for a healthy society?*
History	*What is the meaning of history?*

Each worldview has to address these and other big questions. People form a worldview based on how they answer these questions. The answers they come up with are shaped by their assumptions and preconceptions, as we saw in the last chapter. Here's a quick overview of the five leading worldviews discussed in this course.

Part 1—Worldview Summaries

Secularism is focused on the here and now. It gives no thought of God or the world to come. It is atheistic (God does not exist), materialistic (only the physical world exists), and naturalistic (everything can be explained through natural processes). Secularism believes in science and denies the supernatural. Humans can solve the world's problems through science and reason. There are no institutions ordained by God (church, family, state). There are no moral absolutes handed down by God. Religion shouldn't be allowed to influence modern society. The most intelligent individuals should make the rules for our society.

KARL MARX AND FRIEDRICH ENGELS, BERLIN, GERMANY

Marxism is about replacing a capitalist society with a utopian society (communism) in which the state and economic classes no longer exist. The first step toward communism is socialism. Socialism advocates government or communal ownership of property. Marxists see humanity as evolving biologically and socially. They believe that once communism is achieved, religion will disappear, socioeconomic classes will melt away, government will no longer be necessary, and everyone will own everything in common. Our meaning and purpose don't come from God but from our collective struggle to bring about this communist utopia.

Postmodernism is a reaction against modernism, (the worldview that was dominant from the 1700s through the 1900s). It professes that morality and truth are both relative. Any worldview claiming to have "the truth" is delusional and oppressive. Those in power use their influence to promote their own metanarrative (or grand story of reality) to the exclusion of others. According to the postmodernist, the metanarratives we've been taught—Christianity, secularism, Marxism, and new spirituality—simply enslave us. Believing that we have "the truth" and others don't is what leads to selfishness, discrimination, and death. Understanding the power of metanarratives is the key to freeing ourselves from their grip.

Human beings have no identifiable, unchanging essence or nature. We don't exist as persons created in the image of God. Categories like sane or insane, normal or abnormal, male or female are just social constructs invented by the culture in which we live. We should reject such dichotomies and be whatever we want, living according to how we feel.

New spirituality is historically rooted in Eastern worldviews like Hinduism and Buddhism. It expresses itself in the West today primarily through the new spirituality movement and pop psychology. New spirituality teaches that everyone and everything is god. Reality is ultimately spiritual. Distinctions are an illusion; there are no separate, individual things. Everything and everyone is connected; everything is one and divine.

Our purpose in life is to overcome our ignorance and fully realize our own divinity. Life, death, and reincarnation exist to help people reach this knowledge, or higher consciousness—*a state of awareness in which individuals realize their divinity and the divine connectedness of all things.*

Christianity is based on the life and teachings of Jesus Christ. It teaches about a personal God who has revealed himself through nature and through Scripture. God made humans in his image. We are body (physical) and soul (spiritual). Our disobedience (sin) has broken our fellowship with God, but he made a way back to fellowship with him through his Son. Jesus Christ's sacrifice on the cross enables salvation. Salvation sanctifies us or makes us holy; and sanctification restores our broken relationship with our Creator.

Now let's review the highlights of what the Christian worldview teaches about the seven disciplines discussed.

> **Higher Consciousness**
> A state of awareness in which
> individuals realize their divinity and
> the divine connectedness of all things

Part 2—Christianity in Relation to Seven Disciplines

1. Theology: *Theology* is *the study of God.* Christianity believes in a personal, triune God who made humans in his image so we could have a personal relationship with him (Genesis 1:27). He is the Creator of all things and holds everything together by his all-powerful word (Colossians 1:17).

God makes himself known in two primary ways: 1) general revelation, as displayed throughout nature (Romans 1:19–20), and 2) special revelation, as discovered through supernatural means, such as the Bible and miracles (Hebrews 1:1–2). God is personal, powerful, loving, just, good, and merciful. Because God created us, we owe him our love and obedience. Because he has a purpose for us, what we do matters. Because he loves all people, we must love them too.

2. Philosophy: *Philosophy* is *the study of truth, knowledge, and ultimate reality.* The goal of philosophy is wisdom—the ability to make decisions that glorify God in our relationships with him, ourselves, others, and the earth (Proverbs 9:10). There is a kind of worldly wisdom that is foolish that must be rejected and refuted (Colossians 2:8).

The truth of what is real can be known from what God has revealed in the written Word and the living Word (John 1:1–18). Reality is composed of both the physical world (what can be perceived by our five senses) and the spiritual realm (human souls, angels, and God). Because God made a world that is knowable, we can understand nature and discover its order through science (Psalm 19:1–4). Believing in a God who made an orderly universe and put human beings in it to discover and share his glory gives us a foundation for wise living.

3. Ethics: *Ethics* is *the study of why and how we make moral choices.* It has to do with how we define such concepts as good and evil and right and wrong. Everyone has an inborn sense of right and wrong, what Paul calls *a conscience* (Romans 2:14–15). Christianity says there are universal moral absolutes that are true for all people at all times. These standards are based on God's holy character (1 Peter 1:15–16).

All the laws and principles that guide our ethics can be summed up in two simple commandments: Love God and love our neighbor (Mark 12:28–31). When our conscience reminds us to obey God's moral standards, we are also being reminded to be more loving. When faced with a moral dilemma or hard choice, we should ask, "What's the loving thing to do?" and then seek God's help to do it (Romans 12:9–10).

4. Biology: *Biology* is *the study of living things and their origins.* The two competing theories of the origin and development of life are neo-Darwinism (evolution) and intelligent design (creationism). Neo-Darwinism asserts that new species arise from natural selection, acting over vast periods of time on chance mutations in DNA. Intelligent design believes that the universe is the creation of an intelligent mind (Genesis 1–3).

How did life start in the first place? Biogenesis—the scientifically proven theory that life only comes from preexisting life—means that life cannot generate itself. That's why the Christian worldview insists it takes a living God to make a living universe (Hebrews 11:3). At the pinnacle of his creation are human beings made in his image and given dominion over his creation (Genesis 1:26–31). We are not the product of endless time and random chance. We were created on purpose and for a purpose.

5. Psychology: *Psychology* is *the study of the human mind and the behavior it produces.* The three main approaches to psychology are psychological materialism, psychological spiritualism, and psychological supernaturalism. Psychological materialism says that reality consists only of the material or physical. Psychological spiritualism is the belief that humans are purely spiritual beings whose minds are part of a divine consciousness. Psychological supernaturalism holds that reality is made of both the material and the spiritual (1 Thessalonians 5:23). Christianity's view of psychology can be called *psychological supernaturalism* because it accepts the biblical teaching that humans are both physical and spiritual beings. Adam's body came alive when God breathed into it (Genesis 2:7).

Christian psychology is based on three truths taught in Scripture: 1) we are made in God's image and have infinite value, 2) we have been damaged by sin and the problems it causes, and 3) we can be redeemed and made new through faith in Jesus Christ (2 Corinthians 5:17). Our future hope is that we will be reunited with God in our resurrected, glorified bodies (1 Corinthians 15:35–44).

6. Sociology: *Sociology is the study of human societies and institutions.* According to Scripture, the three key building blocks of society are the family, the church, and the state (government). Each has a specific role to play in how people get along. Christians have dual citizenship. We are citizens of heaven (Philippians 3:20), but we also have a civic responsibility to be good citizens in our communities (Matthew 5:13–16).

Atheistic worldviews are materialistic and naturalistic. They don't have a basis on which to say that humans have value. These worldviews have no moral absolutes. Every society gets to decide its own rules. The Christian worldview, on the other hand, teaches that humans are made in God's image and have intrinsic value. Because of the fall, humans are sinful and selfish (Romans 3:10, 23). This is the primary source of evil in society. When human hearts are changed through God's grace, societies will change.

7. History: *History is the study of the past, with a view to how it affects the present.* The Bible makes specific claims about past events. There are important lessons to learn from the past (1 Corinthians 10:11). Whether it's secular history or biblical history, the same overarching story is being told. This cosmic metanarrative has four parts—creation, fall, redemption, and restoration.

There is abundant evidence for the historical accuracy of the Bible, especially for the life, death, and resurrection of Jesus Christ. This is the foundation of the Christian faith (1 Corinthians 15:14–15). God has a plan and a purpose that can be traced throughout history (Acts 17:26–28). Not only does this plan affect all of humanity, it affects each of us as individuals. We are living in the flow of what God is doing and have a unique part to play (Ephesians 2:10).

Topic 2—Christian Roots and Fruit

From these seven areas of study we can highlight several foundational truths of the Christian worldview, including these beliefs:

† God is personal and knowable.
† God is the Creator and Sustainer of all things.
† Every human has inherent value by virtue of being made in God's image.
† Humans have both a body and a soul.
† Sin has broken fellowship with God and brought a curse on the world.
† There are moral absolutes based on God's holy character that are written on the heart of every person.
† Jesus died and rose again to break the curse of sin and restore all things to God.
† God has ordained family, church, and government as the central institutions of society.
† History is the unfolding of God's plan for humanity. It has a beginning, middle, and end.

Weaving these truths together gives us a picture of reality in which God and his creation are knowable. What we see in nature and Scripture enables us to know God as Creator, Lawgiver, and Redeemer. We can discern from this revelation that God is holy and loving. His character is the basis of moral standards, which are absolute. Because he doesn't change, the standards don't change. This knowledge of right and wrong is written in every human heart (Romans 2:15).

Humans are not unplanned accidents in an unplanned universe. We are made in God's image. We are created with a soul and a body. Humans were given a choice in the garden of Eden and chose to disobey God. This "fall" into sin has affected all people (Jeremiah 17:9).

God's solution was to send his Son, Jesus Christ, to redeem and restore his lost children. Jesus became flesh and offered humanity a way out of its sinful condition (Roman 5:6–8). By acknowledging Jesus as Lord, we can be born again (1 Peter 1:23) and receive the Holy Spirit (Acts 2:38). After this spiritual rebirth, we are to renew our minds so we can understand and follow God's will (Romans 12:1–2).

Part 1—Worldwide Impact

One of the tests of a worldview is the test of real-world application: "Do the ideas of the worldview result in good or bad consequences? When that worldview is lived out, does it make the world better or worse?" This is in accord with what Jesus taught: A good tree produces good fruit, and a bad tree produces bad fruit (Matthew 7:17).

ROMAN PERSECUTION OF CHRISTIANS UNDER TRAJAN DECIUS, AD 250.

After his resurrection, Jesus told his followers to go into all the world and make disciples (Matthew 28:19–20). So, what kind of fruit has been produced since then? As Christ's followers spread out from Jerusalem and Judea to every part of the Roman Empire, they had a dramatic impact on the lives of everyday people. In a few centuries, their influence even reached emperors! As one famed historian notes,

> There is no greater drama in human record than the sight of a few Christians, scorned or oppressed by a succession of emperors, bearing all trial with fiery tenacity, multiplying quietly, building order while their enemies generated chaos, fighting the sword with the word, brutality with hope, and at last defeating the strongest state that history has ever known. Caesar and Christ had met in the arena, and Christ had won.[2]

The Roman Empire eventually fell, but Christianity kept growing. During what became known as *the Dark Ages,* it survived and flourished in churches and monasteries that preserved biblical and secular knowledge. As one journalist says,

> Rome's collapse meant staggering loss. People forgot how to read, how to farm, how to govern themselves, how to build houses, how to trade, and even what it had once meant to be a human being. Behind monastery walls, though, in their chapels, scriptoriums, and refectories, Benedict's monks built lives of peace, order, and learning and spread their network throughout Western Europe.[3]

In the book *What If Jesus Had Never Been Born?*, the authors provide a detailed summary of the ideas and organizations that grew out of the Christian worldview. The list includes:

MEDIEVAL MURAL, 1277, HOSPITAL IN PISTOIA, TUSCANY, ITALY

- The establishment of hospitals
- The founding of universities (from the Middle Ages, many of the world's greatest universities were started for Christian purposes)
- Literacy and education for the masses
- Capitalism and free enterprise
- Representative government, particularly as it was enacted in the US
- Civil liberties
- The abolition of slavery
- Modern science
- The elevation of the social status of women
- Benevolence and charity (the "good Samaritan" ethic)
- Higher standards of justice
- The elevation of the common man
- High regard for human life
- The codification of many of the world's languages
- Greater development of art and music
- The eternal salvation of countless souls [4]

Part 2—Christianity in America

Let's narrow our focus to the United States and trace the positive impact Christianity has had on our own country. Almost two centuries ago, a Frenchman named *Alexis de Tocqueville* visited America to study what made this fledgling nation so great. After spending months in the 1830s traveling across the nation, he wrote,

There is no country in the whole world in which the Christian religion retains a greater influence over the souls of men than in America; and there can be no greater proof of its utility, and of its conformity to human nature, than that its influence is most powerfully felt over the most enlightened and free nation of the earth.[5]

Students today are taught that the idea that life, liberty, and property are inalienable rights comes from John Locke. But Locke based his thinking on a much older tradition about biblical teachings regarding the value of human life. In his major work *Two Treatises of Government*, Locke makes detailed arguments about human rights being derived from the creation account in Genesis.[6]

This understanding of biblical teaching is what led early thinkers to develop the principles of equality that are the basis for the modern idea of human rights. Our own Declaration of Independence has at least four references to the divine:

- The "laws of nature and of nature's God" entitle the United States to independence.
- Men are "endowed by their Creator with certain unalienable rights."
- Congress appeals "to the Supreme Judge of the world for the rectitude of our intentions."
- The signers, "with a firm reliance on the protection of divine Providence," pledge to each other their lives, fortunes, and sacred honor.[7]

Almost 250 years later, America is still considered a Christian country, with two-thirds of American adults saying they are Christians.[8] But in many ways we have turned from this godly heritage. Rather than being salt and light (Matthew 5:13), many Christians have focused on eternal life with Jesus and withdrawn from influencing this one. This has allowed other worldviews to become the dominant influence in America. One contemporary writer offers this sobering overview:

> The [secularists] hold the seats of power: in government, in law, in education, in the media, in medicine, and in the judiciary. They care nothing for our morality. They abhor our "puritanical" values. They chafe against our piety. They despise our non-conformity. But, they applaud our irrelevancy. They appreciate our distraction from the things of this earth. They know that as long as we separate righteousness and justice, they will continue to have free reign. They will be able to continue to reshape life, liberty, and the pursuit of happiness in their own image. They will be able to perpetuate their slaughter of the unborn, their assault on the family, their defamation of all things holy, all things sacred, and all things pure. They will be able to transfer deity and rule from God Almighty to themselves, doing what is right in their own eyes (see Judges 21:25).[9]

Atheistic worldviews like secularism, Marxism, and postmodernism currently have the loudest voice in colleges and universities, public schools, the media, the arts, music, law, business, medicine, psychology, sociology, and government. The challenge for Christians is to confront non-Christian thinking and to reestablish the influence of Christianity on our culture. It will take a rebirth of morality, a revival of spiritual interests, a renewal of intellectual honesty, and a recovery of courage. It will take strengthening the family and reawakening our churches.

Christianity offers a message of hope, inspiring us to engage the culture with God's truth. The philosopher Francis Schaeffer insisted that, "as Christians we are not only to know the right worldview, the worldview that tells us the truth of what is, but consciously to act upon that worldview so as to influence society in all its parts and facets across the whole spectrum of life . . . to the extent of our individual and collective ability."[10]

Part 3—Faith Isn't Blind

Belief in the Christian worldview isn't based on blind faith, but on evidence-based faith. There is evidence in the Bible, science, history, and personal experience.

In Hebrews we see that faith shows the reality of what we hope for; it is the evidence of things we cannot see (Hebrews 1:11). The Greek word for *faith* used here means *firm persuasion*, or *a conviction based upon hearing*. It carries the meaning of forensic proof, the same kind of proof used in a court of law to convince a judge or jury of the guilt or innocence of the defendant. This is underscored by the word *evidence*. Evidence in a court of law is based on solid facts.

THE EVANGELISTS—MATTHEW, MARK, LUKE, AND JOHN

But what kind of facts support our faith? The testimony of eyewitnesses, as we saw in the last lesson. The Gospels contain numerous eyewitness accounts of the life, death, and resurrection of Jesus. The book of Acts and the epistles go on to give eyewitness accounts of the birth and growth of the early church.

The disciples were aware of the power of personal testimony. They shared their experiences of seeing Jesus alive after the resurrection when they spoke to others (1 John 1:1–4). The apostle John gives a detailed account of the disciples sharing a meal with the resurrected Jesus and ends with the words, This disciple is the one who testifies to these events and has recorded them here. And we know that his account of these things is accurate (John 21:24).

This was only one of the post-resurrection encounters. Luke writes, During the forty days after he suffered and died, he appeared to the apostles from time to time, and he proved to them in many ways that he was actually alive. And he talked to them about the Kingdom of God (Acts 1:3). And Paul tells us, After that, he was seen by more than 500 of his followers at one time, most of whom are still alive, though some have died (1 Corinthians 15:6).

As Oxford professor John Lennox writes,

> Mainstream Christianity will insist that faith and evidence are inseparable. Indeed, faith is a response to evidence, not a rejoicing in the absence of evidence. The Christian apostle John writes in his biography of Jesus, "These things are written that you might believe . . ." That is, he understands that what he is writing is to be regarded as part of the evidence on which faith is based. . . . It is no part of the biblical view that things should be believed where there is no evidence. Just as in science, faith, reason and evidence belong together.[11]

Conclusion

Paul preached the gospel throughout the Mediterranean world with one primary purpose: that all nations might believe and obey Jesus (Romans 16:26). True, he was an apostle, but Paul says all Christians are ambassadors: For God was in Christ, reconciling the world to himself, no longer counting people's sins against them. And he gave us this wonderful message of reconciliation. So we are Christ's ambassadors; God is making his appeal through us. We speak for Christ when we plead, "Come back to God! (2 Corinthians 5:19–20).

One Christian writer who lived in a foreign country for a few years put it this way:

> Every day we are called to ambassadorship, no matter where we live. While God does use people like the Apostle Paul to venture into lands where God and His love are unknown, Jesus makes it very clear that we must start on the home front. While eating with his disciples between his resurrection and ascension, Jesus tells his followers that they will be his witnesses in Jerusalem, and in all Judea and Samaria, and to the ends of the earth (Acts 1:8). Their ministry of reconciliation began on the home front, familiar territory, and ours should too![12]

As you finish your school year, the best way to put all this head knowledge into practice is to be an ambassador for Christ. Nearly everyone you meet is on a quest to find meaning and purpose in their lives. You can share with them a worldview that has the most satisfying answers to life's biggest questions. The answers are not about "what" or "why" or "how," but about "who." As Peter tells us, You must worship Christ as Lord of your life. And if someone asks about your hope as a believer, always be ready to explain it. But do this in a gentle and respectful way. Keep your conscience clear. Then if people speak against you, they will be ashamed when they see what a good life you live because you belong to Christ (1 Peter 3:15–16).

ENDNOTES

1 W. Gary Phillips, William E. Brown, and John Stonestreet, *Making Sense of Your World: A Biblical Worldview* (Salem, WI: Sheffield Publishing Company, 2008), 61–90.

2 Will Durant, *Caesar and Christ: A History of Roman Civilization and of Christianity from Their Beginnings to A.D. 325* (New York, NY: Simon and Schuster, 1944), 652.

3 Rod Dreher, "Benedict Option," *The American Conservative*, December 12, 2013, http://www.theamericanconservative.com/articles/benedict-option/.

4 D. James Kennedy and Jerry Newcombe, *What If Jesus Had Never Been Born?* (Nashville, TN: Thomas Nelson, 1994), 3–4.

5 Alexis de Tocqueville, *Democracy in America*, trans. by Henry Reeve (New Rochelle, NY: Arlington House, [1966]), vol. 1, 294.

6 John Locke, *Two Treatises of Government*, ed. by Peter Laslett (Cambridge: Cambridge University Press, 1960), 274.

7 The Claremont Institute, "Nature's God," 2016, http://founding.com/natures-god/.

8 Pew Foundation poll reported in U.S. News & World Report, October 17, 2019, https://www.usnews.com/news/us/articles/2019-10-17/larger-portion-of-americans-has-no-religious-affiliation.

9 George Grant, *Trial and Error: The American Civil Liberties Union and Its Impact on Your Family* (Brentwood, TN: Wolgemuth & Hyatt, 1989), 133.

10 Francis A. Schaeffer, *How Should We Then Live?* (Wheaton, IL: Crossway Books, 1983), 87.

11 John C. Lennox, *God's Undertaker: Has Science Buried God?* (Oxford: Lion Books, 2009), 16.

12 Hailey Domeck, "We Are Ambassadors," CRU, December 2, 2016, https://www.cru.org/us/en/train-and-grow/spiritual-growth/core-christian-beliefs/we-are-ambassadors.html.

Application Story: Interrogation

My dear sister Carol,

Remember when you used to laugh at me and say that if I died it would likely be because of something I said? Well, it looks like that may be the case after all.

I'm writing to you from within a prison of a communist country. Somehow the local police found out I was distributing Bibles. They were waiting for me today and arrested me when I arrived. During the first interrogation, I confessed to being a missionary and even tried to witness to the officer. And. . . that's where my mouth got me in trouble.

I'm sorry, Carol. I know you tried to dissuade me from walking down this path. I know you didn't want to see this happen to your little brother. But remember to put your faith in God. He has never failed me before, and I won't turn my back on him now. Please pray for me.

Oh, I hear footsteps! Someone is coming. I'll finish writing later.

Carol, you will NEVER believe what just happened!

The guards came into the room and led me down the hallway of the prison. They had the barrels of their automatic rifles pressed into the small of my back. They forced me through a doorway at the end of the hall. Sitting behind a large desk was the local police chief. He had a stern look and his uniform was immaculate. The guards forced me to kneel before his desk.

The police chief rose and dismissed the guards. My mind was spinning. My first thought was that he was going to do something so horrible to me he didn't even want his men knowing about it. Once the guards were gone, he crossed to the window and began gazing at the surrounding countryside.

"You may stand," he said simply. I instantly complied. Still gazing out the window, he continued to speak. "Do you know who I am, Mr. Muller? My name is Ino Sidnaka. I am the Deputy Police

Commissioner. It is my duty to keep the peace. And, according to the reports I've received, you are disturbing that peace."

Carol, what could I say? It was obvious someone turned me in. I chose to remain silent.

Commissioner Sidnaka finally turned and resumed his seat at his desk. His cold eyes studied me intently. "Mr. Muller, you should know that I hold your very life in my hands. You have been caught distributing materials that are not sanctioned by the government. If I choose, I could have you simply disappear. No one would ever learn of your fate."

A sudden peace I had never experienced before washed over me. I don't know how else to describe it. "'For me, to live is Christ; to die is gain.' You may kill my body, but you cannot kill my spirit."

Sidnaka's eyes narrowed. I could almost see the wheels turning in his mind. "If nothing else, you certainly have conviction. I admire that. Yet what good will it do you if you are dead?" He leaned back in his chair.

"Perhaps you can explain something to me," he said. "You see, Mr. Muller, I take pride in my intelligence, in my knowledge of the world. In my experience, there are only two ways to control another: external force, or internal willingness. For example, I can have my men drag you back to your cell, or you can go willingly. But there are some things that even force cannot accomplish. It does not foster true conviction. Many in your position would renounce their faith, yet you persist. You might change your mind under torture, but that is not conviction. It is survival."

I won't pretend I wasn't terrified. I don't fear death, but pain and suffering is another matter. I prayed that if it came to that, God would give me the strength to honor him.

Commissioner Sidnaka continued. "Religion is an odd thing. It has the ability to influence a person's thoughts and behaviors in ways no amount of force can. Government can demand compliance externally, but it cannot shape the human heart. Religions, on the other hand, shape behavior and thought through rules and regulations. For the Buddhists, it is the Eightfold Path. For the Muslims, it is the Five Pillars of Islam. For the Jews, it is the Ten Commandments. For the Hindus, it is the Ten Disciplines. They get their followers to comply by convincing them that paradise can be bought by right action.

"But you Christians are different." The Commissioner stared hard at me, as if trying to delve into the depths of my mind. "While you believe in right conduct, it does not ultimately drive your actions. You run *into* the plague. You build hospitals for the sick. You build schools to educate others at great personal expense. Where others seek to make slaves, you seek to free them. No, you are motivated by something much more powerful. Am I right, Mr. Muller?"

Still unsure what he wanted from me; I merely spoke the truth. "Yes, Mr. Sidnaka. You are correct. We are motivated by love for our Savior! We cannot purchase forgiveness; we cannot earn paradise. It is offered freely as a gift from God. Everything we do is in response to the love he has already shown us."

The Commissioner began to smile. "Yes. Love. Do you see this picture?" He held out a picture of two young girls. "These are my granddaughters. I would do anything for them because I love them. Love is the most powerful motivator of all. I must admit, I was a hard father. I disciplined my children harshly. And I have passed that spirit on to my son. Yet when I think of him hurting my sweet granddaughters, I cannot help but see how wrong it is. There must be a better way."

I could not believe my ears! This man could have me executed, yet he was talking to me about his granddaughters. In that moment, I felt a profound sense of pity for him. Where once I had seen a cruel, hardened man, I now saw a lost soul. He had been raised under an evil regime that denied the existence of God. Yet he found him in the faces of his grandchildren.

"And so, Mr. Muller, I come to my point," the Commissioner said at length. "You see, I need your help. My superiors expect for me to produce results. They want order and productivity from those under my authority. They expect me to achieve this through fear—fear of punishment and death. But I've come to understand that while fear may motivate many, it has limited effectiveness. But love knows no bounds.

"In exchange for your freedom, I want you to help me understand how this Jesus of yours is able to inspire his followers to sacrifice everything for him, even to suffer and die. Then, I want you to help me teach that to my officers, then to the people. And maybe, just maybe, to my son. And, if I'm right, the region will flourish as a result."

Can you believe it, Carol? This once cruel man came to see what so many have not yet grasped. Governments rule by fear and cruelty. Religions rule by laws and regulations. But only the love of a suffering Savior and the free gift of salvation can pierce the depths of the heart and inspire true devotion.

With fond love,

Billy

Bible Survey

Lesson 10   Justified by Faith

Getting Started—The Main Ideas

The letter to the Galatians is the fourth letter of the apostle Paul's in the New Testament. It follows Romans and 1 and 2 Corinthians. It was not written to a specific church but to several churches in a specific region. Paul was concerned that those churches were turning away from God by following a different gospel than the one he had preached to them. He wrote to affirm his authority as an apostle and to confirm that salvation, for both Jews and Gentiles, comes through faith in Jesus Christ and not through obedience to Jewish laws.

Paul explained that the false teaching the Galatians had heard would enslave them rather than help them live in freedom. Then he warned the Galatians not to use their freedom to sin. Instead, he urged them to live godly lives empowered by the Holy Spirit.

Topic 1—Called by God

Introduction: Paul began his letter to the Galatians by stating that he was appointed as a minister of the gospel by Jesus himself and by God the Father. He told the Galatians about his conversion and calling, describing how he had met with the apostles and confirmed that the message he had been preaching was in agreement with theirs. Why did Paul give the Galatians so many reasons to believe in his authority? He wanted them to understand that they were being fooled by false teachers, and he wanted to correct their wrong beliefs.

Part 1—Introduction to Galatians

Do you know where the Galatians lived? Can you find Galatia on a map? Unless you are looking at a map of the world in ancient times, you will not find it. The letters of the New Testament were written almost 2,000 years ago, and the names of many territories and cities have changed since then.

Galatia was a part of what today is the country of Turkey. Turkey is in Asia Minor, the part of Asia that is south of the Black Sea and north of the Mediterranean Sea where the continents of Europe and Asia meet. The map on the next page shows where Galatia was in ancient times. Some of the other regions on the map may be familiar to you.

RUINS OF THE ANCIENT CITY OF LYSTRA IN GALATIA

The kingdom of Galatia began around 275 BC. It was conquered and became a province in the Roman Empire around 25 BC. Rome extended Galatian rule to the south, where you see Phrygia on the map. Some scholars think that the letter to the Galatians was written to churches in Northern Galatia around AD 52 or 53, but most now think that it was written to churches in Southern Galatia around AD 47 or 48. This is because Lystra, Derbe, and Iconium, cities in Galatia that are mentioned in Acts (Acts 13:5, 14:6), were in Southern Galatia. Of the three cities, the only one that is still inhabited is Iconium, now known as *Konya*—the seventh-largest city in Turkey.

124   © ⓢ Walking in Truth Grade 8

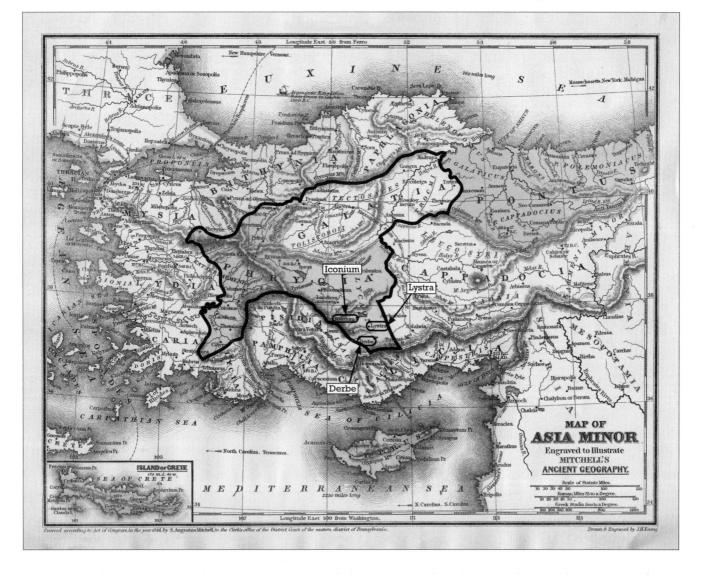

Southern Galatia is on the trade routes to Europe and closer to Jerusalem than Northern Galatia, but Jews lived in both regions. Acts 14 tells us that Paul and Barnabas preached in Iconium, Lystra, and Derbe and founded churches there. After that, they traveled by ship to Antioch of Syria (Acts 14:26). This is what happened next:

[1] While Paul and Barnabas were at Antioch of Syria, some men from Judea arrived and began to teach the believers: "Unless you are circumcised as required by the law of Moses, you cannot be saved." [2] Paul and Barnabas disagreed with them, arguing vehemently. Finally, the church decided to send Paul and Barnabas to Jerusalem, accompanied by some local believers, to talk to the apostles and elders about this question.

Acts 15:1–2

A council was held in Jerusalem to settle the question, and Paul and Barnabas were sent back to the church in Antioch of Syria as official representatives to confirm that Gentiles did not have to follow Jewish laws. Later, Paul traveled to Galatia, where he went from town to town, instructing the believers to follow the decisions made by the apostles and elders in Jerusalem (Acts 16:4). After Paul left, false teachers took advantage of the situation. They questioned Paul's authority and taught that it was necessary for Gentiles to follow Jewish customs. So, Paul wrote to the churches in Galatia to refute this teaching and to defend his authority.

UKRAINIAN MOSAIC
OF THE APOSTLES

Part 2—The Only Good News

Have you ever been asked, or assigned, to do a particular task? If so, you know that being given a responsibility implies that one is also given the authority and resources to carry it out. A police officer shows that she has authority by displaying her badge; a journalist might show his press pass. In a similar way, Paul began his letter to the Galatians by emphasizing his title and credentials. This is what he said:

¹ This letter is from Paul, an apostle. I was not appointed by any group of people or any human authority, but by Jesus Christ himself and by God the Father, who raised Jesus from the dead. Galatians 1:1

Paul was officially appointed by God. There is no higher authority in the universe! He was appointed to be an apostle. The word *apostle*, in Greek, means *messenger*. What was the message that Paul had for the Galatians? He did not take long to get to the point. After praying for the Galatians, Paul wrote:

⁶ I am shocked that you are turning away so soon from God, who called you to himself through the loving mercy of Christ. You are following a different way that pretends to be the Good News ⁷ but is not the Good News at all. You are being fooled by those who deliberately twist the truth concerning Christ. Galatians 1:6–7

Part 3—Paul's Calling

Paul's greeting surely caught the Galatians' attention! He continued his letter by giving the believers more details about his background. Paul wanted the churches to understand that he had been called and taught by Jesus, and that the apostles in Jerusalem had also confirmed his calling. In other words, he wanted the Galatians to realize that he really did have the authority he claimed to have from God.

¹¹ Dear brothers and sisters, I want you to understand that the gospel message I preach is not based on mere human reasoning. ¹² I received my message from no human source, and no one taught me. Instead, I received it by direct revelation from Jesus Christ.

¹³ You know what I was like when I followed the Jewish religion—how I violently persecuted God's church. I did my best to destroy it. ¹⁴ I was far ahead of my fellow Jews in my zeal for the traditions of my ancestors.

¹⁵ But even before I was born, God chose me and called me by his marvelous grace. Then it pleased him ¹⁶ to reveal his Son to me so that I would proclaim the Good News about Jesus to the Gentiles. Galatians 1:11–16

PAUL, WINDOW IN
SLOVAKIAN CHURCH

God knows everything and everyone. Inspired by the Holy Spirit, King David wrote that God knew us, and planned our future, even when we were in our mother's womb (Psalm 139:13–16). Paul testified that God had chosen him, even before he was born, to share Christ with the Gentiles. Although Paul did not realize this when he was a Pharisee, full of zeal and persecuting Christians, when Jesus appeared to him he revealed it to Paul (Acts 9:1–19).

When this happened, I did not rush out to consult with any human being. ¹⁷ Nor did I go up to Jerusalem to consult with those who were apostles before I was. Instead, I went away into Arabia, and later I returned to the city of Damascus.

[18] Then three years later I went to Jerusalem to get to know Peter, and I stayed with
him for fifteen days. [19] The only other apostle I met at that time was James, the
Lord's brother. [20] I declare before God that what I am writing to you is not a lie.

[21] After that visit I went north into the provinces of Syria and Cilicia. [22] And still the
churches in Christ that are in Judea didn't know me personally. [23] All they knew was
that people were saying, "The one who used to persecute us is now preaching the
very faith he tried to destroy!" [24] And they praised God because of me.

Galatians 1:16–24

Peter and Paul, church window in Croatia

Often, people who have done wrong in the past want to hide this fact. But Paul was honest about what he had done. In a letter to the believers in Corinth, he explained, I am the least of all the apostles. In fact, I'm not even worthy to be called an apostle after the way I persecuted God's church. But . . . God poured out his special favor on me (1 Corinthians 15:9–10). Instead of hiding his past, Paul saw his transformation as a reason to praise God. He continued:

[1] Then fourteen years later I went back to Jerusalem again, this time with Barnabas; and Titus came along,
too. [2] I went there because God revealed to me that I should go. While I was there I met privately with those
considered to be leaders of the church and shared with them the message I had been preaching to the Gentiles.
I wanted to make sure that we were in agreement, for fear that all my efforts had been wasted and I was
running the race for nothing. [3] And they supported me and did not even demand that my companion Titus be
circumcised, though he was a Gentile.

[4] Even that question came up only because of some so-called believers
there—false ones, really—who were secretly brought in. They sneaked
in to spy on us and take away the freedom we have in Christ Jesus. They
wanted to enslave us and force us to follow their Jewish regulations. [5] But
we refused to give in to them for a single moment. We wanted to preserve
the truth of the gospel message for you.

Galatians 2:1–5

Paul did not hide the truth about his past, and he did not hide the truth about the dispute that came up in Jerusalem. He told the Galatians what the apostles concluded:

[7] [The leaders of the church] saw that God had given me the responsibility of preaching the gospel to the
Gentiles, just as he had given Peter the responsibility of preaching to the Jews. [8] For the same God who worked
through Peter as the apostle to the Jews also worked through me as the apostle to the Gentiles.

[9] In fact, James, Peter, and John, who were known as pillars of the church, recognized the gift God had given
me, and they accepted Barnabas and me as their co-workers. They encouraged us to keep preaching to the
Gentiles, while they continued their work with the Jews. [10] Their only suggestion was that we keep on helping
the poor, which I have always been eager to do.

Galatians 2:7–10

Topic 2—Superiority of the Gospel

Introduction: Paul told the Galatians that he had fought to keep the truth of the gospel for their sake (Galatians 2:5). What did this mean? In his letter to the church in Rome, Paul wrote that the gospel, or good news, tells us how God makes us right in his sight. This is accomplished from start to finish by faith (Romans 1:17). The false teachers who had confused the Galatians did not believe this. They taught that people could only be saved if they had faith plus obedience to the Law. So Paul had to explain their error. Faith alone brings salvation, not faith plus the Law.

Part 1—Made Right by Faith

You might think, after reading that the apostles recognized Peter as the apostle to the Jews, and Paul as the apostle to the Gentiles, that the two of them would always get along really well. But this was not the case.

[11] But when Peter came to Antioch, I had to oppose him to his face, for what he did was very wrong. [12] When he first arrived, he ate with the Gentile believers, who were not circumcised. But afterward, when some friends of James came, Peter wouldn't eat with the Gentiles anymore. He was afraid of criticism from these people who insisted on the necessity of circumcision. [13] As a result, other Jewish believers followed Peter's hypocrisy, and even Barnabas was led astray by their hypocrisy.   Galatians 2:11–13

When Peter first came to visit with Paul in Antioch, he ate with Gentile believers. But when James' friends came, Peter stopped eating with the Gentiles. He was afraid he would be criticized. Have you ever changed your behavior, or seen someone else change theirs, to get someone else's approval? Peer pressure is *the pressure people feel to be like their social group.* Sometimes peer pressure can be good, if it motivates you toward good behavior. But in Peter's case, it made him act in a way that was against his beliefs. Hypocrisy is *the practice of claiming to be what you are not or pretending to believe something you do not.* Paul explained to the Galatians how he confronted Peter:

[14] When I saw that they were not following the truth of the gospel message, I said to Peter in front of all the others, "Since you, a Jew by birth, have discarded the Jewish laws and are living like a Gentile, why are you now trying to make these Gentiles follow the Jewish traditions?

[15] "You and I are Jews by birth, not 'sinners' like the Gentiles. [16] Yet we know that a person is made right with God by faith in Jesus Christ, not by obeying the law. And we have believed in Christ Jesus, so that we might be made right with God because of our faith in Christ, not because we have obeyed the law. For no one will ever be made right with God by obeying the law."

[17] But suppose we seek to be made right with God through faith in Christ and then we are found guilty because we have abandoned the law. Would that mean Christ has led us into sin? Absolutely not! [18] Rather, I am a sinner if I rebuild the old system of law I already tore down. [19] For when I tried to keep the law, it condemned me. So I died to the law—I stopped trying to meet all its requirements—so that I might live for God. [20] My old self has been crucified with Christ. It is no longer I who live, but Christ lives in me. So I live in this earthly body by trusting in the Son of God, who loved me and gave himself for me. [21] I do not treat the grace of God as meaningless. For if keeping the law could make us right with God, then there was no need for Christ to die.   Galatians 2:14–21

Through his behavior, Peter was sinning. He was implying that there was no need for Christ to die. But Paul reminded him, and the Galatians, that Christ died to save both Jews and Gentiles.

Part 2—Faith or Law?

Paul continued his argument that only faith makes us right with God by asking the Galatians a series of questions.

¹ Oh, foolish Galatians! Who has cast an evil spell on you? For the meaning of Jesus Christ's death was made as clear to you as if you had seen a picture of his death on the cross. ² Let me ask you this one question: Did you receive the Holy Spirit by obeying the law of Moses? Of course not! You received the Spirit because you believed the message you heard about Christ. ³ How foolish can you be? After starting your new lives in the Spirit, why are you now trying to become perfect by your own human effort? ⁴ Have you experienced so much for nothing? Surely it was not in vain, was it?

⁵ I ask you again, does God give you the Holy Spirit and work miracles among you because you obey the law? Of course not! It is because you believe the message you heard about Christ.

Galatians 3:1–5

Paul hoped such questions would make the Galatians realize that faith alone makes people right with God. But the believers with a Jewish background might have needed more convincing. They were proud of being Abraham's descendants, so Paul discussed Abraham too.

⁶ In the same way, "Abraham believed God, and God counted him as righteous because of his faith." ⁷ The real children of Abraham, then, are those who put their faith in God.

⁸ What's more, the Scriptures looked forward to this time when God would make the Gentiles right in his sight because of their faith. God proclaimed this good news to Abraham long ago when he said, "All nations will be blessed through you." ⁹ So all who put their faith in Christ share the same blessing Abraham received because of his faith.

Galatians 3:6–9

The believers with a Jewish background might have objected to Paul's arguments, saying that even though all nations would be blessed through Abraham, this blessing would come through the laws that God gave to his people through Moses. Paul corrected this view.

¹⁰ But those who depend on the law to make them right with God are under his curse, for the Scriptures say, "Cursed is everyone who does not observe and obey all the commands that are written in God's Book of the Law." ¹¹ So it is clear that no one can be made right with God by trying to keep the law. For the Scriptures say, "It is through faith that a righteous person has life." ¹² This way of faith is very different from the way of law, which says, "It is through obeying the law that a person has life."

¹³ But Christ has rescued us from the curse pronounced by the law. When he was hung on the cross, he took upon himself the curse for our wrongdoing. For it is written in the Scriptures, "Cursed is everyone who is hung on a tree." ¹⁴ Through Christ Jesus, God has blessed the Gentiles with the same blessing he promised to Abraham, so that we who are believers might receive the promised Holy Spirit through faith.

Galatians 3:10–14

Paul explained that the blessing that all nations would receive through Abraham did not come from the law, but rather through the Child who would be Abraham's descendant.

¹⁵ Dear brothers and sisters, here's an example from everyday life. Just as no one can set aside or amend an irrevocable agreement, so it is in this case. ¹⁶ God gave the promises to Abraham and his child. And notice that the Scripture doesn't say "to his children," as if it meant many descendants. Rather, it says "to his child"—and that, of course, means Christ. ¹⁷ This is what I am trying to say: The agreement God made with Abraham could not be canceled 430 years later when God gave the law to Moses. God would be breaking his promise. ¹⁸ For if the inheritance could be received by keeping the law, then it would not be the result of accepting God's promise. But God graciously gave it to Abraham as a promise.

¹⁹ Why, then, was the law given? It was given alongside the promise to show people their sins. But the law was designed to last only until the coming of the child who was promised. God gave his law through angels to Moses, who was the mediator between God and the people. ²⁰ Now a mediator is helpful if more than one party must reach an agreement. But God, who is one, did not use a mediator when he gave his promise to Abraham.

²¹ Is there a conflict, then, between God's law and God's promises? Absolutely not! If the law could give us new life, we could be made right with God by obeying it. ²² But the Scriptures declare that we are all prisoners of sin, so we receive God's promise of freedom only by believing in Jesus Christ.

Galatians 3:15–22

Topic 3—Children and Heirs

Introduction: Paul continued his letter to the Jewish and Gentile believers in the churches of Galatia by reminding them that Christ had brought them together. Though the believers had different backgrounds and social standing, in Christ Jesus they were all one and adopted into God's family (Galatians 3:28, 4:5). Paul shared his concern that by listening to false teaching, the believers would enslave themselves instead of living in freedom as God's children. Then he compared the believers' situation to that experienced by Abraham's physical children through Sarah, his wife, and Hagar, his slave.

Part 1—One in Christ

Paul said that the law showed people their sins until Jesus, the Child who was promised, came (Galatians 3:19). He continued his letter by comparing the law to a guardian:

²³ Before the way of faith in Christ was available to us, we were placed under guard by the law. We were kept in protective custody, so to speak, until the way of faith was revealed.

²⁴ Let me put it another way. The law was our guardian until Christ came; it protected us until we could be made right with God through faith. ²⁵ And now that the way of faith has come, we no longer need the law as our guardian.

²⁶ For you are all children of God through faith in Christ Jesus. ²⁷ And all who have been united with Christ in baptism have put on Christ, like putting on new clothes. ²⁸ There is no longer Jew or Gentile, slave or free, male and female. For you are all one in Christ Jesus. ²⁹ And now that you belong to Christ, you are the true children of Abraham. You are his heirs, and God's promise to Abraham belongs to you. Galatians 3:23–29

The law that had blessed the Jews and shaped their identity was superseded, or set aside, in favor of the way of faith. Through Jesus Christ, everyone could become a child of God. It did not matter if you were a boy or a girl or rich or poor. It did not matter what your social, political, religious, or ethnic status had been. This was unheard of in ancient society; it was revolutionary! By being baptized, you became God's child and heir. Paul continued:

¹ Think of it this way. If a father dies and leaves an inheritance for his young children, those children are not much better off than slaves until they grow up, even though they actually own everything their father had. ² They have to obey their guardians until they reach whatever age their father set. ³ And that's the way it was with us before Christ came. We were like children; we were slaves to the basic spiritual principles of this world.

⁴ But when the right time came, God sent his Son, born of a woman, subject to the law. ⁵ God sent him to buy freedom for us who were slaves to the law, so that he could adopt us as his very own children. ⁶ And because we are his children, God has sent the Spirit of his Son into our hearts, prompting us to call out, "Abba, Father." ⁷ Now you are no longer a slave but God's own child. And since you are his child, God has made you his heir. Galatians 4:1–7

Paul said almost the same thing in his letter to the believers in the church in Rome (Romans 8:14–16). And to those in the church in Corinth, he wrote that God has identified us as his own by placing the Holy Spirit in our hearts (1 Corinthians 2:22). The Holy Spirit in our hearts confirms that we belong to God.

Part 2—Admonition to the Galatians

The churches in Galatia were mixed congregations. Whenever Paul and his coworkers went to preach in a new town, he began in the synagogue (Acts 17:2) and then reached out to the Gentiles. Paul had written to both Jewish and Gentile believers, focusing his attention on whether it was necessary to observe Jewish laws, but then he addressed the Gentiles.

TEMPLE OF BAAL SHAMIN IN SYRIA
(DESTROYED BY ISIS IN 2015)

⁸ Before you Gentiles knew God, you were slaves to so-called gods that do not even exist. ⁹ So now that you know God (or should I say, now that God knows you), why do you want to go back again and become slaves once more to the weak and useless spiritual principles of this world? ¹⁰ You are trying to earn favor with God by observing certain days or months or seasons or years. ¹¹ I fear for you. Perhaps all my hard work with you was for nothing. ¹² Dear brothers and sisters, I plead with you to live as I do in freedom from these things, for I have become like you Gentiles— free from those laws.

You did not mistreat me when I first preached to you. ¹³ Surely you remember that I was sick when I first brought you the Good News. ¹⁴ But even though my condition tempted you to reject me, you did not despise me or turn me away. No, you took me in and cared for me as though I were an angel from God or even Christ Jesus himself. ¹⁵ Where is that joyful and grateful spirit you felt then? I am sure you would have taken out your own eyes and given them to me if it had been possible. ¹⁶ Have I now become your enemy because I am telling you the truth?

¹⁷ Those false teachers are so eager to win your favor, but their intentions are not good. They are trying to shut you off from me so that you will pay attention only to them. ¹⁸ If someone is eager to do good things for you, that's all right; but let them do it all the time, not just when I'm with you.

¹⁹ Oh, my dear children! I feel as if I'm going through labor pains for you again, and they will continue until Christ is fully developed in your lives. ²⁰ I wish I were with you right now so I could change my tone. But at this distance I don't know how else to help you.

Galatians 4:8–20

Notice how tenderly Paul spoke to the Gentiles, whom God had especially called him to win. He reminded them of their past kindness to him, emphasizing that he has not forgotten their good work. But he also warned them not to be deceived by false teachers and not to return to their old way of life of endless effort trying to win God's favor, when God has already accepted them in Christ.

Part 3—Two Covenants

What do you call someone who is trained in the law? Usually, a lawyer. We call Paul a missionary or an apostle, forgetting that Paul was trained in Jewish law by Gamaliel, one of the most respected Pharisees of his day (Acts 5, 34, 22:3). Paul did not just know the law, like a lawyer. He sought to enforce the law—like police officers and prosecuting attorneys do today (Acts 22:4). Paul was also a Roman citizen, and

he knew the laws of the Roman Empire well enough to use them to his advantage (Acts 16:37, 22:25). To continue his arguments to the Galatians, Paul drew on his knowledge and experience as a legal scholar.

²¹ Tell me, you who want to live under the law, do you know what the law actually says? ²² The Scriptures say that Abraham had two sons, one from his slave wife and one from his freeborn wife. ²³ The son of the slave wife was born in a human attempt to bring about the fulfillment of God's promise. But the son of the freeborn wife was born as God's own fulfillment of his promise.

24 These two women serve as an illustration of God's two covenants. The first woman, Hagar, represents Mount Sinai where people received the law that enslaved them. 25 And now Jerusalem is just like Mount Sinai in Arabia, because she and her children live in slavery to the law. 26 But the other woman, Sarah, represents the heavenly Jerusalem. She is the free woman, and she is our mother. 27 As Isaiah said,

"Rejoice, O childless woman,
    you who have never given birth!
Break into a joyful shout,
    you who have never been in labor!
For the desolate woman now has more children
    than the woman who lives with her husband!"

ABRAHAM AND SARAH
CAST OUT HAGAR, BY
ADRIEN VAN DER WERFF

28 And you, dear brothers and sisters, are children of the promise, just like Isaac. 29 But you are now being persecuted by those who want you to keep the law, just as Ishmael, the child born by human effort, persecuted Isaac, the child born by the power of the Spirit.

30 But what do the Scriptures say about that? "Get rid of the slave and her son, for the son of the slave woman will not share the inheritance with the free woman's son." 31 So, dear brothers and sisters, we are not children of the slave woman; we are children of the free woman.

Galatians 4:21–31

Topic 4—Freedom

Introduction: Paul's letter to the believers of the churches in Galatia was probably difficult for them to read and receive with a humble heart. After all, Paul offered one argument after another showing how the teachings they had been following were wrong. Many people find it very hard to change their minds, admit they made a mistake, and change their behavior. God, who knows and loves everyone, inspired Paul to reaffirm his love for the Galatians and to encourage them to move forward.

Part 1—Freedom in Christ

What does it really mean to be free? In the times of the Roman Empire, many people were enslaved. Scholars estimate that at least a third of the population of the Roman Empire were slaves. Paul's audience had a keen understanding of the difference that freedom, or the lack of it, had for one's status and opportunity in society. But by following false teaching, the Galatians had been enslaving themselves, and Paul encouraged them to be free.

1 Christ has truly set us free. Now make sure that you stay free, and don't get tied up again in slavery to the law.

7 You were running the race so well. Who has held you back from following the truth? 8 It certainly isn't God, for he is the one who called you to freedom. 9 This false teaching is like a little yeast that spreads through the whole batch of dough! 10 I am trusting the Lord to keep you from believing false teachings. God will judge that person, whoever he is, who has been confusing you.

¹³ You have been called to live in freedom, my brothers and sisters. But don't use your freedom to satisfy your sinful nature. Instead, use your freedom to serve one another in love. ¹⁴ For the whole law can be summed up in this one command: "Love your neighbor as yourself." ¹⁵ But if you are always biting and devouring one another, watch out! Beware of destroying one another.

Galatians 5:1, 7–10, 13–15

Loving our brothers and sisters is the way we obey God and demonstrate our faith. Paul put it this way: What is important is faith expressing itself in love (Galatians 5:6). Paul wanted the Galatians to take care not to constantly argue, but instead to serve and encourage one another.

Part 2—Life by the Spirit

If the Galatians did not have to follow Jewish laws and regulations, did that mean they were free to do anything they liked? No. Paul had already made clear that sin itself makes everyone a prisoner (Galatians 3:22). So he encouraged the believers not to give in to sin and instead live holy lives.

¹⁶ So I say, let the Holy Spirit guide your lives. Then you won't be doing what your sinful nature craves. ¹⁷ The sinful nature wants to do evil, which is just the opposite of what the Spirit wants. And the Spirit gives us desires that are the opposite of what the sinful nature desires. These two forces are constantly fighting each other, so you are not free to carry out your good intentions. ¹⁸ But when you are directed by the Spirit, you are not under obligation to the law of Moses.

¹⁹ When you follow the desires of your sinful nature, the results are very clear: sexual immorality, impurity, lustful pleasures, ²⁰ idolatry, sorcery, hostility, quarreling, jealousy, outbursts of anger, selfish ambition, dissension, division, ²¹ envy, drunkenness, wild parties, and other sins like these. Let me tell you again, as I have before, that anyone living that sort of life will not inherit the Kingdom of God.

²² But the Holy Spirit produces this kind of fruit in our lives: love, joy, peace, patience, kindness, goodness, faithfulness, ²³ gentleness, and self-control. There is no law against these things!

Galatians 5:16–23

How do you know that you are following God's will and doing what he wants you to do? You know it by the fruit that is evident in your life. Jesus taught the same thing to his followers:

⁴³ "A good tree can't produce bad fruit, and a bad tree can't produce good fruit. ⁴⁴ A tree is identified by its fruit. Figs are never gathered from thornbushes, and grapes are not picked from bramble bushes. ⁴⁵ A good person produces good things from the treasury of a good heart, and an evil person produces evil things from the treasury of an evil heart. What you say flows from what is in your heart.

Luke 6:43–45

So if you want to have a good heart and produce good fruit, you must trust in Jesus and rely on his Spirit to help you.

²⁴ Those who belong to Christ Jesus have nailed the passions and desires of their sinful nature to his cross and crucified them there. ²⁵ Since we are living by the Spirit, let us follow the Spirit's leading in every part of our lives.

Galatians 5:24–25

Paul knew that the Galatians had been fighting. In their zeal to worship God, they had been arguing among themselves about the need to obey the law. Paul warned them, If you are always biting and devouring one another, watch out! Beware of destroying one another (Galatians 5:15). Do you think, considering what had been going on, that the Galatians needed this warning? It might have been tempting for some of the Galatian believers to think that they were right and others were wrong, that they followed the Holy Spirit's leading but that the brothers and sisters with whom they disagreed were sinning. So Paul added, let us not become conceited, or provoke one another, or be jealous of one another (Galatians 5:26). Then he described how the Galatians should treat a believer who sinned.

¹ Dear brothers and sisters, if another believer is overcome by some sin, you who are godly should gently and humbly help that person back onto the right path. And be careful not to fall into the same temptation yourself. ² Share each other's burdens, and in this way obey the law of Christ. ³ If you think you are too important to help someone, you are only fooling yourself. You are not that important.

⁴ Pay careful attention to your own work, for then you will get the satisfaction of a job well done, and you won't need to compare yourself to anyone else. ⁵ For we are each responsible for our own conduct.

⁶ Those who are taught the word of God should provide for their teachers, sharing all good things with them.

⁷ Don't be misled—you cannot mock the justice of God. You will always harvest what you plant. ⁸ Those who live only to satisfy their own sinful nature will harvest decay and death from that sinful nature. But those who live to please the Spirit will harvest everlasting life from the Spirit. ⁹ So let's not get tired of doing what is good. At just the right time we will reap a harvest of blessing if we don't give up. ¹⁰ Therefore, whenever we have the opportunity, we should do good to everyone—especially to those in the family of faith.
Galatians 6:1–10

Paul encouraged the Galatians to serve one another in love and to do good to everyone, especially those in the church, their brothers and sisters in Christ. Then he added:

¹¹ NOTICE WHAT LARGE LETTERS I USE AS I WRITE THESE CLOSING WORDS IN MY OWN HANDWRITING.
Galatians 6:11

Elsewhere Paul explained, here is my greeting in my own handwriting—Paul. I do this in all my letters to prove they are from me (2 Thessalonians 3:17). Remember that the Galatians had been questioning Paul's teaching and authority? Paul was not taking any chances. He wanted the Galatians to know for sure that the letter they held in their hands really came from him.

¹⁴ As for me, may I never boast about anything except the cross of our Lord Jesus Christ. Because of that cross, my interest in this world has been crucified, and the world's interest in me has also died. ¹⁵ It doesn't matter whether we have been circumcised or not. What counts is whether we have been transformed into a new creation. ¹⁶ May God's peace and mercy be upon all who live by this principle; they are the new people of God.

[18] Dear brothers and sisters, may the grace of our Lord Jesus Christ be with your spirit. Amen.

Galatians 6:14–16, 18

Paul prayed for the Galatians and encouraged them to live in peace, rejoicing in their new identity as children of God, made new and righteous through faith. Instead of boasting about how much they obeyed the Law and tried to be perfect through their own efforts (Galatians 3:3), Paul modeled a life of boasting only in the cross of Christ that gave them all freedom.

Riches in Christ

Getting Started—The Main Ideas

The book of Ephesians follows Paul's letter to the Galatians in the New Testament. Like Romans, Galatians, and 1 and 2 Corinthians, Ephesians is an epistle, or letter. It may have been meant for a single congregation (the book of Acts indicates that Paul visited the church there), but it was probably circulated to several house churches in and around Ephesus. Paul heard of the faith of the believers in the area, but had not personally met all of them.

In the letter, Paul explained the wonderful riches that believers have received through Christ. He referred to the church as a family, a house or temple, a bride, and a soldier outfitting himself with armor. These analogies were written to illustrate the unity of purpose of the church and to show how individual members must work together. Paul spoke to the need to put away gossip, criticism, lying, jealousy, grudge holding, and anger, because these are barriers to unity in the body of Christ. He also discussed the need for submission—*the act of yielding to the will or authority of another person out of love or respect for that person.*

> **Submission**
> The act of yielding to the will or authority of another person out of love or respect for that person

Topic 1—Blessings in Christ

Introduction: Ephesians is notable for several reasons. First, along with Philippians, Colossians, and Philemon, it is one of Paul's prison epistles, written in about AD 60 while Paul was under house arrest in Rome. Although Paul was not free to come and go, he was able to write letters and to receive visitors. One such visitor, Tychicus, may have been sent to Paul from the Ephesian church. In Paul's closing remarks to the church, or churches, he indicated that he sent Tychicus back to the church with the letter and his personal encouragement. Also noteworthy is that although many of Paul's epistles deal with

false teaching and problems in the local church, Ephesians does not include a reference to specific people or doctrinal issues in the city of Ephesus. Ephesians deals with topics at the very core of what it means to be a Christian—both in faith and in practice.

Part 1—Introduction to Ephesians

Ephesus was located near the western shores of modern-day Turkey, where the Aegean Sea meets the former estuary of the River Kaystros, about 80 kilometers south of Izmir, near modern-day Selçuk. It is currently

uninhabited and is an archaeological site, but in Paul's day, it was the Mediterranean's main commercial center and major port. Today, it is about six miles from the sea due to a buildup of silt from the river.

The Lydian King Croesus, who ruled from 560 to 547 BC, was famous for funding the temple of Artemis in Ephesus. Artemis was the goddess of the hunt, chastity, childbirth, wild animals, and the wilderness. She was the patroness of Ephesus. Artemis' temple was one of the Seven Wonders of the Ancient World, but today only a single column stands in the nearby ruins that remain from the once-magnificent pagan temple.

FOURTH-CENTURY
BAPTISTERY IN TURKEY

It is possible that the church in Ephesus was started by Paul but led by Priscilla and Aquila, a Jewish couple who knew the doctrines of the Christian faith (Acts 18:26), and who were left in Ephesus by Paul on his second missionary journey (Acts 18:18–19). It was in Ephesus that Priscilla and Aquila met Apollos, a Jewish evangelist, and taught him about God's plan of salvation as well as the baptism of the Holy Spirit (Acts 18:24–26). Later Paul traveled to Ephesus and preached there for three years (Acts 19:8–10, 20:31).

The church in Ephesus included both Jewish and Gentile converts to Christianity. In introducing himself as the author of the letter, Paul referred to ehis role as an *apostle*, someone sent on a mission, and he called the Ephesians *God's holy people*, regardless of their former beliefs.

¹ This letter is from Paul, chosen by the will of God to be an apostle of Christ Jesus.

I am writing to God's holy people in Ephesus, who are faithful followers of Christ Jesus. ² May God our Father and the Lord Jesus Christ give you grace and peace.

Ephesians 1:1–2

Paul began his letters with the words "grace and peace." God's grace gives us peace!

Part 2—Redemption through Christ

The church in Ephesus probably included many slaves given the enormous slave population in the first-century Roman Empire. Some historians estimate that as many as one-third of the people in the empire were slaves. So, when Paul talked about Christ having purchased our freedom with his blood, enslaved members of the church would have been comforted by the message. Those who were free, both Jews and Gentiles, would also have understood the analogy. We were slaves to the consequences of our sin; Christ freed us!

³ All praise to God, the Father of our Lord Jesus Christ, who has blessed us with every spiritual blessing in the heavenly realms because we are united with Christ. ⁴ Even before he made the world, God loved us and chose us in Christ to be holy and without fault in his eyes. ⁵ God decided in advance to adopt us into his own family by bringing us to himself through Jesus Christ. This is what he wanted to do, and it gave him great pleasure. ⁶ So we praise God for the glorious grace he has poured out on us who belong to his dear Son. ⁷ He is so rich in kindness and grace that he purchased our freedom with the blood of his Son and forgave our sins. ⁸ He has showered his kindness on us, along with all wisdom and understanding.

Ephesians 1:3–8

Paul went on to describe the mystery that God had hidden until he sent his Son into the world; God's plan to bring about our salvation! Through Christ's atonement, all the relationships of creation, in heaven and on the earth, will be restored.

⁹ God has now revealed to us his mysterious will regarding Christ—which is to fulfill his own good plan. ¹⁰ And this is the plan: At the right time he will bring everything together under the authority of Christ—everything in heaven and on earth. ¹¹ Furthermore, because we are united with Christ, we have received an inheritance from God, for he chose us in advance, and he makes everything work out according to his plan.

Ephesians 1:9–11

There are very few guarantees in life, especially when it comes to making plans. However, God's plans are perfect because he is perfect. The Holy Spirit's presence in our heart is a guarantee that we will see God's plans come to fruition. Notice that all of God's plans for our lives are ultimately for his glory.

¹² God's purpose was that we Jews who were the first to trust in Christ would bring praise and glory to God. ¹³ And now you Gentiles have also heard the truth, the Good News that God saves you. And when you believed in Christ, he identified you as his own by giving you the Holy Spirit, whom he promised long ago. ¹⁴ The Spirit is God's guarantee that he will give us the inheritance he promised and that he has purchased us to be his own people. He did this so we would praise and glorify him.

Ephesians 1:12–14

Part 3—Praying for Spiritual Wisdom

Have you ever wondered why some people seem to have all the answers and others are clueless? When it comes to spiritual insight and wisdom, we don't have to wonder. God is more than willing to help us grow in the knowledge of him and of his will. Paul said that he prayed for the Ephesians constantly. He mentioned specifically that he prayed for them to grow in their faith. Why do you think Paul prayed for the believers' spiritual understanding?

¹⁵ Ever since I first heard of your strong faith in the Lord Jesus and your love for God's people everywhere, ¹⁶ I have not stopped thanking God for you. I pray for you constantly, ¹⁷ asking God, the glorious Father of our Lord Jesus Christ, to give you spiritual wisdom and insight so that you might grow in your knowledge of God. ¹⁸ I pray that your hearts will be flooded with light so that you can understand the confident hope he has given to those he called—his holy people who are his rich and glorious inheritance.

¹⁹ I also pray that you will understand the incredible greatness of God's power for us who believe him. This is the same mighty power ²⁰ that raised Christ from the dead and seated him in the place of honor at God's right hand in the heavenly realms. ²¹ Now he is far above any ruler or authority or power or leader or anything else—not only in this world but also in the world to come. ²² God has put all things under the authority of Christ and has made him head over all things for the benefit of the church. ²³ And the church is his body; it is made full and complete by Christ, who fills all things everywhere with himself.

Ephesians 1:15–23

Topic 2—The Gift of Grace

Introduction: No single teaching of any religion sets Christianity apart more than the doctrine of grace—God's unmerited (unearned) favor. Other worldviews rest on human beings reaching out to God, trying to earn his favor, or trying to become more godlike themselves, or they ignore God. In Christianity, we understand that we are unable to do anything to earn God's favor. Paul described us as being "dead" in our sins (Ephesians 2:1), and the dead cannot do anything to help themselves. The only hope for our redemption and reconciliation with God is through faith in the gift of Christ's atoning work on the cross.

[1] Once you were dead because of your disobedience and your many sins. [2] You used to live in sin, just like the rest of the world, obeying the devil—the commander of the powers in the unseen world. He is the spirit at work in the hearts of those who refuse to obey God. [3] All of us used to live that way, following the passionate desires and inclinations of our sinful nature. By our very nature we were subject to God's anger, just like everyone else.

[4] But God is so rich in mercy, and he loved us so much, [5] that even though we were dead because of our sins, he gave us life when he raised Christ from the dead. (It is only by God's grace that you have been saved!) [6] For he raised us from the dead along with Christ and seated us with him in the heavenly realms because we are united with Christ Jesus. [7] So God can point to us in all future ages as examples of the incredible wealth of his grace and kindness toward us, as shown in all he has done for us who are united with Christ Jesus.

[8] God saved you by his grace when you believed. And you can't take credit for this; it is a gift from God. [9] Salvation is not a reward for the good things we have done, so none of us can boast about it. [10] For we are God's masterpiece. He has created us anew in Christ Jesus, so we can do the good things he planned for us long ago.

Ephesians 2:1–10

Topic 3—One in Christ

Introduction: Recall that the church in Ephesus was made up of both Jewish and Gentile Christians. Pious Jews considered all non-Jews as "unclean" people. They considered themselves clean because of their heritage and their strict observance of the Law, especially the law of circumcision. Paul pointed out that Jews and Gentiles were both sinners before God and needed to be cleansed by Christ. Whenever we feel separated, excluded, or alienated from others, we should reread these verses to realize that no one is ever separated from God's love or from the body of believers.

[11] Don't forget that you Gentiles used to be outsiders. You were called "uncircumcised heathens" by the Jews, who were proud of their circumcision, even though it affected only their bodies and not their hearts. [12] In those days you were living apart from Christ. You were excluded from citizenship among the people of Israel, and you did not know the covenant promises God had made to them. You lived in this world without God and without hope. [13] But now you have been united with Christ Jesus. Once you were far away from God, but now you have been brought near to him through the blood of Christ.

[14] For Christ himself has brought peace to us. He united Jews and Gentiles into one people when, in his own body on the cross, he broke down the wall of hostility that separated us. [15] He did this by ending the system of

law with its commandments and regulations. He made peace between Jews and Gentiles by creating in himself one new people from the two groups. [16] Together as one body, Christ reconciled both groups to God by means of his death on the cross, and our hostility toward each other was put to death.

[17] He brought this Good News of peace to you Gentiles who were far away from him, and peace to the Jews who were near. [18] Now all of us can come to the Father through the same Holy Spirit because of what Christ has done for us.

Ephesians 2:11–18

Paul closed this section in his epistle by comparing the church to a family. He also compared it to a house, with the cornerstone being Christ himself. Think about your house and the blessings you have as a member of a family as you read Paul's words.

[19] So now you Gentiles are no longer strangers and foreigners. You are citizens along with all of God's holy people. You are members of God's family. [20] Together, we are his house, built on the foundation of the apostles and the prophets. And the cornerstone is Christ Jesus himself. [21] We are carefully joined together in him, becoming a holy temple for the Lord. [22] Through him you Gentiles are also being made part of this dwelling where God lives by his Spirit.

Ephesians 2:19–22

Topic 4—God's Plan

Introduction: Even though Paul was under house arrest in Rome, and supervised by soldiers, he was free to move from room to room. He may have been chained to a soldier at night to prevent escape, but Paul never saw Caesar as his jailer; he called himself a "prisoner of Christ" because Jesus was his Lord, and he served Christ primarily on behalf of the Gentiles who did not know the riches of faith in Christ. Paul didn't hesitate to preach God's eternal plan of salvation which God had revealed to him and the other apostles. This revelation united both believing Jews and believing Gentiles together as fellow heirs of salvation.

Part 1—The Mystery

Perhaps you have been entrusted to keep a secret, such as the time and location of a surprise birthday party or the contents of a package under the Christmas tree. Maybe you've been bursting to tell someone and found it difficult to keep quiet. Paul knew the biggest secret of all time—God's plan to reconcile the world to himself.

[1] When I think of all this, I, Paul, a prisoner of Christ Jesus for the benefit of you Gentiles . . . [2] assuming, by the way, that you know God gave me the special responsibility of extending his grace to you Gentiles. [3] As I briefly wrote earlier, God himself revealed his mysterious plan to me. [4] As you read what I have written, you will understand my insight into this plan regarding Christ. [5] God did not reveal it to previous generations, but now by his Spirit he has revealed it to his holy apostles and prophets.

[6] And this is God's plan: Both Gentiles and Jews who believe the Good News share equally in the riches inherited by God's children. Both are part of the same body, and both enjoy the promise of blessings because they belong to Christ Jesus. [7] By God's grace and mighty power, I have been given the privilege of serving him by spreading this Good News.

⁸ Though I am the least deserving of all God's people, he graciously gave me the privilege of telling the Gentiles about the endless treasures available to them in Christ. ⁹ I was chosen to explain to everyone this mysterious plan that God, the Creator of all things, had kept secret from the beginning.

¹⁰ God's purpose in all this was to use the church to display his wisdom in its rich variety to all the unseen rulers and authorities in the heavenly places. ¹¹ This was his eternal plan, which he carried out through Christ Jesus our Lord.

¹² Because of Christ and our faith in him, we can now come boldly and confidently into God's presence. ¹³ So please don't lose heart because of my trials here. I am suffering for you, so you should feel honored.   Ephesians 3:1–13

You might be wondering why God kept his plan a secret for so many centuries. Jewish believers understood that salvation for the Gentiles would come through Israel (Isaiah 11:10, 49:6), but they had a hard time accepting Gentiles as equal partakers of God's riches and coheirs of God's kingdom. Most thought a non-Jew could only be saved by becoming a Jew. As an apostle to the Gentiles, Paul explained that all people are saved through faith in Christ Jesus. God called him to reveal this mystery even though Paul had previously persecuted God's people (1 Corinthians 15:9).

Part 2—Praying for Spiritual Growth

Paul declared that God's love reaches every corner of existence. Lasting longer than our lives, it is wider than our understanding, higher than our thoughts, and deeper than our feelings. Paul prayed that the Ephesians would come to understand God's love, because without experiencing God's love, they were incomplete. There are four distinct requests Paul prayed for the believers: for inner spiritual strength, the indwelling of Christ in their hearts, the power to understand the dimensions of God's love, and to personally experience that love.

Because we read in English and live in an individualistic society, we can get the mistaken impression that Paul used the pronouns "you" and "your" as if he were addressing only individual believers. But in Greek, all the pronouns Paul used in his prayer were plural. So, Paul prayed for the entire body of believers to be made complete with all the fullness of life and power that came from God.

¹⁴ When I think of all this, I fall to my knees and pray to the Father, ¹⁵ the Creator of everything in heaven and on earth. ¹⁶ I pray that from his glorious, unlimited resources he will empower you with inner strength through his Spirit. ¹⁷ Then Christ will make his home in your hearts as you trust in him. Your roots will grow down into God's love and keep you strong. ¹⁸ And may you have the power to understand, as all God's people should, how wide, how long, how high, and how deep his love is. ¹⁹ May you experience the love of Christ, though it is too great to understand fully. Then you will be made complete with all the fullness of life and power that comes from God.   Ephesians 3:14–19

Paul ended this section of his epistle with a brief doxology—a statement of praise. The remaining chapters of Ephesians transition to new themes and practical matters within the church.

²⁰ Now all glory to God, who is able, through his mighty power at work within us, to accomplish infinitely more than we might ask or think. ²¹ Glory to him in the church and in Christ Jesus through all generations forever and ever! Amen.   Ephesians 3:20–21

Topic 5—Unity in Christ

Introduction: In the first three chapters of Ephesians, Paul explained the mystery of God's plan to unite both Jews and Gentiles into one body through the atoning work of Christ. In the next three chapters, Paul discussed how to live in unity as children of light in a dark world.

Part 1—One Body, One Spirit

Even though Paul penned the words we read today in Ephesians chapter 4 nearly 2,000 years ago, they apply to Christian behavior today. As you read these verses, consider how your behavior compares to what Paul said Christians ought to do.

[1] Therefore I, a prisoner for serving the Lord, beg you to lead a life worthy of your calling, for you have been called by God. [2] Always be humble and gentle. Be patient with each other, making allowance for each other's faults because of your love. [3] Make every effort to keep yourselves united in the Spirit, binding yourselves together with peace. [4] For there is one body and one Spirit, just as you have been called to one glorious hope for the future.

[5] There is one Lord, one faith, one baptism,
[6] one God and Father of all,
  who is over all, in all, and living through all.

Ephesians 4:1–6

Did you notice how many times Paul used the word "one"? Our oneness in Christ is the basis of unity in the church. Yet, even though we are *unified*, we are not *uniform*. God has given each Christian at least one spiritual gift to fulfill different functions within the church—with the ultimate goal of glorifying God.

[7] However, he has given each one of us a special gift through the generosity of Christ. [8] That is why the Scriptures say,

"When he ascended to the heights,
  he led a crowd of captives
  and gave gifts to his people."

[9] Notice that it says "he ascended." This clearly means that Christ also descended to our lowly world. [10] And the same one who descended is the one who ascended higher than all the heavens, so that he might fill the entire universe with himself.

[11] Now these are the gifts Christ gave to the church: the apostles, the prophets, the evangelists, and the pastors and teachers. [12] Their responsibility is to equip God's people to do his work and build up the church, the body of Christ. [13] This will continue until we all come to such unity in our faith and knowledge of God's Son that we will be mature in the Lord, measuring up to the full and complete standard of Christ.

[14] Then we will no longer be immature like children. We won't be tossed and blown about by every wind of new teaching. We will not be influenced when people try to trick us with lies so clever they sound like the truth. [15] Instead, we will speak the truth in love, growing in every way more and more like Christ, who is the

head of his body, the church. ¹⁶ He makes the whole body fit together perfectly. As each part does its own special work, it helps the other parts grow, so that the whole body is healthy and growing and full of love.

Ephesians 4:7–16

Part 2—Children of Light

Perhaps at this point, the Ephesians wondered how to live as redeemed people. So, Paul said, in effect, "Now that you know what Christ has done for you, here's what you ought to do for Christ." We have a holy calling to live a life of purity and faith. He emphasized things believers should do, including being humble, gentle, patient, and forgiving. He commanded believers to stop living for pleasure, lying, letting anger control behavior, stealing, or any type of sinful behavior.

¹⁷ With the Lord's authority I say this: Live no longer as the Gentiles do, for they are hopelessly confused. ¹⁸ Their minds are full of darkness; they wander far from the life God gives because they have closed their minds and hardened their hearts against him. ¹⁹ They have no sense of shame. They live for lustful pleasure and eagerly practice every kind of impurity.

²⁰ But that isn't what you learned about Christ. ²¹ Since you have heard about Jesus and have learned the truth that comes from him, ²² throw off your old sinful nature and your former way of life, which is corrupted by lust and deception. ²³ Instead, let the Spirit renew your thoughts and attitudes. ²⁴ Put on your new nature, created to be like God—truly righteous and holy.

²⁵ So stop telling lies. Let us tell our neighbors the truth, for we are all parts of the same body. ²⁶ And "don't sin by letting anger control you." Don't let the sun go down while you are still angry, ²⁷ for anger gives a foothold to the devil.

²⁸ If you are a thief, quit stealing. Instead, use your hands for good hard work, and then give generously to others in need.   Ephesians 4:17–28

The saying, "Sticks and stones can break my bones, but words will never hurt me" is a lie. Words do hurt! Paul grouped foul language (cussing, swearing, and using crude words) with abusive language because both types of words can and do destroy relationships. Insults can do more damage than fists. Paul commanded the believers only to speak what is helpful. He urged them to encourage or edify one another by their words.

²⁹ Don't use foul or abusive language. Let everything you say be good and helpful, so that your words will be an encouragement to those who hear them.   Ephesians 4:29

As a personal Being, God has feelings. Paul not only reminded the believers of this fact, but warned them that by their behavior, they can bring sorrow to God's heart, like disobedient, disrespectful children grieve their parents.

³⁰ And do not bring sorrow to God's Holy Spirit by the way you live. Remember, he has identified you as his own, guaranteeing that you will be saved on the day of redemption.

³¹ Get rid of all bitterness, rage, anger, harsh words, and slander, as well as all types of evil behavior. ³² Instead, be kind to each other, tenderhearted, forgiving one another, just as God through Christ has forgiven you.

Ephesians 4:30–32

Topic 6—The Spirit-Led Life

Introduction: You do not need to look far to find a multitude of problems in today's culture. In fact, you may look at our culture's problems and say, "What a mess!" But the sin we see in the world today is nothing new. In the first-century world of Ephesus, immorality, cruelty, slavery, broken relationships, and abuse of all kinds were commonplace. Paul's solution to the problems in the home and society was regeneration through Christ—a life filled with love and submission to Christ and to one another.

Part 1—Live Pure Lives

How can anyone hope to live a God-pleasing life in such a dark world? Paul's answer was to imitate Christ. Becoming like Christ means getting rid of things that keep us from imitating him. Christ loved us and offered himself as a sacrifice for us. Sin has no place among God's people.

[1] Imitate God, therefore, in everything you do, because you are his dear children. [2] Live a life filled with love, following the example of Christ. He loved us and offered himself as a sacrifice for us, a pleasing aroma to God.

[3] Let there be no sexual immorality, impurity, or greed among you. Such sins have no place among God's people. [4] Obscene stories, foolish talk, and coarse jokes—these are not for you. Instead, let there be thankfulness to God. [5] You can be sure that no immoral, impure, or greedy person will inherit the Kingdom of Christ and of God. For a greedy person is an idolater, worshiping the things of this world.

[6] Don't be fooled by those who try to excuse these sins, for the anger of God will fall on all who disobey him. [7] Don't participate in the things these people do. [8] For once you were full of darkness, but now you have light from the Lord. So live as people of light! [9] For this light within you produces only what is good and right and true.

Ephesians 5:1–9

Not only did Paul call on the Ephesians to get rid of certain things, but he challenged them to take on new attitudes and actions.

[10] Carefully determine what pleases the Lord. [11] Take no part in the worthless deeds of evil and darkness; instead, expose them. [12] It is shameful even to talk about the things that ungodly people do in secret. [13] But their evil intentions will be exposed when the light shines on them, [14] for the light makes everything visible. This is why it is said,

"Awake, O sleeper,
　rise up from the dead,
　and Christ will give you light."

[15] So be careful how you live. Don't live like fools, but like those who are wise. [16] Make the most of every opportunity in these evil days. [17] Don't act thoughtlessly, but understand what the Lord wants you to do. [18] Don't be drunk with wine, because that will ruin your life. Instead, be filled with the Holy Spirit, [19] singing psalms and hymns and spiritual songs among yourselves, and making music to the Lord in your hearts. [20] And give thanks for everything to God the Father in the name of our Lord Jesus Christ.

Ephesians 5:10–20

grateful
thankful
blessed

Part 2—Husbands and Wives

Paul went on to discuss relationships in the home. He stated that the home should mirror the relationship Christ has with the church. This can only happen if both spouses are controlled by the Spirit, husbands love their wives, and wives respect their husbands.

21 And further, submit to one another out of reverence for Christ.

22 For wives, this means submit to your husbands as to the Lord. 23 For a husband is the head of his wife as Christ is the head of the church. He is the Savior of his body, the church. 24 As the church submits to Christ, so you wives should submit to your husbands in everything.

25 For husbands, this means love your wives, just as Christ loved the church. He gave up his life for her 26 to make her holy and clean, washed by the cleansing of God's word. 27 He did this to present her to himself as a glorious church without a spot or wrinkle or any other blemish. Instead, she will be holy and without fault. 28 In the same way, husbands ought to love their wives as they love their own bodies. For a man who loves his wife actually shows love for himself. 29 No one hates his own body but feeds and cares for it, just as Christ cares for the church. 30 And we are members of his body.

31 As the Scriptures say, "A man leaves his father and mother and is joined to his wife, and the two are united into one." 32 This is a great mystery, but it is an illustration of the way Christ and the church are one. 33 So again I say, each man must love his wife as he loves himself, and the wife must respect her husband.

Ephesians 5:21–33

Topic 7—Godly Relationships

Introduction: Do you find it easy to be a Christian on Sunday yet difficult to follow Christ the rest of the week? Perhaps you should look at the way you conduct yourself in your relationships. Children, parents, teachers, students, classmates, and teammates all engage in relationships. The topic was as important to first-century Christians as it is to us today. Paul devoted a substantial portion of his epistle to defining how we ought to treat one another within our relationships. We already saw how he addressed marriage. Paul also wrote about parents and children, masters and slaves.

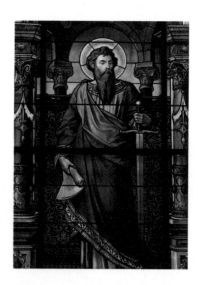

1 Children, obey your parents because you belong to the Lord, for this is the right thing to do. 2 "Honor your father and mother." This is the first commandment with a promise: 3 If you honor your father and mother, "things will go well for you, and you will have a long life on the earth."

4 Fathers, do not provoke your children to anger by the way you treat them. Rather, bring them up with the discipline and instruction that comes from the Lord.

5 Slaves, obey your earthly masters with deep respect and fear. Serve them sincerely as you would serve Christ. 6 Try to please them all the time, not just when they are watching you. As slaves of Christ, do the will of God with all your heart. 7 Work with enthusiasm, as though you were working for the Lord rather than for people. 8 Remember that the Lord will reward each one of us for the good we do, whether we are slaves or free.

⁹Masters, treat your slaves in the same way. Don't threaten them; remember, you both have the same Master in heaven, and he has no favorites.

Ephesians 6:1–9

It is important to remember that when Paul told slaves to obey their masters, he was not justifying or promoting the institution of slavery. Slavery was an inherent evil in a godless society. Christianity was new, limited in size and lacking any authority, so the church was powerless to make sweeping and immediate changes in the culture. Change, of course, happened within the church: the cultural and societal distinctions between its members were stripped away by God's amazing grace. Eventually, the church became the primary institution for social change.

Topic 8—The Armor of God

Introduction: Remember that Paul was under house arrest in Rome at the time he wrote the letter to the Ephesians. Although he was probably free during the day to move about, he was likely chained to a soldier at night. The Roman soldier was fitted with the armor he needed for defense and the weapons he needed for offense. Paul used the Roman soldier's equipment as an analogy for the Christian life.

The idea of spiritual warfare is intimidating. Christians face three opponents: the world, our own flesh, and the devil. The "world" is the society around us that is opposed to God, our flesh is our sinful nature, and the devil is Satan. He is our enemy, tempter (Matthew 4:3), accuser (Revelation 12:7–11) and a liar (John 8:44). Satan and his demons launch attacks against God's children, yet we are not powerless. Paul described the weapons we have at our disposal in order to battle evil.

¹⁰A final word: Be strong in the Lord and in his mighty power. ¹¹Put on all of God's armor so that you will be able to stand firm against all strategies of the devil. ¹²For we are not fighting against flesh-and-blood enemies, but against evil rulers and authorities of the unseen world, against mighty powers in this dark world, and against evil spirits in the heavenly places.

¹³Therefore, put on every piece of God's armor so you will be able to resist the enemy in the time of evil. Then after the battle you will still be standing firm. ¹⁴Stand your ground, putting on the belt of truth and the body armor of God's righteousness. ¹⁵For shoes, put on the peace that comes from the Good News so that you will be fully prepared. ¹⁶In addition to all of these, hold up the shield of faith to stop the fiery arrows of the devil. ¹⁷Put on salvation as your helmet, and take the sword of the Spirit, which is the word of God. Ephesians 6:10–17

Paul continued his letter with the admonition to pray and news of his situation.

¹⁸Pray in the Spirit at all times and on every occasion. Stay alert and be persistent in your prayers for all believers everywhere.

Ephesians 6:18

Did you notice how all-compassing this verse is? Paul instructed believers to pray for each other all the time and in every place. Christians do not need to pray only at special times of day or in special places; God is pleased whenever and wherever we pray.

What kinds of prayers should we make? Two examples in the letter to the Ephesians are Paul's prayer for the believers to have spiritual wisdom (Ephesians 1:15–23) and for their spiritual growth (Ephesians 3:14–21). But at the end of his letter, Paul asks the Ephesians to pray that he would have boldness to proclaim the Good News:

¹⁹ And pray for me, too. Ask God to give me the right words so I can boldly explain God's mysterious plan that the Good News is for Jews and Gentiles alike. ²⁰ I am in chains now, still preaching this message as God's ambassador. So pray that I will keep on speaking boldly for him, as I should.

²¹ To bring you up to date, Tychicus will give you a full report about what I am doing and how I am getting along. He is a beloved brother and faithful helper in the Lord's work. ²² I have sent him to you for this very purpose—to let you know how we are doing and to encourage you.

Ephesians 6:19–22

Finally, Paul closed his letter with a blessing:

²³ Peace be with you, dear brothers and sisters, and may God the Father and the Lord Jesus Christ give you love with faithfulness. ²⁴ May God's grace be eternally upon all who love our Lord Jesus Christ.

Ephesians 6:23–24

Joyful Living

Getting Started—The Main Ideas

Philippians is one of the letters that Paul wrote with Timothy's assistance while he was in prison (the others are Ephesians, Colossians, and Philemon). Paul wrote to encourage the believers in Philippi to continue spreading the good news and to hold fast to their faith in Christ. He wanted believers to share his determination and to rejoice with him that, despite persecution, more people were learning about Jesus.

RUINS OF PHILIPPI IN GREECE

The book of Philippians has one of the loveliest and most important passages about Jesus in all of Scripture (Philippians 2:6–11). Scholars think that it was one of the hymns sung by Christians in the early church. Paul wanted his readers to imitate Jesus' selfless attitude and to serve one another. In doing so, they would honor Jesus. Paul emphasized that knowing Christ is more important and valuable than anything else in life.

Through every circumstance that Paul and the Philippians faced—imprisonment, persecution, disagreements, trouble, financial needs, and much more—Paul wanted the Philippians to remember that God worked in and among them (Philippians 1:6, 2:13) and would help them (Philippians 4:19). Therefore, they did not need to be anxious. Instead, they could experience contentment, which is *an attitude of happiness, satisfaction, and peace with one's present circumstances*. Trusting in God, they could then rejoice as they pressed onward in faith.

> **Contentment**
> An attitude of happiness, satisfaction, and peace with one's present circumstances

Topic 1—Joy in Suffering

Introduction: Who were the Philippians? When did Paul meet them? What kind of relationship did they have? The book of Acts describes how the church at Philippi began when Paul journeyed there with Luke and several others who accompanied him on his second missionary journey. They traveled to Macedonia, the region where the city of Philippi was, in obedience to a vision that the Holy Spirit had given to Paul (Acts 16:9–10). In writing the letter to the Philippians, Paul was not writing to strangers but to close friends at a church he started.

Part 1—Introduction to Philippians

Picture a fast-running stream. Fertile land. A short distance to the sea. Gold mines in the mountains nearby. Does this sound like a good location for a city? Philip II of Macedon certainly thought so. He conquered it and named it after himself in 356 BC. When the Macedonians were defeated by the Romans in 167 BC, Philippi became more important. It became a strategic and commercial center when the Romans built the Via Egnatia, the major road in the area, connecting what today are the countries of Albania, Macedonia,

Greece, and Turkey. Philippi was later the site of one of the most important battles in the history of the Roman Empire. Its population increased when many solders settled there after the war. It was very patriotic.

Philippi is mentioned many times in the book of Acts, which was written by Luke, one of Paul's traveling companions. This is how Luke described the time that Paul first traveled there:

[11] We boarded a boat at Troas and sailed straight across to the island of Samothrace, and the next day we landed at Neapolis. [12] From there we reached Philippi, a major city of that district of Macedonia and a Roman colony. And we stayed there several days.

Acts 16:11–12

Paul's custom was to visit the local synagogue and preach there first (Acts 17:2). But there were not many Jews in Philippi, so the city did not have a synagogue. Luke said:

[13] On the Sabbath we went a little way outside the city to a riverbank, where we thought people would be meeting for prayer, and we sat down to speak with some women who had gathered there. [14] One of them was Lydia from Thyatira, a merchant of expensive purple cloth, who worshiped God. As she listened to us, the Lord opened her heart, and she accepted what Paul was saying. [15] She and her household were baptized, and she asked us to be her guests. "If you agree that I am a true believer in the Lord," she said, "come and stay at my home." And she urged us until we agreed.

Acts 16:13–15

LYDIA OF THYATIRA

BAPTISTERY OF ST. LYDIA NEAR PHILIPPI, GREECE

Lydia was the first convert in Europe. Her hospitality allowed Paul and his group to stay in Philippi and preach. The remainder of Acts 16 tells about Paul and Silas' encounter with a demon-possessed slave girl, the riot incited by her masters when she was freed in Jesus' name, how Paul and Silas were beaten and thrown into prison, and how an earthquake enabled Paul and Silas to share the gospel with the jailer and his family, who all believed in Jesus. Paul and Silas left Philippi shortly afterward, but it is thought that Luke stayed behind and helped the church to grow, until he rejoined Paul's group several years later (Acts 20:6).

Philippians was written by Paul from prison (Philippians 1:13), probably when he was in Rome, between AD 61 and 63. Timothy may have acted as a scribe for Paul. The letter was probably carried from Rome to the church in Philippi by Epaphroditus, a Christian from Philippi who visited Paul in prison and brought him aid from the church (Philippians 2:25–30).

Part 2—Greetings and Gratitude

Paul's letter to the Philippian church is not sad. It is cheerful. In fact, Paul used some form of the word *joy* sixteen times in this short letter. He was excited to write to his friends.

[1] This letter is from Paul and Timothy, slaves of Christ Jesus.

I am writing to all of God's holy people in Philippi who belong to Christ Jesus, including the church leaders and deacons.

[2] May God our Father and the Lord Jesus Christ give you grace and peace.

[3] Every time I think of you, I give thanks to my God. [4] Whenever I pray, I make my requests for all of you with joy, [5] for you have been my partners in spreading the Good News about Christ from the time you first heard it until now. [6] And I am certain that God, who began the good work within you, will continue his work until it is finally finished on the day when Christ Jesus returns.

⁷ So it is right that I should feel as I do about all of you, for you have a special place in my heart. You share with me the special favor of God, both in my imprisonment and in defending and confirming the truth of the Good News. ⁸ God knows how much I love you and long for you with the tender compassion of Christ Jesus.

⁹ I pray that your love will overflow more and more, and that you will keep on growing in knowledge and understanding. ¹⁰ For I want you to understand what really matters, so that you may live pure and blameless lives until the day of Christ's return. ¹¹ May you always be filled with the fruit of your salvation—the righteous character produced in your life by Jesus Christ—for this will bring much glory and praise to God.

Philippians 1:1–11

Paul rejoiced that his friends partnered with him in spreading the good news of Jesus Christ. He saw God's grace in the Philippians' lives, and he prayed confidently for them.

Part 3—Paul's Calling

Paul's friends were probably happy and grateful to hear from him. But they might also have been concerned about his being in prison. So Paul hurried to tell them how he was doing:

¹² And I want you to know, my dear brothers and sisters, that everything that has happened to me here has helped to spread the Good News. ¹³ For everyone here, including the whole palace guard, knows that I am in chains because of Christ. ¹⁴ And because of my imprisonment, most of the believers here have gained confidence and boldly speak God's message without fear.

PAINTING OF PAUL IN PRISON BY REMBRANDT

¹⁵ It's true that some are preaching out of jealousy and rivalry. But others preach about Christ with pure motives. ¹⁶ They preach because they love me, for they know I have been appointed to defend the Good News. ¹⁷ Those others do not have pure motives as they preach about Christ. They preach with selfish ambition, not sincerely, intending to make my chains more painful to me. ¹⁸ But that doesn't matter. Whether their motives are false or genuine, the message about Christ is being preached either way, so I rejoice. And I will continue to rejoice. ¹⁹ For I know that as you pray for me and the Spirit of Jesus Christ helps me, this will lead to my deliverance. Philippians 1:12–19

Even though Paul hoped to be freed from prison, he knew he could be executed, so he talked about his death:

²⁰ I fully expect and hope that I will never be ashamed, but that I will continue to be bold for Christ, as I have been in the past. And I trust that my life will bring honor to Christ, whether I live or die. ²¹ For to me, living means living for Christ, and dying is even better. ²² But if I live, I can do more fruitful work for Christ. So I really don't know which is better. ²³ I'm torn between two desires: I long to go and be with Christ, which would be far better for me. ²⁴ But for your sakes, it is better that I continue to live.

²⁵ Knowing this, I am convinced that I will remain alive so I can continue to help all of you grow and experience the joy of your faith. ²⁶ And when I come to you again, you will have even more reason to take pride in Christ Jesus because of what he is doing through me.

Philippians 1:20–26

Paul did not want his friends in Philippi to worry. When he wrote that living means living for Christ, and dying is even better (Philippians 1:21), he was reiterating the good news that he had preached to them and to others. He had written something similar to the church in Corinth: Yes, we are fully confident, and we would rather be away from these earthly bodies, for then we will be at home with the Lord. So whether we are here in this body or away from this body, our goal is to please him. (2 Corinthians 5:8–9). Paul admonished the Philippians the same way.

²⁷ Above all, you must live as citizens of heaven, conducting yourselves in a manner worthy of the Good News about Christ. Then, whether I come and see you again or only hear about you, I will know that you are standing together with one spirit and one purpose, fighting together for the faith, which is the Good News.   Philippians 1:27

You might remember that Philippi was a patriotic Roman colony inhabited by soldiers and their descendants. This meant that its citizens were expected to worship Roman gods. Refusing to do that was considered treason, because it could make the gods angry enough to bring disaster to the city. When Paul told the Philippians to live as citizens of heaven, he was encouraging them to do something dangerous and subversive, and they knew it. He continued:

²⁸ Don't be intimidated in any way by your enemies. This will be a sign to them that they are going to be destroyed, but that you are going to be saved, even by God himself. ²⁹ For you have been given not only the privilege of trusting in Christ but also the privilege of suffering for him. ³⁰ We are in this struggle together. You have seen my struggle in the past, and you know that I am still in the midst of it.   Philippians 1:28–30

Paul encouraged the Philippians to remain faithful to Christ and to see that their suffering for Christ, like Paul's own suffering for Christ, provided an opportunity for them to be courageous and testify to the truth of the gospel. For Paul, the important thing was that the gospel of Jesus Christ continue to spread, no matter who preached it, even as the church faced persecution. Paul's priority was Christ and living for him.

Topic 2—Joy in Serving

Introduction: In view of the persecution the Philippians faced for their allegiance to Christ, Paul encouraged them to stand united in love and humility. He described Jesus' own willingness to give up his privilege and position to fulfill the Father's will and die for us on the cross. Paul added that the Philippians should have the same mindset that Jesus had. They should not complain or argue but instead live holy lives that would be a testimony to their neighbors.

Part 1—Christ's Humility

Because the Philippians were suffering similar struggles as Paul was (Philippians 1:29–30), it was important that they be united not only with Christ, through faith, but with one another. When you are going through trouble, it helps to have the support of others who are facing the same thing with you.

Paul wrote: [1] Is there any encouragement from belonging to Christ? Any comfort from his love? Any fellowship together in the Spirit? Are your hearts tender and compassionate? [2] Then make me truly happy by agreeing wholeheartedly with each other, loving one another, and working together with one mind and purpose.

[3] Don't be selfish; don't try to impress others. Be humble, thinking of others as better than yourselves. [4] Don't look out only for your own interests, but take an interest in others, too.   Philippians 2:1–4

The supreme example of someone who valued others above himself is Jesus Christ, who died on the cross so that we could be reconciled to God. So Paul continued his appeal for unity by quoting the lyrics of a hymn the Philippians probably used in worship:

[5] You must have the same attitude that Christ Jesus had.

[6] Though he was God,
   he did not think of equality with God
   as something to cling to.
[7] Instead, he gave up his divine privileges;
   he took the humble position of a slave
   and was born as a human being.
 When he appeared in human form,
[8]   he humbled himself in obedience to God
   and died a criminal's death on a cross.   Philippians 2:5–8

Jesus was, and is, divine. He is God the Son, part of the Trinity along with God the Father and God the Holy Spirit. To save us from our sins, he came to Earth as a helpless human baby to fulfill the plan of salvation announced long ago (Isaiah 7:14, 53:2–12). Dying on a cross was considered a shameful way to die; it was how the Romans executed criminals. But Jesus humbled himself because of his great love for us (1 John 3:16). Paul continued:

[9] Therefore, God elevated him to the place of highest honor
   and gave him the name above all other names,
[10] that at the name of Jesus every knee should bow,
   in heaven and on earth and under the earth,
[11] and every tongue declare that Jesus Christ is Lord,
   to the glory of God the Father.   Philippians 2:9–11

Part 2—Shine for Christ

Paul continued his appeal by stating that the same God who exalted Jesus for his obedience was at work in the Philippians, even when Paul could not be with them. God would help them.

[12] Dear friends, you always followed my instructions when I was with you. And now that I am away, it is even more important. Work hard to show the results of your salvation, obeying God with deep reverence and fear. [13] For God is working in you, giving you the desire and the power to do what pleases him.   Philippians 2:12–13

When Paul wrote that God was working in the Philippians, he used the Greek word *energōn*. God was energizing the Philippians to joyfully live holy lives, following Jesus' example. Paul continued:

14 Do everything without complaining and arguing, 15 so that no one can criticize you. Live clean, innocent lives as children of God, shining like bright lights in a world full of crooked and perverse people.

Philippians 2:12–15

Paul's instruction to the believers in Philippi to shine for God echoed Jesus' own teaching. In the Sermon on the Mount, Jesus said:

15 No one lights a lamp and then puts it under a basket. Instead, a lamp is placed on a stand, where it gives light to everyone in the house. 16 In the same way, let your good deeds shine out for all to see, so that everyone will praise your heavenly Father.

Matthew 5:15–16

Paul challenged the members of the church in Philippi to show the good news about Jesus Christ through their unity and purpose. He knew that he could be killed, and they could be persecuted. Yet he was glad to serve the Lord as long as he lived, and he wanted them to be glad too.

16 Hold firmly to the word of life; then, on the day of Christ's return, I will be proud that I did not run the race in vain and that my work was not useless. 17 But I will rejoice even if I lose my life, pouring it out like a liquid offering to God, just like your faithful service is an offering to God. And I want all of you to share that joy. 18 Yes, you should rejoice, and I will share your joy.

Philippians 2:16–18

Topic 3—Joy in Christ

Introduction: Paul did not want the believers in Philippi to be troubled by his being in jail. He did not want them to be worried about persecution or to be fighting among themselves. He also did not want them to be influenced by false teachers. Instead of focusing on these things, Paul urged believers to look at Christ and recognize that he was their treasure and joy. Paul directed the church in Philippi to focus on the positive and to pray. Finally, Paul thanked the believers for their generosity and encouraged them to trust in God's provision.

Part 1—Rejoice in the Lord

You may remember from Galatians that there were teachers who taught it was necessary to follow Jewish regulations in order to be made right with God (Galatians 2:4). Those regulations included male circumcision. False teachers tried to influence the church in Philippi, and Paul opposed them. One of Paul's purposes in keeping in touch with the believers in the churches he planted was to help them keep their faith pure so they could grow and mature in the Lord.

1 Whatever happens, my dear brothers and sisters, rejoice in the Lord. I never get tired of telling you these things, and I do it to safeguard your faith.

2 Watch out for those dogs, those people who do evil, those mutilators who say you must be circumcised to be saved. 3 For we who worship by the Spirit of God are the ones who are truly circumcised. We rely on what Christ Jesus has done for us. We put no confidence in human effort, 4 though I could have confidence in my own effort if anyone could. Indeed, if others have reason for confidence in their own efforts, I have even more!

⁵ I was circumcised when I was eight days old. I am a pure-blooded citizen of Israel and a member of the tribe of Benjamin—a real Hebrew if there ever was one! I was a member of the Pharisees, who demand the strictest obedience to the Jewish law. ⁶ I was so zealous that I harshly persecuted the church. And as for righteousness, I obeyed the law without fault.

⁷ I once thought these things were valuable, but now I consider them worthless because of what Christ has done. ⁸ Yes, everything else is worthless when compared with the infinite value of knowing Christ Jesus my Lord. For his sake I have discarded everything else, counting it all as garbage, so that I could gain Christ ⁹ and become one with him. I no longer count on my own righteousness through obeying the law; rather, I become righteous through faith in Christ. For God's way of making us right with himself depends on faith. ¹⁰ I want to know Christ and experience the mighty power that raised him from the dead. I want to suffer with him, sharing in his death, ¹¹ so that one way or another I will experience the resurrection from the dead! Philippians 3:1–11

Paul stressed that the only way we can be made right with God is through Jesus. Our human achievements pale compared to knowing him. He is the Way, the Truth, and the Life we need (John 14:6). In comparison, everything else is worthless. Christ gives us not only righteousness but the promise of the resurrection and eternal life.

Part 2—Press Onward

When Paul spoke about how much he valued Christ, or how much he was willing to suffer for him, he did not want the Philippians to think that he was boasting. Therefore, he explained:

¹² I don't mean to say that I have already achieved these things or that I have already reached perfection. But I press on to possess that perfection for which Christ Jesus first possessed me. ¹³ No, dear brothers and sisters, I have not achieved it, but I focus on this one thing: Forgetting the past and looking forward to what lies ahead, ¹⁴ I press on to reach the end of the race and receive the heavenly prize for which God, through Christ Jesus, is calling us.

¹⁵ Let all who are spiritually mature agree on these things. If you disagree on some point, I believe God will make it plain to you. ¹⁶ But we must hold on to the progress we have already made.

¹⁷ Dear brothers and sisters, pattern your lives after mine, and learn from those who follow our example. ¹⁸ For I have told you often before, and I say it again with tears in my eyes, that there are many whose conduct shows they are really enemies of the cross of Christ. ¹⁹ They are headed for destruction. Their god is their appetite, they brag about shameful things, and they think only about this life here on earth. ²⁰ But we are citizens of heaven, where the Lord Jesus Christ lives. And we are eagerly waiting for him to return as our Savior. ²¹ He will take our weak mortal bodies and change them into glorious bodies like his own, using the same power with which he will bring everything under his control. Philippians 2:12–21

Paul's letter to the Philippians echoes what he wrote to the church in Corinth. He told the Corinthian believers to imitate him, just as he imitated Christ (1 Corinthians 11:1). Paul did not think he was perfect, or that he was the only one whose life the Philippians might imitate. He cared about the believers in Philippi and wanted them to consider their own conduct and persevere in pursuing the Lord. He hoped that this pursuit would bring them joy and peace.

⁴ Always be full of joy in the Lord. I say it again—rejoice! ⁵ Let everyone see that you are considerate in all you do. Remember, the Lord is coming soon.

⁶ Don't worry about anything; instead, pray about everything. Tell God what you need, and thank him for all he has done. ⁷ Then you will experience God's peace, which exceeds anything we can understand. His peace will guard your hearts and minds as you live in Christ Jesus.

⁸ And now, dear brothers and sisters, one final thing. Fix your thoughts on what is true, and honorable, and right, and pure, and lovely, and admirable. Think about things that are excellent and worthy of praise. ⁹ Keep putting into practice all you learned and received from me—everything you heard from me and saw me doing. Then the God of peace will be with you.   Philippians 4:4–9

Part 3—Contentment and Giving

One of the reasons that Paul wrote to the Philippians was to thank them for the gifts they sent through a man called *Epaphroditus*. That man almost died trying to help Paul (Philippians 2:25–30). Epaphroditus was planning to return to Philippi, and Paul wanted him not only to give the believers thanks on his behalf but to reassure them that he would be okay, no matter what happened. Paul also wanted to reassure the Philippians that they would be okay, too, because God would care for them.

¹⁰ How I praise the Lord that you are concerned about me again. I know you have always been concerned for me, but you didn't have the chance to help me. ¹¹ Not that I was ever in need, for I have learned how to be content with whatever I have. ¹² I know how to live on almost nothing or with everything. I have learned the secret of living in every situation, whether it is with a full stomach or empty, with plenty or little. ¹³ For I can do everything through Christ, who gives me strength. ¹⁴ Even so, you have done well to share with me in my present difficulty.   Philippians 4:10–14

Remember, contentment is an attitude of happiness, satisfaction, and peace with one's present circumstances. It is not always easy. Paul described it as something he had to learn. God requires his people to learn and do hard things so that their character might be transformed (Romans 5:3–5). But he also provides the help necessary to face every circumstance. And sometimes he uses believers to bless their brothers and sisters, like he used the Philippians to bless Paul.

¹⁵ As you know, you Philippians were the only ones who gave me financial help when I first brought you the Good News and then traveled on from Macedonia. No other church did this. ¹⁶ Even when I was in Thessalonica you sent help more than once. ¹⁷ I don't say this because I want a gift from you. Rather, I want you to receive a reward for your kindness.

[18] At the moment I have all I need—and more! I am generously supplied with the gifts you sent me with Epaphroditus. They are a sweet-smelling sacrifice that is acceptable and pleasing to God. [19] And this same God who takes care of me will supply all your needs from his glorious riches, which have been given to us in Christ Jesus.

[20] Now all glory to God our Father forever and ever! Amen.   Philippians 4:15–20

Paul had reassured the believers in Philippi that he was all right, even in prison. He thanked them for their gifts. He encouraged them to love and serve one another with the same mindset Christ had. And he assured them God would help them, answer their prayers, and supply all their needs. Paul did all this repeatedly mentioning how much joy he had, and how much he wanted them to share his joy. How do you think the Philippians might have felt after reading Paul's letter? They surely realized they had many reasons to rejoice!

Lesson 13   God's Rescue Mission

Getting Started—The Main Ideas

The letter to the Colossians is the seventh letter of Paul's in the New Testament. It follows Romans, 1 and 2 Corinthians, Galatians, Ephesians, and Philippians. Paul was under house arrest in Rome when he wrote the epistle during the same time period as he penned the letters of Ephesians, Philippians, and Philemon. Timothy, Paul's young student and coworker, was with Paul at least part of the time during this confinement because Paul and Timothy are both mentioned as the authors of the letter to the Colossians. Timothy probably took dictation from Paul.

Paul's purpose in writing was to remind the believers of God's plan to save all those who place their faith in Christ. Paul underscored the gospel message that salvation is only through faith in Jesus Christ. He emphasized that the Person of Jesus Christ must be understood accurately because, as he affirmed, Christ is the visible image of the invisible God. He existed before anything was created and is supreme over all creation. For God in all his fullness was pleased to live in Christ (Colossians 1:15, 19).

When Jesus died on the cross, Paul explained, he accomplished the greatest rescue mission ever attempted and carried out. Paul assured believers that they can trust in the finished work of God who has rescued us from the kingdom of darkness and transferred us into the Kingdom of his dear Son, who purchased our freedom and forgave our sins (Colossians 1:13–14).

Paul's epistle not only taught the Christians correct doctrine about Christ's nature and purpose, but it also provided instruction about living a new life in Christ. This new life produces a Christlike character, affection, forgiveness, peace, worship, ministry, devotion to Christ, and thankfulness in everything.

Topic 1—Rescued from Darkness

Introduction: In the southwestern state of Arizona, visitors can experience total darkness. The Coronado Cave is part of the Coronado National Memorial Park in Hereford, Arizona. The cave is absolutely pitch black, and, without a light source, hikers can easily become disoriented. In the first-century Roman world, most people were spiritually disoriented—turned away from God and hardened against him in their hearts. The Colossian believers needed to live as light in the dark world around them.

Part 1—Introduction to Colossians

The Colossian church was founded by Epaphras during the time Paul was living in Ephesus. (You can read about Paul's sojourn there in Acts 19:10.) Bible scholars do not know why Epaphras decided to start a church in Colossae—perhaps it was his hometown. We also do not know how Epaphras became a Christian, but we do know that he was familiar with Paul. Later, the church experienced problems that Epaphras told Paul about when he visited Paul during his imprisonment in Rome between AD 61 and AD 63.

Recall that Paul's letters to the churches of the New Testament were written almost 2,000 years ago, and the names of regions and cities have changed since then. So, you won't find Colossae, or Colosse, as it is sometimes spelled, on a modern map of Turkey. However, the site of Ephesus is known, and archaeologists say the site of Colossae is about 120 miles east of Ephesus in the Lycus River Valley. Although no one lives there now, Colossae was one of three major cities in the area (the other two were Laodicea and Hierapolis), at the foot of Mount Cadmus. Abundant pastureland made the area ideal for raising sheep, and Colossae was a center for trade in wool and woolen goods. It was also famous for its purple dye made from the cyclamen flower. Philemon lived in this city, and Paul later addressed another of his epistles to him.

As we know from Colossians 2:1, Paul never visited the church in Colossae, but he knew (from Epaphras) about the false teachers and empty philosophies that were taking hold in the congregation, so he addressed issues of faith and conduct directly. Tychicus—who also carried the letter of Ephesians—brought Paul's words to Colossae and probably stayed on for a while to offer instruction and counsel.

Part 2—Paul Commends the Colossians

Paul began his letter by saying that he was pleased when he heard of the Colossians' faith and love for all God's people as a gift of the Holy Spirit. Paul, Timothy, and Epaphras prayed ardently on behalf of the believers, especially that they would grow in spiritual wisdom and understanding. Paul used two familiar analogies to encourage the believers—first that they would produce good fruit, and second that they would be lights in a dark world.

[1] This letter is from Paul, chosen by the will of God to be an apostle of Christ Jesus, and from our brother Timothy.

[2] We are writing to God's holy people in the city of Colosse, who are faithful brothers and sisters in Christ.

May God our Father give you grace and peace.

[3] We always pray for you, and we give thanks to God, the Father of our Lord Jesus Christ. [4] For we have heard of your faith in Christ Jesus and your love for all of God's people, [5] which come from your confident hope of what God has reserved for you in heaven. You have had this expectation ever since you first heard the truth of the Good News.

[6] This same Good News that came to you is going out all over the world. It is bearing fruit everywhere by changing lives, just as it changed your lives from the day you first heard and understood the truth about God's wonderful grace.

[7] You learned about the Good News from Epaphras, our beloved co-worker. He is Christ's faithful servant, and he is helping us on your behalf. [8] He has told us about the love for others that the Holy Spirit has given you.

[9] So we have not stopped praying for you since we first heard about you. We ask God to give you complete knowledge of his will and to give you spiritual wisdom and understanding. [10] Then the way you live will always honor and please the Lord, and your lives will produce every kind of good fruit. All the while, you will grow as you learn to know God better and better.

[11] We also pray that you will be strengthened with all his glorious power so you will have all the endurance and patience you need. May you be filled with joy, [12] always thanking the Father. He has enabled you to share in the inheritance that belongs to his people, who live in the light. [13] For he has rescued us from the kingdom of darkness and transferred us into the Kingdom of his dear Son, [14] who purchased our freedom and forgave our sins.   Colossians 1:1–14

Part 3—The Supremacy of Christ

Paul continued his letter with what was probably an early Christian hymn about the supremacy, sufficiency, and lordship of Christ. Supremacy is *the quality or state of being highest in rank or authority*. Paul affirmed that Christ is fully human and fully divine, the Son of God, and Ruler over all creation. He is the source of creation and the one who reconciles and brings peace to everything in heaven and on Earth.

As you read this section of Scripture, think about it as a hymn of praise. Read it again, and let it sink into your mind and your heart.

[15] Christ is the visible image of the invisible God.
   He existed before anything was created and is supreme over all creation,
[16] for through him God created everything

   in the heavenly realms and on earth.
He made the things we can see
   and the things we can't see—
such as thrones, kingdoms, rulers, and authorities in the unseen world.
   Everything was created through him and for him.
[17] He existed before anything else,
   and he holds all creation together.
[18] Christ is also the head of the church,
   which is his body.
   He is the beginning,
      supreme over all who rise from the dead.
   So he is first in everything.
[19] For God in all his fullness
   was pleased to live in Christ,
[20] and through him God reconciled
   everything to himself.
   He made peace with everything in heaven and on earth
   by means of Christ's blood on the cross.   Colossians 1:15–20

Paul turned his attention to the Gentile believers and challenged them to continue in their faith in Jesus as Lord. They were reconciled to God through Christ and able to stand in the very presence of almighty God!

However, there were forces of wickedness, both physical and spiritual, that would pry the Colossians away from their relationship with God. Paul warned the believers that they must be firm in the truth and not "drift away" by believing teachings contrary to the good news of God's Word.

²¹ This includes you who were once far away from God. You were his enemies, separated from him by your evil thoughts and actions. ²² Yet now he has reconciled you to himself through the death of Christ in his physical body. As a result, he has brought you into his own presence, and you are holy and blameless as you stand before him without a single fault.

²³ But you must continue to believe this truth and stand firmly in it. Don't drift away from the assurance you received when you heard the Good News. The Good News has been preached all over the world, and I, Paul, have been appointed as God's servant to proclaim it.   Colossians 1:21–23

> **Supremacy**
> The quality or state of being highest
> in rank or authority

Part 4—Paul's Labor

Recall that Paul was in prison in Rome when he wrote to the Colossian church. He was chained to a soldier at night to prevent his escape, but he endured other physical pain as well, perhaps from a previous beating (Acts 21:32) and stoning (Acts 14:19). Although Paul was in pain, he remarked that his affliction, or *great suffering*, was for the good of the whole church.

One of Paul's purposes in addressing this congregation of believers was to make sure that they understood the secret or mystery that God had kept hidden for centuries but now revealed: God wanted both Jews and Gentiles to share equally in God's riches because Christ lived in them.

²⁴ I am glad when I suffer for you in my body, for I am participating in the sufferings of Christ that continue for his body, the church. ²⁵ God has given me the responsibility of serving his church by proclaiming his entire message to you. ²⁶ This message was kept secret for centuries and generations past, but now it has been revealed to God's people. ²⁷ For God wanted them to know that the riches and glory of Christ are for you Gentiles, too. And this is the secret: Christ lives in you. This gives you assurance of sharing his glory.

²⁸ So we tell others about Christ, warning everyone and teaching everyone with all the wisdom God has given us. We want to present them to God, perfect in their relationship to Christ. ²⁹ That's why I work and struggle so hard, depending on Christ's mighty power that works within me.   Colossians 1:24–29

> **Affliction**
> Great suffering

Topic 2—Complete in Christ

Introduction: Gnosticism, a worldview of various cults in the early Christian centuries, held that matter is evil, so Christ could not have been a human being. Paul wrote again and again about the dual nature of Christ, emphasizing Christ's supremacy. Paul may have had gnostic teaching in mind when he warned the Colossians about being deceived by "high-sounding nonsense" (Colossians 2:8).

Another false teaching that was prevalent in the first-century church was the teaching that a Gentile must first become a Jew before becoming a Christian. As you learned in the book of Galatians, faith alone was all that was needed for salvation, not faith plus obedience to the Law.

Rhetoric (the art of public speaking) was prized by people in the first century. They especially enjoyed listening to learned and sophisticated speakers who could expound on philosophy and religion. Some false teachers encouraged believers to seek mystical or even occult experiences. Each false teacher pulled believers further from the truth. Paul explained that Christians were raised to life because of their faith and trust in the mighty power of God, who raised Christ from the dead. Christ's death gave us new life through the forgiveness of our sins. Christians must refuse and resist all substitutes for the sufficiency of faith in Christ.

[1] I want you to know how much I have agonized for you and for the church at Laodicea, and for many other believers who have never met me personally. [2] I want them to be encouraged and knit together by strong ties of love. I want them to have complete confidence that they understand God's mysterious plan, which is Christ himself. [3] In him lie hidden all the treasures of wisdom and knowledge.

[4] I am telling you this so no one will deceive you with well-crafted arguments. [5] For though I am far away from you, my heart is with you. And I rejoice that you are living as you should and that your faith in Christ is strong.

[6] And now, just as you accepted Christ Jesus as your Lord, you must continue to follow him. [7] Let your roots grow down into him, and let your lives be built on him. Then your faith will grow strong in the truth you were taught, and you will overflow with thankfulness.

[8] Don't let anyone capture you with empty philosophies and high-sounding nonsense that come from human thinking and from the spiritual powers of this world, rather than from Christ. [9] For in Christ lives all the fullness of God in a human body. [10] So you also are complete through your union with Christ, who is the head over every ruler and authority.

Colossians 2:1–10

Jesus, who was fully human and fully God, was the only Person able to accomplish the sanctifying work of cutting away our old nature and canceling the record of our sins. Not only did Paul affirm to the Colossians that their sinful selves were buried with Christ in baptism, but he also announced that spiritual rulers and authorities (demonic agents) no longer had power over them.

[11] When you came to Christ, you were "circumcised," but not by a physical procedure. Christ performed a spiritual circumcision—the cutting away of your sinful nature. [12] For you were buried with Christ when you were baptized. And with him you were raised to new life because you trusted the mighty power of God, who raised Christ from the dead.

[13] You were dead because of your sins and because your sinful nature was not yet cut away. Then God made you alive with Christ, for he forgave all our sins. [14] He canceled the record of the charges against us and took it away by nailing it to the cross. [15] In this way, he disarmed the spiritual rulers and authorities. He shamed them publicly by his victory over them on the cross.

Colossians 2:11–15

The Colossian church was flooded with criticism about what its Gentiles members ate and drank, what holy days they observed, and what points of Jewish law they followed. Instead of being truly free in Christ, they were going backward—mixing the Old Testament system of righteousness through sacrifice and obedience to the Law with new life in Christ. This mix of doctrine and practices, known as *syncretism*, diluted the gospel! Paul encouraged the believers to live like free and forgiven people.

Paul also reminded the Colossians that following human teachings and regulations does not make people holy. If following the Law could do that, there would be no need for Christ to die. It is only by staying connected to Christ and relying on the Holy Spirit to change us from the inside that we can overcome our sinful, selfish desires.

[16] So don't let anyone condemn you for what you eat or drink, or for not celebrating certain holy days or new moon ceremonies or Sabbaths. [17] For these rules are only shadows of the reality yet to come. And Christ himself is that reality. [18] Don't let anyone condemn you by insisting on pious self-denial or the worship of angels, saying they have had visions about these things. Their sinful minds have made them proud, [19] and they are not connected to Christ, the head of the body. For he holds the whole body together with its joints and ligaments, and it grows as God nourishes it.

[20] You have died with Christ, and he has set you free from the spiritual powers of this world. So why do you keep on following the rules of the world, such as, [21] "Don't handle! Don't taste! Don't touch!"? [22] Such rules are mere human teachings about things that deteriorate as we use them. [23] These rules may seem wise because they require strong devotion, pious self-denial, and severe bodily discipline. But they provide no help in conquering a person's evil desires.

Colossians 2:16–23

Topic 3—Principles for Holy Living

Introduction: Gnostic beliefs held that matter was evil and earthly, so it didn't matter what someone did with his or her body if his or her spirit was focused on God. In contrast, Paul taught the Colossians that the Christian worldview should impact on their lives in very practical ways. It did matter what they did with their bodies. And it mattered how they treated others, especially members of their own families.

Part 1—Christian Living

Paul explained that living the new life starts with having a new mindset. Instead of being distracted by competing religious philosophies, believers needed to think about how to live life as sanctified people. They needed to set their sights on God's will and to the task of the church on Earth: to call people to eternal life.

¹ Since you have been raised to new life with Christ, set your sights on the realities of heaven, where Christ sits in the place of honor at God's right hand. ² Think about the things of heaven, not the things of earth. ³ For you died to this life, and your real life is hidden with Christ in God. ⁴ And when Christ, who is your life, is revealed to the whole world, you will share in all his glory.

Colossians 3:1–4

"Impurity" refers to anything unclean, unwholesome, or unedifying. This includes anything that would corrupt our minds, especially sexually suggestive material. Looking at this type of material can be disastrous to a healthy Christian life now and to any future relationship you may have with your future husband or wife. Paul urged the Colossians to "put to death" all impurity. Then he urged the believers to put on a new nature and to be renewed by their Creator.

⁵ So put to death the sinful, earthly things lurking within you. Have nothing to do with sexual immorality, impurity, lust, and evil desires. Don't be greedy, for a greedy person is an idolater, worshiping the things of this world. ⁶ Because of these sins, the anger of God is coming. ⁷ You used to do these things when your life was still part of this world. ⁸ But now is the time to get rid of anger, rage, malicious behavior, slander, and dirty language. ⁹ Don't lie to each other, for you have stripped off your old sinful nature and all its wicked deeds. ¹⁰ Put on your new nature, and be renewed as you learn to know your Creator and become like him. ¹¹ In this new life, it doesn't matter if you are a Jew or a Gentile, circumcised or uncircumcised, barbaric, uncivilized, slave, or free. Christ is all that matters, and he lives in all of us.

Colossians 3:5–11

Paul told the believers to get rid of negative behaviors, including uncontrolled anger and rage, acts of intentional harm to others, and careless words. Then he encouraged the believers to take up new behaviors, such as forgiving others and being kind to them, to produce a pattern of the Spirit-filled, Christ-honoring lives we should have as God's image-bearers.

¹² Since God chose you to be the holy people he loves, you must clothe yourselves with tenderhearted mercy, kindness, humility, gentleness, and patience. ¹³ Make allowance for each other's faults, and forgive anyone who offends you. Remember, the Lord forgave you, so you must forgive others. ¹⁴ Above all, clothe yourselves with love, which binds us all together in perfect harmony. ¹⁵ And let the peace that comes from Christ rule in your hearts. For as members of one body you are called to live in peace. And always be thankful.

¹⁶ Let the message about Christ, in all its richness, fill your lives. Teach and counsel each other with all the wisdom he gives. Sing psalms and hymns and spiritual songs to God with thankful hearts. ¹⁷ And whatever you do or say, do it as a representative of the Lord Jesus, giving thanks through him to God the Father.

Colossians 3:12–17

Part 2—Godly Households

When Christ is Lord of our life, pleasing him will be the deciding factor in what we think and in all our decisions. In a Christian home, decisions are made by husbands and wives in loving submission to each other and to Christ, who is their example. Recall that you learned in the book of Philippians that even though Jesus was equal in nature, divinity, power, glory, and authority with his Father, he humbled himself and submitted to God's plan of redemption (Philippians 2:5–8). Wives were to follow a similar pattern in submitting to their husbands. Likewise, husbands were given the responsibility to love their wives with *agape* love—the unselfish, sacrificial love Jesus has for the church. Children were to obey their loving fathers and mothers, who were obligated to set standards, provide guidance, encourage, and lovingly discipline their children.

¹⁸ Wives, submit to your husbands, as is fitting for those who belong to the Lord.

¹⁹ Husbands, love your wives and never treat them harshly.

²⁰ Children, always obey your parents, for this pleases the Lord. ²¹ Fathers, do not aggravate your children, or they will become discouraged.

Colossians 3:18–21

Remember that Paul did not advocate the institution of slavery when he told slaves to obey their masters. Slavery was an evil that existed throughout the Roman Empire, and many people had household workers who did various tasks for the family. But Paul was not endorsing the status quo; he taught that Christian slaves and Christian masters are accountable to God for the way they treat each other. Paul said:

²² Slaves, obey your earthly masters in everything you do. Try to please them all the time, not just when they are watching you. Serve them sincerely because of your reverent fear of the Lord. ²³ Work willingly at whatever you do, as though you were working for the Lord rather than for people. ²⁴ Remember that the Lord will give you an inheritance as your reward, and that the Master you are serving is Christ. ²⁵ But if you do what is wrong, you will be paid back for the wrong you have done. For God has no favorites.

¹ Masters, be just and fair to your slaves. Remember that you also have a Master—in heaven.

Colossians 3:22–4:1

Remember that the principles of working honestly and diligently apply to you—now, as a student, and later as an employee.

Part 3—Further Instructions

Not only did the Christians in Colossae need advice with family relationships, but they also needed advice on how to conduct themselves with those both inside and outside the church. Paul explained that people are not won to Christ just by kind actions; they need to hear the message of salvation and see a change in the lives of believers. As everyday missionaries, Christians must be on the lookout for opportunities to share the gospel.

² Devote yourselves to prayer with an alert mind and a thankful heart. ³ Pray for us, too, that God will give us many opportunities to speak about his mysterious plan concerning Christ. That is why I am here in chains. ⁴ Pray that I will proclaim this message as clearly as I should.

⁵ Live wisely among those who are not believers, and make the most of every opportunity. ⁶ Let your conversation be gracious and attractive so that you will have the right response for everyone.   Colossians 4:2–6

Finally, Paul added some personal notes. Tychicus and Aristarchus were Gentile coworkers. Tychicus was mentioned in Acts 20:4 as being from Asia Minor; Aristarchus was from Thessalonica, and he shared some harrowing ministry experiences with Paul, including a shipwreck (Acts 27:14–28:1). Aristarchus may have been under house arrest with Paul.

1886 WOODCUT OF A
READING OF PAUL'S LETTER

Onesimus, as you can learn from the book of Philemon, was a runaway slave from Colossae. He later became a Christian. Paul sent him back to his master, Philemon, to be a faithful servant and beloved brother in Christ.

Mark and Luke were writers of the Gospels bearing their names, and Luke also wrote the book of Acts. Epaphras and Justus visited Paul while he was in Rome. Paul signed the letter because Timothy likely penned the letter. We don't know what kind of ministry Paul was talking about when he encouraged Archippus; perhaps it was church planting or pastoring.

[7] Tychicus will give you a full report about how I am getting along. He is a beloved brother and faithful helper who serves with me in the Lord's work. [8] I have sent him to you for this very purpose—to let you know how we are doing and to encourage you. [9] I am also sending Onesimus, a faithful and beloved brother, one of your own people. He and Tychicus will tell you everything that's happening here.

[10] Aristarchus, who is in prison with me, sends you his greetings, and so does Mark, Barnabas's cousin. As you were instructed before, make Mark welcome if he comes your way. [11] Jesus (the one we call Justus) also sends his greetings. These are the only Jewish believers among my co-workers; they are working with me here for the Kingdom of God. And what a comfort they have been!

[12] Epaphras, a member of your own fellowship and a servant of Christ Jesus, sends you his greetings. He always prays earnestly for you, asking God to make you strong and perfect, fully confident that you are following the whole will of God. [13] I can assure you that he prays hard for you and also for the believers in Laodicea and Hierapolis.

ARISTARCHUS

[14] Luke, the beloved doctor, sends his greetings, and so does Demas. [15] Please give my greetings to our brothers and sisters at Laodicea, and to Nympha and the church that meets in her house.

[16] After you have read this letter, pass it on to the church at Laodicea so they can read it, too. And you should read the letter I wrote to them.

[17] And say to Archippus, "Be sure to carry out the ministry the Lord gave you."

[18] HERE IS MY GREETING IN MY OWN HANDWRITING—PAUL.

Remember my chains.

May God's grace be with you.

Colossians 4:7–18

Hope in Christ's Return

Getting Started—The Main Ideas

St. Paul's Cathedral in Thessaloniki, Greece

The first and second letters to the Thessalonians were written by Paul and his companions, Silas and Timothy, to believers in the city of Thessalonica. Now known as *Thessaloniki*, it is the second-largest city in Greece, right after the capital, Athens.

Paul's letters to the Thessalonians are the eighth and ninth letters in the New Testament. Most scholars believe that 1 Thessalonians was written around AD 50 or 51 and that 2 Thessalonians was written only two or three months later.

The first thing that Paul did in 1 Thessalonians was express his concern for the church. He had been worried about how their faith would fare under persecution, but he heard wonderful reports of their faithfulness to the Lord. After commending them and praying for them, he encouraged them to live holy and pure lives, to stay away from sexual immorality, and to work hard. Then Paul taught the Thessalonians what happened to believers who died, and reminded them of the hope they had in the second coming, which is *the belief that Jesus will personally and visibly return from heaven to Earth*. In view of Jesus' return, Paul urged the Thessalonians to encourage one another and to stay alert.

> **The Second Coming**
> The belief that Jesus will personally and visibly return from heaven to Earth

Topic 1—Faithfulness to the Lord

Introduction: You recall that Paul and Silas founded the church in Philippi. God performed a miracle by freeing a slave girl from an evil spirit. Her masters were unhappy and had Paul and Silas thrown in jail. The city officials worried when they learned that Paul and Silas were Roman citizens. They begged them to leave the city. So, Paul and Silas then traveled through the towns of Amphipolis and Apollonia and came to Thessalonica (Acts 17:1). In Acts, Luke described how they founded a church there. The first chapter of 1 Thessalonians gives Paul's perspective on how this happened. It also says that the believers in Thessalonica became well-known to others because of their faith.

Part 1—Introduction to the Thessalonians

Do you remember that Philippi was founded by Philip II of Macedon? Well, Philip had a daughter, Thessalonike, who married a general, Cassander. Forty years after Philippi was founded, in 316 BC, Cassander founded the city of Thessalonica, and naming it after his wife. Later, the kingdom of Macedon was conquered by the Romans. Thessalonica was occupied by the Romans in 168 BC. In 148 BC, it became the capital and eventually the largest city of the province. It had its own harbor and was on the Egnatian Way, the great Roman trade route that was built in 130 BC. So, it was an important commercial and cultural center. Unlike Phillipi, it had a large enough Jewish population that it had a synagogue. And when Paul and his companions arrived in Thessalonica, that is where they went to preach the gospel.

RUINS OF THE ROMAN FORUM
AND ANCIENT MARKETPLACE
IN THESSALONIKI

Part 2—Paul's Previous Visit

The book of Acts tells how Paul's visit to Thessalonica took place and how the church in that city began.

¹ Paul and Silas . . . came to Thessalonica, where there was a Jewish synagogue. ² As was Paul's custom, he went to the synagogue service, and for three Sabbaths in a row he used the Scriptures to reason with the people. ³ He explained the prophecies and proved that the Messiah must suffer and rise from the dead. He said, "This Jesus I'm telling you about is the Messiah." ⁴ Some of the Jews who listened were persuaded and joined Paul and Silas, along with many God-fearing Greek men and quite a few prominent women.

NERO CAESAR
AUGUSTUS GERMANICUS,
AD 37–68

⁵ But some of the Jews were jealous, so they gathered some troublemakers from the marketplace to form a mob and start a riot. They attacked the home of Jason, searching for Paul and Silas so they could drag them out to the crowd. ⁶ Not finding them there, they dragged out Jason and some of the other believers instead and took them before the city council. "Paul and Silas have caused trouble all over the world," they shouted, "and now they are here disturbing our city, too. ⁷ And Jason has welcomed them into his home. They are all guilty of treason against Caesar, for they profess allegiance to another king, named Jesus."

⁸ The people of the city, as well as the city council, were thrown into turmoil by these reports. ⁹ So the officials forced Jason and the other believers to post bond, and then they released them.

¹⁰ That very night the believers sent Paul and Silas to Berea.   Acts 17:1–10

From almost the very start, the believers in Thessalonica faced persecution for their beliefs and faced it courageously. Though Paul and his companions had only been able to teach them about Jesus for a little while, the Thessalonians who believed were firm in their faith. But Paul was concerned about them, so he sent Timothy to visit them to strengthen and encourage them (1 Thessalonians 3:2). When Timothy returned with news of the church, Paul wrote back with thanks and prayers for their well-being.

² We always thank God for all of you and pray for you constantly. ³ As we pray to our God and Father about you, we think of your faithful work, your loving deeds, and the enduring hope you have because of our Lord Jesus Christ.

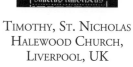

TIMOTHY, ST. NICHOLAS
HALEWOOD CHURCH,
LIVERPOOL, UK

⁴ We know, dear brothers and sisters, that God loves you and has chosen you to be his own people. . . . ⁶ You received the message with joy from the Holy Spirit in spite of the severe suffering it brought you. In this way, you imitated both us and the Lord. ⁷ As a result, you have become an example to all the believers in Greece—throughout both Macedonia and Achaia.

8 And now the word of the Lord is ringing out from you to people everywhere, even beyond Macedonia and Achaia, for wherever we go we find people telling us about your faith in God. We don't need to tell them about it, 9 for they keep talking about the wonderful welcome you gave us and how you turned away from idols to serve the living and true God. 10 And they speak of how you are looking forward to the coming of God's Son from heaven—Jesus, whom God raised from the dead. He is the one who has rescued us from the terrors of the coming judgment.   1 Thessalonians 1:2–10

The Thessalonian believers had become famous for their faith, and their story was encouraging other believers, both near and far. Sometimes people today see faith as a strictly private affair, not as something you discuss with others. But that is not the way Paul and others saw it. They were excited and joyful when they heard of the work God had done in Thessalonica.

2 God gave us the courage to declare his Good News to you boldly, in spite of great opposition. 3 So you can see we were not preaching with any deceit or impure motives or trickery.

4 For we speak as messengers approved by God to be entrusted with the Good News. Our purpose is to please God, not people. He alone examines the motives of our hearts. 5 Never once did we try to win you with flattery, as you well know. And God is our witness that we were not pretending to be your friends just to get your money! 6 As for human praise, we have never sought it from you or anyone else.

7 As apostles of Christ we certainly had a right to make some demands of you, but instead we were like children among you. Or we were like a mother feeding and caring for her own children. 8 We loved you so much that we shared with you not only God's Good News but our own lives, too.

9 Don't you remember, dear brothers and sisters, how hard we worked among you? Night and day we toiled to earn a living so that we would not be a burden to any of you as we preached God's Good News to you. 10 You yourselves are our witnesses—and so is God—that we were devout and honest and faultless toward all of you believers. 11 And you know that we treated each of you as a father treats his own children. 12 We pleaded with you, encouraged you, and urged you to live your lives in a way that God would consider worthy. For he called you to share in his Kingdom and glory.   1 Thessalonians 2:2–12

Paul and Silas, along with Timothy, worked hard to establish the church in Thessalonica. God knew their motives. They cared deeply for the people there. In fact, Paul referred to them using family relationships. Besides calling the Thessalonians his brothers and sisters, Paul said that he and his companions were like children to them, and also like their mother and father. He loved the Thessalonians so much he could hardly describe how he felt! And the people responded to the gospel message:

13 Therefore, we never stop thanking God that when you received his message from us, you didn't think of our words as mere human ideas. You accepted what we said as the very word of God—which, of course, it is. And this word continues to work in you who believe.   1 Thessalonians 2:13

Topic 2—Persecution

PAUL PREACHES IN ATHENS

Introduction: After starting the church in Thessalonica, Paul, Silas, and Timothy had to leave town quickly to avoid the Jews who were making trouble for them. They traveled to Berea, but the Jews from Thessalonica followed them. The believers in Berea took action immediately to protect Paul, escorting him to Athens (Acts 17:10–15). Paul sent Timothy back to Thessalonica and received his report on the church. Paul preached in Athens and then traveled to Corinth, were Silas and Timothy later joined him.

[1] Finally, when we could stand it no longer, we decided to stay alone in Athens, [2] and we sent Timothy to visit you. He is our brother and God's co-worker in proclaiming the Good News of Christ. We sent him to strengthen you, to encourage you in your faith, [3] and to keep you from being shaken by the troubles you were going through. But you know that we are destined for such troubles. [4] Even while we were with you, we warned you that troubles would soon come—and they did, as you well know. [5] That is why, when I could bear it no longer, I sent Timothy to find out whether your faith was still strong. I was afraid that the tempter had gotten the best of you and that our work had been useless.

1 Thessalonians 3:1–5

When Paul warned the Thessalonian believers that they would face trouble, he was telling them the same thing that Jesus had told his disciples (John 16:33) and Paul himself (Acts 9:16). Trusting in Christ does not mean that believers will not ever face troubles, trials, disappointment, or sorrow. But it does mean that despite all these things, overwhelming victory is ours through Christ, who loved us (Romans 8:37). Paul learned that the Thessalonians remained strong in their faith:

[6] But now Timothy has just returned, bringing us good news about your faith and love. He reports that you always remember our visit with joy and that you want to see us as much as we want to see you. [7] So we have been greatly encouraged in the midst of our troubles and suffering, dear brothers and sisters, because you have remained strong in your faith. [8] It gives us new life to know that you are standing firm in the Lord.

1 Thessalonians 3:6–8

YOUTH USING AMERICAN SIGN LANGUAGE FOR "LOVE"

The Thessalonians' faithfulness made Paul glad and grateful.

[9] How we thank God for you! Because of you we have great joy as we enter God's presence. [10] Night and day we pray earnestly for you, asking God to let us see you again to fill the gaps in your faith.

[11] May God our Father and our Lord Jesus bring us to you very soon. [12] And may the Lord make your love for one another and for all people grow and overflow, just as our love for you overflows. [13] May he, as a result, make your hearts strong, blameless, and holy as you stand before God our Father when our Lord Jesus comes again with all his holy people. Amen.

1 Thessalonians 3:9–13

Topic 3—Living to Please God

Introduction: After learning that the believers in Thessalonica had remained faithful even when facing persecution, Paul prayed for them to grow in love and holiness. Then he did what he often did in his letters: he reminded his readers of things he had already taught them. Paul did not mind repeating himself. When he wrote to the Philippians, Paul said, I never get tired of telling you these things, and I do it to safeguard your faith (Philippians 3:1). He continued:

¹ Finally, dear brothers and sisters, we urge you in the name of the Lord Jesus to live in a way that pleases God, as we have taught you. You live this way already, and we encourage you to do so even more. ² For you remember what we taught you by the authority of the Lord Jesus. ³ God's will is for you to be holy, so stay away from all sexual sin. ⁴ Then each of you will control his own body and live in holiness and honor— ⁵ not in lustful passion like the pagans who do not know God and his ways.

1 Thessalonians 4:1–5

Notice the order that is given in this Scripture passage. When a believer stays away from sin, instead of flirting with it and obsessing about it, he or she is then able to exercise self-control. Elsewhere, the Bible explains that desires give birth to sinful actions. And when sin is allowed to grow, it gives birth to death (James 1:15). If you do not want sin in your life, don't give it a chance to grow. Stay away from it! Paul continued:

⁶ Never harm or cheat a fellow believer in this matter by violating his wife, for the Lord avenges all such sins, as we have solemnly warned you before. ⁷ God has called us to live holy lives, not impure lives. ⁸ Therefore, anyone who refuses to live by these rules is not disobeying human teaching but is rejecting God, who gives his Holy Spirit to you.

1 Thessalonians 4:6–8

Sexual sin is a serious matter. It harms and cheats others. A believer who engages in sexual sin dishonors and rejects the holy God who saved and indwells him or her. By treating people as if they were objects, or abusing them, a believer dishonors the One who made every person in God's image. This does not mean that the Bible is against sex in its proper context. After all, God created men and women as sexual beings. It also does not mean that God, who is Love, forbids love. Paul added:

⁹ But we don't need to write to you about the importance of loving each other, for God himself has taught you to love one another. ¹⁰ Indeed, you already show your love for all the believers throughout Macedonia. Even so, dear brothers and sisters, we urge you to love them even more.

1 Thessalonians 4:9–10

How do you love others? You care about their needs. You pray for them. You encourage them. Finally, keeping in mind the opposition that the Thessalonians faced, Paul wrote:

¹¹ Make it your goal to live a quiet life, minding your own business and working with your hands, just as we instructed you before. ¹² Then people who are not believers will respect the way you live, and you will not need to depend on others.

1 Thessalonians 4:11–12

Paul had taught the Thessalonians, by his own example, to work hard to support themselves so as not to burden others (1 Thessalonians 2:9). In addition to his work planting churches, Paul made a living as a tentmaker (Acts 18:3). Remember what Paul taught elsewhere: Work willingly at whatever you do, as though you were working for the Lord rather than for people (Colossians 3:23). Working with one's hands is not dishonorable or something to be looked down upon. Paul hoped that the Thessalonians' hard work would be a good witness to those around them.

Topic 4–The Lord's Coming

Introduction: When Paul wrote this letter to the Thessalonians, Timothy had just returned and given him a report on how the church was thriving despite persecution. Although some people had already died as martyrs for the faith—such as Stephen, whose stoning Paul had witnessed (Acts 7:54, 57–60), and the apostle James (Acts 12:1–2)—the persecution in Thessalonica had not reached the level it had in Jerusalem. But in his letter, Paul next addressed the topic of what happens to believers who die. Perhaps Timothy brought news that some beloved members of the church had died. Or perhaps Paul, inspired by the Holy Spirit, felt it was important to prepare the church for what was to come.

[13] And now, dear brothers and sisters, we want you to know what will happen to the believers who have died so you will not grieve like people who have no hope. [14] For since we believe that Jesus died and was raised to life again, we also believe that when Jesus returns, God will bring back with him the believers who have died.

[15] We tell you this directly from the Lord: We who are still living when the Lord returns will not meet him ahead of those who have died. [16] For the Lord himself will come down from heaven with a commanding shout, with the voice of the archangel, and with the trumpet call of God. First, the believers who have died will rise from their graves. [17] Then, together with them, we who are still alive and remain on the earth will be caught up in the clouds to meet the Lord in the air. Then we will be with the Lord forever. [18] So encourage each other with these words.

1 Thessalonians 4:13–18

Paul taught that the believers in Thessalonica should be encouraged by the hope of the resurrection. Because Jesus lives, those who believe in him also have eternal life. They will not remain in their graves but will rise to meet the Lord Jesus in the air when he returns in glory. This is what Jesus himself taught his disciples:

[30] All the peoples of the earth . . . will see the Son of Man coming on the clouds of heaven with power and great glory. [31] And he will send out his angels with the mighty blast of a trumpet, and they will gather his chosen ones from all over the world—from the farthest ends of the earth and heaven.

Matthew 24:30–31

Remember, the second coming is the belief that Jesus will personally and visibly return from heaven to Earth. When Jesus comes back, he will judge the living and the dead and establish his kingdom. As the believers in Thessalonica faced all kinds of trials, remembering that Jesus would return was surely an encouragement. Paul continued:

[1] Now concerning how and when all this will happen, dear brothers and sisters, we don't really need to write you. [2] For you know quite well that the day of the Lord's return will come unexpectedly, like a thief in the night. [3] When people are saying, "Everything is peaceful and secure," then disaster will fall on them as suddenly as a pregnant woman's labor pains begin. And there will be no escape.

1 Thessalonians 5:1–3

Paul taught what Jesus had taught. When Jesus spoke to his disciples about what the day of the Lord's return would be like, he said it would come unexpectedly. He too used the image of a thief in the night, as well as the images of a master away on business and a delayed bridegroom (Matthew 24:42–44, 45–50, 25:1–13). Jesus repeatedly warned the disciples to be prepared. Paul reiterated this message in his letter to the Thessalonians.

⁴But you aren't in the dark about these things, dear brothers and sisters, and you won't be surprised when the day of the Lord comes like a thief. ⁵For you are all children of the light and of the day; we don't belong to darkness and night. ⁶So be on your guard, not asleep like the others. Stay alert and be clearheaded. ⁷Night is the time when people sleep and drinkers get drunk. ⁸But let us who live in the light be clearheaded, protected by the armor of faith and love, and wearing as our helmet the confidence of our salvation.

⁹For God chose to save us through our Lord Jesus Christ, not to pour out his anger on us. ¹⁰Christ died for us so that, whether we are dead or alive when he returns, we can live with him forever. ¹¹So encourage each other and build each other up, just as you are already doing.

1 Thessalonians 5:4–11

People who do not know God or the Scriptures, and even many who do not understand them well, may imagine God as someone full of wrath and displeasure, eager to punish people. But Paul emphasized God's

desire to save people through Jesus rather than to pour out his anger on them. In another letter, the apostle Peter affirmed: The Lord is not slow in keeping his promise [about the day of his return]. Instead he is patient with you, not wanting anyone to perish, but everyone to come to repentance (2 Peter 3:9). We can encourage each other in faith by remembering and proclaiming that the God we worship is not only just, but wonderfully loving and patient. He wants us all to know Christ and live with him forever.

Topic 5—Paul's Advice

Introduction: Paul urged the Thessalonians to live holy lives as they waited for Jesus' return. He gave the believers practical advice with many short, direct sentences.

¹²Dear brothers and sisters, honor those who are your leaders in the Lord's work. They work hard among you and give you spiritual guidance. ¹³Show them great respect and wholehearted love because of their work. And live peacefully with each other.

¹⁴Brothers and sisters, we urge you to warn those who are lazy. Encourage those who are timid. Take tender care of those who are weak. Be patient with everyone.

¹⁵See that no one pays back evil for evil, but always try to do good to each other and to all people.

¹⁶Always be joyful. ¹⁷Never stop praying. ¹⁸Be thankful in all circumstances, for this is God's will for you who belong to Christ Jesus.

1 Thessalonians 5:12–18

It is not always easy to be joyful or to pray or to give thanks. A well-known story about a famous Welsh preacher named *Matthew Henry* says that after being robbed of his wallet, he prayed to God, saying, "I thank Thee first because I was never robbed before; second, because although they took my purse they did not take my life; third, because although they took my all, it was not much; and fourth because it was I who was robbed, and not I who robbed."[1]

Giving thanks in all circumstances is difficult, but God can help us do so. Perhaps that is why Paul's next words encouraged the believers to remember God was at work in their midst.

[19] Do not stifle the Holy Spirit. [20] Do not scoff at prophecies, [21] but test everything that is said. Hold on to what is good. [22] Stay away from every kind of evil.

1 Thessalonians 5:19–22

Do you remember who was praised for following these commands? After Paul left Thessalonica, and before he wrote this letter, he traveled to another city. The Bible says, The people of Berea were more open-minded

than those in Thessalonica, and they listened eagerly to Paul's message. They searched the Scriptures day after day to see if Paul and Silas were teaching the truth (Acts 17:3). They tested what the missionaries said to see if it was true. They did not ignore the promptings of the Holy Spirit. He was working in their hearts. They did not scoff at the strange message these people had about a man named *Jesus* who rose from the dead. Instead, they listened and compared what was said with the Scriptures. The Holy Spirit, who is God, uses both the natural and supernatural gifts he has given, and the Bible, to guide his people.

Staying away from evil is important for anyone who wants to follow Jesus. In another letter, Paul wrote: Let the Holy Spirit guide your lives. Then you won't be doing what your sinful nature craves. The sinful nature wants to do evil, which is just the opposite of what the Spirit wants (Galatians 5:16–17). So, Paul concluded his letter to the Thessalonians with a prayer that they would be holy:

[23] Now may the God of peace make you holy in every way, and may your whole spirit and soul and body be kept blameless until our Lord Jesus Christ comes again. [24] God will make this happen, for he who calls you is faithful.

[25] Dear brothers and sisters, pray for us.

[26] Greet all the brothers and sisters with a sacred kiss.

[27] I command you in the name of the Lord to read this letter to all the brothers and sisters.

[28] May the grace of our Lord Jesus Christ be with you.

1 Thessalonians 5:23–28

Topic 6—Hope and Encouragement

Introduction: Paul followed up his first letter to the believers in Thessalonica with a second letter, which became the book of 2 Thessalonians in the New Testament. Recall that most scholars think 2 Thessalonians was sent only a few months after the first letter, in AD 50 or 51. Because of this, the situation had not changed that much. The believers were still facing persecution and looking forward to the time when God would make things right. They were still looking forward to the second coming.

[1] This letter is from Paul, Silas, and Timothy.

We are writing to the church in Thessalonica, to you who belong to God our Father and the Lord Jesus Christ.

[2] May God our Father and the Lord Jesus Christ give you grace and peace.

[3] Dear brothers and sisters, we can't help but thank God for you, because your faith is flourishing and your love for one another is growing. [4] We proudly tell God's other churches about your endurance and faithfulness

in all the persecutions and hardships you are suffering. ⁵ And God will use this persecution to show his justice and to make you worthy of his Kingdom, for which you are suffering. ⁶ In his justice he will pay back those who persecute you.

⁷ And God will provide rest for you who are being persecuted and also for us when the Lord Jesus appears from heaven. He will come with his mighty angels, ⁸ in flaming fire, bringing judgment on those who don't know God and on those who refuse to obey the Good News of our Lord Jesus. ⁹ They will be punished with eternal destruction, forever separated from the Lord and from his glorious power. ¹⁰ When he comes on that day, he will receive glory from his holy people—praise from all who believe. And this includes you, for you believed what we told you about him.

JUDGMENT DAY FRESCO, VORONET MONASTERY, ROMANIA

¹¹ So we keep on praying for you, asking our God to enable you to live a life worthy of his call. May he give you the power to accomplish all the good things your faith prompts you to do. ¹² Then the name of our Lord Jesus will be honored because of the way you live, and you will be honored along with him. This is all made possible because of the grace of our God and Lord, Jesus Christ.   2 Thessalonians 1:1–12

Paul commended the believers' love, endurance, and faithfulness. He assured them that God was aware of their suffering and would punish those who persecuted them. Paul prayed for God to empower the believers to live according to their faith so that Jesus would be honored.

Topic 7—Before Christ's Return

Introduction: Paul learned that some believers misunderstood what he had written about the second coming and the day of the Lord's return. He wrote to correct them and to explain how those who believe in Jesus should live while they wait for Jesus to come back.

¹ Now, dear brothers and sisters, let us clarify some things about the coming of our Lord Jesus Christ and how we will be gathered to meet him. ² Don't be so easily shaken or alarmed by those who say that the day of the Lord has already begun. Don't believe them, even if they claim to have had a spiritual vision, a revelation, or a letter supposedly from us. ³ Don't be fooled by what they say. For that day will not come until there is a great rebellion against God and the man of lawlessness is revealed—the one who brings destruction. ⁴ He will exalt himself and defy everything that people call god and every object of worship. He will even sit in the temple of God, claiming that he himself is God.

⁵ Don't you remember that I told you about all this when I was with you? ⁶ And you know what is holding him back, for he can be revealed only when his time comes. ⁷ For this lawlessness is already at work secretly, and it will remain secret until the one who is holding it back steps out of the way. ⁸ Then the man of lawlessness will be revealed, but the Lord Jesus will slay him with the breath of his mouth and destroy him by the splendor of his coming.

⁹ This man will come to do the work of Satan with counterfeit power and signs and miracles. ¹⁰ He will use every kind of evil deception to fool those on their way to destruction, because they refuse to love and accept the truth that would save them. ¹¹ So God will cause them to be greatly deceived, and they will believe these lies. ¹² Then they will be condemned for enjoying evil rather than believing the truth.   2 Thessalonians 2:1–12

The appearance of the man of lawlessness was prophesied in the Old Testament. When Jesus taught his disciples what would happen in the end times, he referred to a prophecy from Daniel to warn his followers to pay attention; Jesus added that the disciples should not be deceived by false prophets but should stand strong to the end (Matthew 24:11–15). Paul taught the Thessalonians that there would be many signs before the Lord returned, so they did not need to fear that they had missed the second coming.

Topic 8—Standing Firm

Introduction: If the Thessalonian believers did not have to worry about the end times, what did they need to do? Paul continued his letter to the believers by rejoicing in their salvation and encouraging them to stand firm in their faith. He reminded them that due to their belief, they would be made holy and share in Christ's glory.

¹³ As for us, we can't help but thank God for you, dear brothers and sisters loved by the Lord. We are always thankful that God chose you to be among the first to experience salvation—a salvation that came through the Spirit who makes you holy and through your belief in the truth. ¹⁴ He called you to salvation when we told you the Good News; now you can share in the glory of our Lord Jesus Christ.

¹⁵ With all these things in mind, dear brothers and sisters, stand firm and keep a strong grip on the teaching we passed on to you both in person and by letter.

¹⁶ Now may our Lord Jesus Christ himself and God our Father, who loved us and by his grace gave us eternal comfort and a wonderful hope, ¹⁷ comfort you and strengthen you in every good thing you do and say.

2 Thessalonians 2:13–17

After praying for them, Paul then asked the Thessalonians to pray also.

¹ Finally, dear brothers and sisters, we ask you to pray for us. Pray that the Lord's message will spread rapidly and be honored wherever it goes, just as when it came to you. ² Pray, too, that we will be rescued from wicked and evil people, for not everyone is a believer. ³ But the Lord is faithful; he will strengthen you and guard you from the evil one. ⁴ And we are confident in the Lord that you are doing and will continue to do the things we commanded you. ⁵ May the Lord lead your hearts into a full understanding and expression of the love of God and the patient endurance that comes from Christ.

2 Thessalonians 3:1–5

Before ending his letter, Paul dealt with a problem. Because some believers thought the second coming would happen right away, they had stopped working and started gossiping. Their behavior was a burden to their brothers and sisters.

⁶ And now, dear brothers and sisters, we give you this command in the name of our Lord Jesus Christ: Stay away from all believers who live idle lives and don't follow the tradition they received from us. ⁷ For you know that you ought to imitate us. We were not idle when we were with you. ⁸ We never accepted food from anyone without paying for it. We worked hard day and night so we would not be a burden to any of you. ⁹ We certainly had the right to ask you to feed us, but we wanted to give you an example to follow. ¹⁰ Even while we were with you, we gave you this command: "Those unwilling to work will not get to eat."

[11] Yet we hear that some of you are living idle lives, refusing to work and meddling in other people's business. [12] We command such people and urge them in the name of the Lord Jesus Christ to settle down and work to earn their own living. [13] As for the rest of you, dear brothers and sisters, never get tired of doing good.

[14] Take note of those who refuse to obey what we say in this letter. Stay away from them so they will be ashamed. [15] Don't think of them as enemies, but warn them as you would a brother or sister.

2 Thessalonians 3:6–15

Paul gave the Thessalonians advice similar to what he said to other churches. In writing to the Galatians, he said, Let us not become weary in doing good, for at the proper time we will reap a harvest if we do not give up (Galatians 6:9). And in writing to the Corinthians, he warned, Do not be misled: "Bad company corrupts good character" (1 Corinthians 15:33). It can be very hard to admit that a friend or a brother or sister is lazy or disobedient, but it is important not to let feelings cloud your judgment. Do not let such people influence you. Don't copy them and gossip about them either. Honestly tell them about your concerns and see how they respond. Choose to spend time with others who encourage you to move forward and who help you grow. Strive to be the kind of person who helps others be the best they can be, too.

[16] Now may the Lord of peace himself give you his peace at all times and in every situation. The Lord be with you all.

[17] HERE IS MY GREETING IN MY OWN HANDWRITING— PAUL. I DO THIS IN ALL MY LETTERS TO PROVE THEY ARE FROM ME.

[18] May the grace of our Lord Jesus Christ be with you all.

2 Thessalonians 3:16–18

Paul finished his second letter to the Thessalonians in the same way he started it, by praying that Jesus' grace would be with each believer there. And his prayer was answered. Church history tells how the Christian faith grew in Thessalonica and the surrounding regions, until many more people came to know Jesus as their Lord and Savior.

ENDNOTES
1 Cited by Randy Alcorn in *Happiness* (Carol Stream, IL: Tyndale House Publishers, 2015), 362.

Getting Started—The Main Ideas

The first and second letters to Timothy were written by Paul to his young student and coworker Timothy. These two books, along with Titus, are called *pastoral epistles*, meaning they were written from one pastor to another. Bible scholars place the date of 1 Timothy at about AD 64. Paul wrote 2 Timothy in about AD 67, just before history tells us he was executed by Caesar Nero. It was probably his last letter.

Timothy was one of Paul's closest companions. You may recall that Timothy was with Paul during his first imprisonment in Rome and probably wrote down the letter to the Colossians as Paul dictated it. Sometime during or just after his imprisonment, Paul had sent Timothy to pastor the church at Ephesus during a difficult time. First Timothy is not only a personal encouragement but also contains Paul's practical advice about ministry.

Paul's purpose in writing his second letter was to urge Timothy to visit one final time. From the somber nature of 2 Timothy, Paul knew that his work was done and that his life was nearly at an end (2 Timothy 4:6–8).

CELSUS LIBRARY IN EPHESUS

Topic 1—Paul Advises Timothy

Introduction: Paul's first letter to Timothy affirmed Paul's apostleship and his relationship to Timothy as a father figure and mentor, or *a trusted counselor*. Paul first called on God the Father to bless Timothy. Then he gave Timothy a stern warning about false teachers who were infiltrating the church with heresy—*any teaching that does not agree with biblical truth*. Most of their heresies sounded logical and were cunningly convincing, but they misled believers because they contradicted the instruction the apostles had received directly from Jesus. So, Paul sent Timothy to Ephesus to combat heretical teachings by preaching sound doctrine and salvation through faith in Christ alone.

Mentor
A trusted counselor

Heresy
Any teaching that does not agree with biblical truth

Part 1—Introduction to 1 and 2 Timothy

Timothy probably became a Christian after Paul's first missionary visit to Lystra (Acts 16:1–5). He already had solid training in the Hebrew Scriptures from his mother and grandmother, who were Jewish. By Paul's second visit, Timothy had grown into a mature disciple (Acts 16:2), and Paul and Silas did not hesitate to take Timothy along on their missionary journey. Because Timothy was of mixed Greek-Jewish ancestry, he had not been circumcised. Knowing how important it was to reach both Jewish and non-Jewish people with the gospel, Timothy submitted to the rite of circumcision to avoid any potential problems with the Jews (Acts 16:3).

Although completely dedicated to preaching the gospel, Timothy seemed to struggle because he was young and timid. But Paul saw great potential in this young man and entrusted him with important responsibilities. Paul sent Timothy to Corinth when the church was going through a difficult time (1 Corinthians 4:17). Timothy continued to travel with Paul, seeing many people come to faith in Christ. He also sent Timothy to Thessalonica (1 Thessalonians 3:1–2) to encourage the believers there. During the time of Paul's imprisonment, Timothy was Paul's right hand.

The second epistle to Timothy was Paul's last letter before his death under Caesar Nero. Written about three years after his first letter, 2 Timothy contains practical advice, commands and challenges, and personal remarks that shed light on Paul's character and the source of his strength: the Lord Jesus Christ.

Part 2—Sound Doctrine

Paul first visited Ephesus on his second missionary journey (Acts 18:19–21). Later, on Paul's third missionary journey (Acts 19:20), Paul stayed in Ephesus for almost three years. He warned the Ephesian leaders to be on their guard against false teachers who would inevitably come after he left (Acts 20:17–31).

The church at Ephesus was plagued by at least two heresies: first, that a person must submit to the Law before becoming a Christian; second, that a person had to discover hidden knowledge or worship angels to be a true believer. (Remember that angel worship was something Paul denounced in the book of Colossians.) Regardless of the type of heresy the false teachers preached, they were motivated by personal interests. They kept the believers involved in endless discussions of irrelevant issues, pulling people away from the truth and from the mission of the church: reaching others for Christ.

[1] This letter is from Paul, an apostle of Christ Jesus, appointed by the command of God our Savior and Christ Jesus, who gives us hope.

[2] I am writing to Timothy, my true son in the faith. May God the Father and Christ Jesus our Lord give you grace, mercy, and peace.

[3] When I left for Macedonia, I urged you to stay there in Ephesus and stop those whose teaching is contrary to the truth. [4] Don't let them waste their time in endless discussion of myths and spiritual pedigrees. These things only lead to meaningless speculations, which don't help people live a life of faith in God.

[5] The purpose of my instruction is that all believers would be filled with love that comes from a pure heart, a clear conscience, and genuine faith. [6] But some people have missed this whole point. They have turned away from these things and spend their time in meaningless discussions. [7] They want to be known as teachers of the law of Moses, but they don't know what they are talking about, even though they speak so confidently.

[8] We know that the law is good when used correctly. [9] For the law was not intended for people who do what is right. It is for people who are lawless and rebellious, who are ungodly and sinful, who consider nothing sacred and defile what is holy, who kill their father or mother or commit other murders. [10] The law is for people who are sexually immoral, or who practice homosexuality, or are slave traders, liars, promise breakers, or who do anything else that contradicts the wholesome teaching [11] that comes from the glorious Good News entrusted to me by our blessed God.

1 Timothy 1:1–11

After condemning lawless, rebellious, sinful, and ungodly people, Paul went on to remind Timothy that he, Paul, was the lowest of all sinners; he had persecuted the church, Jesus' people. Jesus Christ came into the world to save the lost and change their hearts.

[12] I thank Christ Jesus our Lord, who has given me strength to do his work. He considered me trustworthy and appointed me to serve him, [13] even though I used to blaspheme the name of Christ. In my insolence, I persecuted his people. But God had mercy on me because I did it in ignorance and unbelief. [14] Oh, how generous and gracious our Lord was! He filled me with the faith and love that come from Christ Jesus.

[15] This is a trustworthy saying, and everyone should accept it: "Christ Jesus came into the world to save sinners"—and I am the worst of them all. [16] But God had mercy on me so that Christ Jesus could use me as a prime example of his great patience with even the worst sinners. Then others will realize that they, too, can believe in him and receive eternal life. [17] All honor and glory to God forever and ever! He is the eternal King, the unseen one who never dies; he alone is God. Amen.

[18] Timothy, my son, here are my instructions for you, based on the prophetic words spoken about you earlier. May they help you fight well in the Lord's battles.

1 Timothy 1:12–18

Topic 2—Instruction for Leaders

Introduction: Two of the personal qualities of God that you have learned are that he is omnipotent and omniscient. You may wonder: If God is all-powerful and all-knowing, why do we need to pray? Doesn't God act without our prayers? Of course he does! However, prayer is integral to the Christian life. As one church father, Martin Luther, said, "To be a Christian without prayer is no more possible than to be alive without breathing."[1]

Paul reminded Timothy that prayer should be his highest priority. Paul counseled Timothy to intercede on behalf of all people because God wants everyone to be saved. To intercede is *to act as a go-between*. When we pray for God to help others, we are acting as intercessors. Paul compared our intercession to Christ, our Mediator, reconciling God and human beings.

Part 1—Intercession

[1] I urge you, first of all, to pray for all people. Ask God to help them; intercede on their behalf, and give thanks for them. [2] Pray this way for kings and all who are in authority so that we can live peaceful and quiet lives marked by godliness and dignity. [3] This is good and pleases God our Savior, [4] who wants everyone to be saved and to understand the truth. [5] For,

> There is one God and one Mediator who can reconcile God and humanity—the man Christ Jesus. [6] He gave his life to purchase freedom for everyone.

This is the message God gave to the world at just the right time. [7] And I have been chosen as a preacher and apostle to teach the Gentiles this message about faith and truth. I'm not exaggerating—just telling the truth.

1 Timothy 2:1–7

Part 2—Church Leaders

If you have studied the book of Acts, you learned that Paul established churches and then left them in the capable hands of church leaders. Paul gave Timothy the task of leading the Ephesian church, which was no easy job. As the church grew, it was important for Timothy to appoint overseers to manage various aspects of ministry, just as Peter and John selected trustworthy deacons to serve the Jerusalem church (Acts 6:3) when it grew. Such believers had proven they had the character and qualities to serve others in this capacity. Paul advised Timothy about how to choose church leaders who would bear the heavy responsibility of making decisions for God's church.

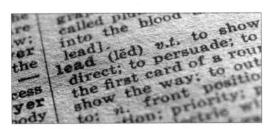

[1] This is a trustworthy saying: "If someone aspires to be a church leader, he desires an honorable position." [2] So a church leader must be a man whose life is above reproach. He must be faithful to his wife. He must exercise self-control, live wisely, and have a good reputation. He must enjoy having guests in his home, and he must be able to teach. [3] He must not be a heavy drinker or be violent. He must be gentle, not quarrelsome, and not love money. [4] He must manage his own family well, having children who respect and obey him. [5] For if a man cannot manage his own household, how can he take care of God's church?

[6] A church leader must not be a new believer, because he might become proud, and the devil would cause him to fall. [7] Also, people outside the church must speak well of him so that he will not be disgraced and fall into the devil's trap.

[8] In the same way, deacons must be well respected and have integrity. They must not be heavy drinkers or dishonest with money. [9] They must be committed to the mystery of the faith now revealed and must live with a clear conscience. [10] Before they are appointed as deacons, let them be closely examined. If they pass the test, then let them serve as deacons.

[11] In the same way, their wives must be respected and must not slander others. They must exercise self-control and be faithful in everything they do.

[12] A deacon must be faithful to his wife, and he must manage his children and household well. [13] Those who do well as deacons will be rewarded with respect from others and will have increased confidence in their faith in Christ Jesus.

1 Timothy 3:1–13

As adopted sons and daughters of God through faith in Christ, we are part of the family or household of God. Just as there are rules and expectations for behavior in our own families, there are also expectations of how we are to conduct ourselves as members of God's family.

Paul ended this section of his letter to Timothy with a short hymn of praise, underscoring the humanity and divinity of Christ. False teachers spread a heresy that misrepresented Jesus as not having a human body.

[14] I am writing these things to you now, even though I hope to be with you soon, [15] so that if I am delayed, you will know how people must conduct themselves in the household of God. This is the church of the living God, which is the pillar and foundation of the truth.

[16] Without question, this is the great mystery of our faith:

Christ was revealed in a human body
and vindicated by the Spirit.
He was seen by angels
and announced to the nations.
He was believed in throughout the world
and taken to heaven in glory.

1 Timothy 3:14–16

Topic 3—Instructions for Timothy

Introduction: Everyone knows that exercise has benefits for our health. When we get in shape, we have more stamina and strength and maintain a healthy weight. Without exercise, we can even become depressed! But what about our faith? Paul told Timothy that it's not okay to have "flabby faith." Spiritual discipline is even more important than physical training. Physical training may prevent injuries in this life; faith not only sustains us through crises, but gives us hope for the life to come. Our faith grows as we rely on the Holy Spirit and use our spiritual gifts in service to the church (1 Timothy 4:14–16).

For Timothy and the Ephesian church, it was important to establish spiritual truth and stability. Timothy's conduct had to be irreproachable because he would face resistance from people in the church as well as from those outside it.

Part 1—A Worthy Servant

[1] Now the Holy Spirit tells us clearly that in the last times some will turn away from the true faith; they will follow deceptive spirits and teachings that come from demons. [2] These people are hypocrites and liars, and their consciences are dead.

[3] They will say it is wrong to be married and wrong to eat certain foods. But God created those foods to be eaten with thanks by faithful people who know the truth. [4] Since everything God created is good, we should not reject any of it but receive it with thanks. [5] For we know it is made acceptable by the word of God and prayer.

[6] If you explain these things to the brothers and sisters, Timothy, you will be a worthy servant of Christ Jesus, one who is nourished by the message of faith and the good teaching you have followed. [7] Do not waste time arguing over godless ideas and old wives' tales. Instead, train yourself to be godly. [8] "Physical training is good, but training for godliness is much better, promising benefits in this life and in the life to come." [9] This is a trustworthy saying, and everyone should accept it. [10] This is why we work hard and continue to struggle, for our hope is in the living God, who is the Savior of all people and particularly of all believers.   1 Timothy 4:1–10

Timothy's ordination as a church leader was confirmed by prophecy and by the laying on of hands by the leaders of the church (1 Timothy 4:14). Timothy was not self-appointed nor self-seeking. Paul knew he could be intimidated by older members of the church. Paul urged him to set an example for others and to encourage all members of the congregation, regardless of age.

[11] Teach these things and insist that everyone learn them. [12] Don't let anyone think less of you because you are young. Be an example to all believers in what you say, in the way you live, in your love, your faith, and your purity. [13] Until I get there, focus on reading the Scriptures to the church, encouraging the believers, and teaching them.

[14] Do not neglect the spiritual gift you received through the prophecy spoken over you when the elders of the church laid their hands on you. [15] Give your complete attention to these matters. Throw yourself into your tasks so that everyone will see your progress. [16] Keep a close watch on how you live and on your teaching. Stay true to what is right for the sake of your own salvation and the salvation of those who hear you.   1 Timothy 4:11–16

Part 2—Respecting Others

A large part of setting a good example is showing respect for others. Paul advised Timothy saying never speak harshly to an older man, but appeal to him respectfully as you would to your own father. Talk to younger men as you would to your own brothers. Treat older women as you would your mother, and treat younger women with all purity as you would your own sisters (1 Timothy 5:1–2).

The church, too, is called to show respect, especially to its leaders. Modern churches have a variety of positions and titles for people in leadership. Some of the names you may be familiar with include pastors or ministers, elders, deacons, council members, trustees, bishops, overseers, and others. In his first letter to Timothy, Paul used the term *elders* to describe those who preach and teach for a salary. This term does not refer to the physical age of a leader; rather, an elder is a mature and qualified servant who preaches or teaches God's Word.

[17] Elders who do their work well should be respected and paid well, especially those who work hard at both preaching and teaching. [18] For the Scripture says, "You must not muzzle an ox to keep it from eating as it treads out the grain." And in another place, "Those who work deserve their pay!"

¹⁹ Do not listen to an accusation against an elder unless it is confirmed by two or three witnesses. ²⁰ Those who sin should be reprimanded in front of the whole church; this will serve as a strong warning to others.

²¹ I solemnly command you in the presence of God and Christ Jesus and the highest angels to obey these instructions without taking sides or showing favoritism to anyone.

²² Never be in a hurry about appointing a church leader. Do not share in the sins of others. Keep yourself pure.   1 Timothy 5:17–22

Topic 4—Contentment

Introduction: Recall that the Ephesian church was distracted by heresies. These included false teachings about the necessity of becoming a Jew before becoming a Christian, the worship of angels or finding "hidden" knowledge, and inaccurate teachings about the nature of Christ. Jewish believers doted on their genealogies, possibly thinking that their ancestry would somehow help their salvation. All these false ideas promoted dissension in the church; something which Paul told Timothy that he must stop at all costs.

Another distraction to the believers was worldliness and a lack of contentment. As in today's culture, many Christians placed a high priority on wealth. Paul reminded Timothy that chasing after money can lead people away from the true faith.

³ Some people may contradict our teaching, but these are the wholesome teachings of the Lord Jesus Christ. These teachings promote a godly life. ⁴ Anyone who teaches something different is arrogant and lacks understanding. Such a person has an unhealthy desire to quibble over the meaning of words. This stirs up arguments ending in jealousy, division, slander, and evil suspicions. ⁵ These people always cause trouble. Their minds are corrupt, and they have turned their backs on the truth. To them, a show of godliness is just a way to become wealthy.

⁶ Yet true godliness with contentment is itself great wealth. ⁷ After all, we brought nothing with us when we came into the world, and we can't take anything with us when we leave it. ⁸ So if we have enough food and clothing, let us be content.

⁹ But people who long to be rich fall into temptation and are trapped by many foolish and harmful desires that plunge them into ruin and destruction. ¹⁰ For the love of money is the root of all kinds of evil. And some people, craving money, have wandered from the true faith and pierced themselves with many sorrows.   1 Timothy 6:3–10

Check out the verbs Paul used in the last section of his first letter to Timothy: run, pursue righteousness, fight, hold tight, and obey. Do Paul's words grant permission for spiritual complacency, or are they a call to action? Did Timothy need to be ready to move? He most certainly did! And, as Christians in today's world, we are also called to move. We take our marching orders from Christ himself.

¹¹ But you, Timothy, are a man of God; so run from all these evil things. Pursue righteousness and a godly life, along with faith, love, perseverance, and gentleness. ¹² Fight the good fight for the true faith. Hold tightly to

the eternal life to which God has called you, which you have declared so well before many witnesses. ¹³ And I charge you before God, who gives life to all, and before Christ Jesus, who gave a good testimony before Pontius Pilate, ¹⁴ that you obey this command without wavering. Then no one can find fault with you from now until our Lord Jesus Christ comes again. ¹⁵ For,

At just the right time Christ will be revealed from heaven by the blessed and only almighty God, the King of all kings and Lord of all lords. ¹⁶ He alone can never die, and he lives in light so brilliant that no human can approach him. No human eye has ever seen him, nor ever will. All honor and power to him forever! Amen.

¹⁷ Teach those who are rich in this world not to be proud and not to trust in their money, which is so unreliable. Their trust should be in God, who richly gives us all we need for our enjoyment. ¹⁸ Tell them to use their money to do good. They should be rich in good works and generous to those in need, always being ready to share with others. ¹⁹ By doing this they will be storing up their treasure as a good foundation for the future so that they may experience true life.

²⁰ Timothy, guard what God has entrusted to you. Avoid godless, foolish discussions with those who oppose you with their so-called knowledge. ²¹ Some people have wandered from the faith by following such foolishness.

May God's grace be with you all.   1 Timothy 6:11–21

Topic 5—Be Faithful

Introduction: Paul's second letter to Timothy was written in AD 66 or 67 from Rome. At the time of the letter, Paul was under arrest, this time under Caesar Nero, who had stepped up his persecution of Christians, blaming them for a massive fire in Rome in July of AD 65. When Paul was first under arrest in Rome, he was confined to his house but was able to have visitors. This time, however, Paul was almost alone, except for Luke. He had made an appeal for his freedom in court, but no one came along to witness for his defense. From his words to Timothy, we can see that Paul was lonely. He might have been arrested so suddenly that he was unable to gather his belongings. His environment was probably a cold, damp dungeon, so he asked Timothy to bring him his cloak and his scrolls and documents. However, Paul's most important assignment for Timothy was for him to remain faithful to the truth of the gospel.

This epistle is Paul's last letter to Timothy and to all Christians. It is a call to us to stand courageously for the truth, to know and obey God's Word, and to allow ourselves to be empowered by the Holy Spirit, for God has not given us a spirit of fear and timidity, but of power, love, and self-discipline (2 Timothy 1:7). **Paul continued:**

⁸ So never be ashamed to tell others about our Lord. And don't be ashamed of me, either, even though I'm in prison for him. With the strength God gives you, be ready to suffer with me for the sake of the Good News. ⁹ For God saved us and called us to live a holy life. He did this, not because we deserved it, but because that was his plan from before the beginning of time—to show us his grace through Christ Jesus. ¹⁰ And now he has made all of this plain to us by the appearing of Christ Jesus, our Savior. He broke the power of death and illuminated the way to life and immortality through the Good News. ¹¹ And God chose me to be a preacher, an apostle, and a teacher of this Good News.

¹² That is why I am suffering here in prison. But I am not ashamed of it, for I know the one in whom I trust, and I am sure that he is able to guard what I have entrusted to him until the day of his return.

¹³ Hold on to the pattern of wholesome teaching you learned from me—a pattern shaped by the faith and love that you have in Christ Jesus. ¹⁴ Through the power of the Holy Spirit who lives within us, carefully guard the precious truth that has been entrusted to you.

¹⁵ As you know, everyone from the province of Asia has deserted me—even Phygelus and Hermogenes.

¹⁶ May the Lord show special kindness to Onesiphorus and all his family because he often visited and encouraged me. He was never ashamed of me because I was in chains. ¹⁷ When he came to Rome, he searched everywhere until he found me. ¹⁸ May the Lord show him special kindness on the day of Christ's return. And you know very well how helpful he was in Ephesus.

2 Timothy 1:8–18

Paul used analogies to make his points clear. He urged Timothy to be like a good soldier, one who followed orders with the goal of victory. Paul compared Christians to athletes, enduring training to win a prize. And he reminded Timothy that hardworking farmers kept their focus on producing a bountiful crop. Athletes, soldiers, and farmers all needed to keep their eyes on the goal—and for Christians, the goal is to glorify God in all we do.

¹ Timothy, my dear son, be strong through the grace that God gives you in Christ Jesus. ² You have heard me teach things that have been confirmed by many reliable witnesses. Now teach these truths to other trustworthy people who will be able to pass them on to others.

³ Endure suffering along with me, as a good soldier of Christ Jesus. ⁴ Soldiers don't get tied up in the affairs of civilian life, for then they cannot please the officer who enlisted them. ⁵ And athletes cannot win the prize unless they follow the rules. ⁶ And hardworking farmers should be the first to enjoy the fruit of their labor. ⁷ Think about what I am saying. The Lord will help you understand all these things.

⁸ Always remember that Jesus Christ, a descendant of King David, was raised from the dead. This is the Good News I preach. ⁹ And because I preach this Good News, I am suffering and have been chained like a criminal. But the word of God cannot be chained. ¹⁰ So I am willing to endure anything if it will bring salvation and eternal glory in Christ Jesus to those God has chosen.

¹¹ This is a trustworthy saying:

> If we die with him,
>   we will also live with him.
> ¹² If we endure hardship,
>   we will reign with him.
> If we deny him,
>   he will deny us.
> ¹³ If we are unfaithful,
>   he remains faithful,
>   for he cannot deny who he is.

¹⁴ Remind everyone about these things, and command them in God's presence to stop fighting over words. Such arguments are useless, and they can ruin those who hear them.   2 Timothy 2:1–14

Because Paul knew his death was imminent, he wanted to be sure to pass the torch of leadership on to Timothy. Timothy needed to work hard, remember his call, use his spiritual gifts boldly, keep his eyes on the truth, prepare others to succeed him in ministry, be self-disciplined, prepare to endure hardship, get along with difficult people, and keep his life pure. These same qualities are essential for ministers in the church today.

¹⁵ Work hard so you can present yourself to God and receive his approval. Be a good worker, one who does not need to be ashamed and who correctly explains the word of truth. ¹⁶ Avoid worthless, foolish talk that only leads to more godless behavior. ¹⁷ This kind of talk spreads like cancer as in the case of Hymenaeus and Philetus. ¹⁸ They have left the path of truth, claiming that the resurrection of the dead has already occurred; in this way, they have turned some people away from the faith.

¹⁹ But God's truth stands firm like a foundation stone with this inscription: "The LORD knows those who are his," and "All who belong to the LORD must turn away from evil."

²⁰ In a wealthy home some utensils are made of gold and silver, and some are made of wood and clay. The expensive utensils are used for special occasions, and the cheap ones are for everyday use. ²¹ If you keep yourself pure, you will be a special utensil for honorable use. Your life will be clean, and you will be ready for the Master to use you for every good work.   2 Timothy 2:15–21

Timothy's life was in transition. He had been Paul's star student, a worthy pupil who knew what it was to endure hardship and to stand strong for the truth of the gospel. However, Timothy was a young man, and Paul knew that he could be tempted into impure relationships. So, Paul advised Timothy not just to avoid lustful thoughts but to run from them—physically, if need be! In addition, Paul recommended that Timothy make friends with like-minded Christians who worshipped and served with pure hearts. Young Christians today would do well to follow Paul's advice.

²² Run from anything that stimulates youthful lusts. Instead, pursue righteous living, faithfulness, love, and peace. Enjoy the companionship of those who call on the Lord with pure hearts.

²³ Again I say, don't get involved in foolish, ignorant arguments that only start fights. ²⁴ A servant of the Lord must not quarrel but must be kind to everyone, be able to teach, and be patient with difficult people. ²⁵ Gently instruct those who oppose the truth. Perhaps God will change those people's hearts, and they will learn the truth. ²⁶ Then they will come to their senses and escape from the devil's trap. For they have been held captive by him to do whatever he wants.   2 Timothy 2:22–26

Topic 6—Advice for the Future

Introduction: Chapter 3 marks a transition in Paul's second letter to Timothy. After reflecting on the past and commenting on the current situation, Paul urged Timothy to face the future. Without doubting the power of God, Paul declared, "There will be difficult times." Persecution from outside the church under Caesar Nero had already begun in earnest. Nero sent many Christians to their deaths.

Paul warned Timothy that persecution within the church would come in the form of impostors claiming to have knowledge of God. They would try to deceive many people, but ultimately their behavior would give them away.

Even though we do not live under threat of martyrdom, as did many Christians in the first century, Christians in other countries do face persecution and even death. Persecution can take many forms: from insults, ridicule, and harassment to beatings, confinement, and worse. Whatever we might face as a result of our convictions, our commitment to Christ must come before our personal comfort (Luke 9:62).

Part 1—Remain Faithful

[1] You should know this, Timothy, that in the last days there will be very difficult times. [2] For people will love only themselves and their money. They will be boastful and proud, scoffing at God, disobedient to their parents, and ungrateful. They will consider nothing sacred. [3] They will be unloving and unforgiving; they will slander others and have no self-control. They will be cruel and hate what is good. [4] They will betray their friends, be reckless, be puffed up with pride, and love pleasure rather than God. [5] They will act religious, but they will reject the power that could make them godly. Stay away from people like that! 2 Timothy 3:1–5

It may take a little detective work to discern an impostor. First, the behavior of an impostor betrays an attitude of pride. But it's also important to check out the imposter's words. Do they align with Scripture? Is the focus on Christ's finished work on the cross? Do the imposter's words introduce a teaching that is obviously or even subtly opposed to God's Word? If so, refuse to listen to them. And remember: all sin has consequences, and no one will get away with it forever.

[10] But you, Timothy, certainly know what I teach, and how I live, and what my purpose in life is. You know my faith, my patience, my love, and my endurance. [11] You know how much persecution and suffering I have endured. You know all about how I was persecuted in Antioch, Iconium, and Lystra—but the Lord rescued me from all of it. [12] Yes, and everyone who wants to live a godly life in Christ Jesus will suffer persecution. [13] But evil people and impostors will flourish. They will deceive others and will themselves be deceived.

[14] But you must remain faithful to the things you have been taught. You know they are true, for you know you can trust those who taught you. [15] You have been taught the holy Scriptures from childhood, and they have given you the wisdom to receive the salvation that comes by trusting in Christ Jesus. 2 Timothy 3:10–15

The whole Bible is God's inspired Word and therefore trustworthy. We should read it and apply it to our lives. It's a standard for testing everything that claims to be true, our safeguard against false worldviews, and our source of knowledge about how to be saved.

[16] All Scripture is inspired by God and is useful to teach us what is true and to make us realize what is wrong in our lives. It corrects us when we are wrong and teaches us to do what is right. [17] God uses it to prepare and equip his people to do every good work. 2 Timothy 3:16–17

Part 2—Preach the Word

[1] I solemnly urge you in the presence of God and Christ Jesus, who will someday judge the living and the dead when he comes to set up his Kingdom: [2] Preach the word of God. Be prepared, whether the time is favorable or not. Patiently correct, rebuke, and encourage your people with good teaching.

[3] For a time is coming when people will no longer listen to sound and wholesome teaching. They will follow their own desires and will look for teachers who will tell them whatever their itching ears want to hear. [4] They will reject the truth and chase after myths.

[5] But you should keep a clear mind in every situation. Don't be afraid of suffering for the Lord. Work at telling others the Good News, and fully carry out the ministry God has given you.

[6] As for me, my life has already been poured out as an offering to God. The time of my death is near. [7] I have fought the good fight, I have finished the race, and I have remained faithful. [8] And now the prize awaits me—the crown of righteousness, which the Lord, the righteous Judge, will give me on the day of his return. And the prize is not just for me but for all who eagerly look forward to his appearing.

2 Timothy 4:1–8

ENDNOTES
1 Martin Luther, quoted by George Sweeting in *Talking It Over* (Moody Press, 1979), 88.

Getting Started—The Main Ideas

Traditionally, it was believed that Paul authored the epistle to the Hebrews. However, as early as the fourth century—and possibly earlier—scholars began to question whether Paul indeed penned this letter. While there is evidence to support Paul's authorship as well as the authorship of someone other than Paul, most scholars today believe the writer of Hebrews is unknown. The book of Hebrews can be found after the letters that Paul wrote to churches (such as the church in Corinth or the churches in Galatia) and to individuals (Titus, Timothy, and Philemon).

The epistle is called *the letter to the Hebrews* because it was meant to encourage Jewish believers who were in danger of losing their faith. The writer of the letter used many different arguments to discuss why the gospel of Jesus Christ superseded the faith of their Jewish ancestors. The letter to the Hebrews showed why Jesus is superior to angels and to Moses. It taught that Jesus, the Son of God through whom God created the universe (Hebrews 1:2), put his status aside for a little while to die for human beings (Hebrews 2:9, 17). Then Jesus became a High Priest in heaven, standing before God, ready to help those who believe in him.

The writer of Hebrews compared Jesus to angels and to Moses. That writer also compared the Jewish Christians to the people of Israel, warning them to recognize that their ancestors angered God so much that he did not allow them to enter his rest (Hebrews 4:1–3). Instead of imitating their ancestors, the Jewish Christians needed to believe in God and in his Son.

Topic 1—Greatness of the Son

Introduction: The letter to the Hebrews is very different from the letters in the New Testament that you have already studied. It does not start with a greeting, and it includes many quotes from the Hebrew Scriptures. But the message of Hebrews agrees with what the apostles taught. For example, John said that God created everything through Jesus (John 1:3); so does Hebrews (Hebrews 1:2). Peter taught that the risen Jesus is in heaven at God's right hand and rules the angels (1 Peter 3:22). Hebrews teaches the same thing, using many references to psalms that Christians with a Jewish background knew.

Part 1—Introduction to Hebrews

Hebrews is unique among the letters of the New Testament because it does not tell who wrote it or who was supposed to receive it. The author was probably a Jewish man. In the Greek, verb endings and adjectives change depending on gender, and the author used a male word in speaking about himself (Hebrews 11:32).

He also wrote that "God spoke . . . to our ancestors through the prophets" (Hebrews 1:1), so he was probably not a Gentile convert.

Many people thought Paul wrote the letter, but most scholars today disagree. They think that Hebrews may have been written by Barnabas, the apostle from Cyprus who traveled with Paul on his first missionary journey (Acts 4:36–37, 11:20–15:39); by Apollos, an eloquent speaker from Egypt who taught in Corinth and in other churches (Acts 18:24, 1 Corinthians 3:1–6); or by someone else. No one knows for sure who the author was.

This epistle came to be known as *the letter to the Hebrews* based on its content. The writer assumed that the intended readers know the Hebrew Scriptures well. The letter argued against going back to the old covenant that God had with the Jewish people. It encouraged believers who had suffered for Christ not to throw away their faith but to stick with the new covenant offered in Christ (Hebrews 10:32–36).

Since the writer of Hebrews mentioned that believers from Italy, who had moved to a different country, sent their greetings (Hebrews 13:24), the letter is thought to have been written to believers still living in Italy. The writer of Hebrews also stated that his readers had been persecuted but had not yet given [their] lives in [their] struggle against sin (Hebrews 12:4). Because of this, scholars believe that Hebrews was written before the persecution of Christians sanctioned by the Roman emperor Nero in AD 64, or before the Domitian persecution starting in AD 81. It was certainly written before AD 96, when Clement, the bishop of Rome, referred to it in one of his letters.

Part 2—Christ Is Superior

Most letters in the New Testament follow the letter-writing conventions of the Roman Empire: they tell who wrote the letter, to whom, and add a greeting, exhortation or a short prayer. Hebrews does not begin that way. Instead, it says:

¹ Long ago God spoke many times and in many ways to our ancestors through the prophets. ² And now in these final days, he has spoken to us through his Son. God promised everything to the Son as an inheritance, and through the Son he created the universe. ³ The Son radiates God's own glory and expresses the very character of God, and he sustains everything by the mighty power of his command. When he had cleansed us from our sins, he sat down in the place of honor at the right hand of the majestic God in heaven. ⁴ This shows that the Son is far greater than the angels, just as the name God gave him is greater than their names.   Hebrews 1:1–4

This description of Jesus might sound familiar because it echoes what was written to the church in Colossae. That letter describes God's Son as the visible image of the invisible God [who] is supreme over all creation . . . existed before anything else [who] holds all creation together, and through [whom] God reconciled everything to himself (Colossians 1:15–20). Both Hebrews and Colossians emphasize Jesus' position of preeminence. A person who is preeminent is *more important, powerful, or better than others in a specific way.*

The author of the letter to the Hebrews argued that Jesus was more important than angels. Why was important to make this point? Perhaps the Hebrew believers were troubled, like the church in Colossae, by people insisting . . . on the worship of angels, saying they . . . had visions about these things (Colossians 2:18).

We do not know exactly what was going on, but we do know that the author of Hebrews used verses from the Psalms and other parts of the Old Testament to show the many ways that Jesus is superior to angels.

⁵ For God never said to any angel what he said to Jesus:

"You are my Son.
    Today I have become your Father."

God also said,

"I will be his Father,
    and he will be my Son."

⁶ And when he brought his supreme Son into the world, God said,

"Let all of God's angels worship him."

⁷ Regarding the angels, he says,

"He sends his angels like the winds,
    his servants like flames of fire."

⁸ But to the Son he says,

"Your throne, O God, endures forever and ever.
    You rule with a scepter of justice.
⁹ You love justice and hate evil.
    Therefore, O God, your God has anointed you,
    pouring out the oil of joy on you more than on anyone else."

JESUS WORSHIPPED BY ANGELS,
ST. PETERSBURG, RUSSIA

TRINITY, CHURCH OF
THE HOLY SEPULCHRE,
JERUSALEM, ISRAEL

¹⁰ He also says to the Son,

"In the beginning, Lord, you laid the foundation of the earth
    and made the heavens with your hands.
¹¹ They will perish, but you remain forever.
    They will wear out like old clothing.
¹² You will fold them up like a cloak
    and discard them like old clothing.
    But you are always the same;
    you will live forever."

¹³ And God never said to any of the angels,

"Sit in the place of honor at my right hand
    until I humble your enemies,
    making them a footstool under your feet."

¹⁴ Therefore, angels are only servants—spirits sent to care for people who will inherit salvation.

Hebrews 1:5–14

Jesus' preeminence over angels set the stage for the next topics that the author of Hebrews discussed.

Topic 2—The Incarnation

Introduction: The writer of Hebrews knew the Hebrew Scriptures well. He cited several passages to show that Jesus was more important than angels. In the next section of the letter, he warned the Hebrews to take Jesus' message of salvation seriously. Then he continued contrasting Jesus with angels and explaining that Jesus had to become human to fulfill the promises in Psalms and in Isaiah.

Part 1—A Warning

Remember that the author of Hebrews said that Jesus was superior to angels and that angels were only servants? According to Jewish tradition, based on an alternative translation of Deuteronomy 33:2 which says that God came from Mount Sinai with myriads of holy ones, from the south, from his mountain slopes, angels were present when Moses received the Ten Commandments. The author of Hebrews affirmed this tradition and compared it to the good news spoken by Jesus.

[1] So we must listen very carefully to the truth we have heard, or we may drift away from it. [2] For the message God delivered through angels has always stood firm, and every violation of the law and every act of disobedience was punished. [3] So what makes us think we can escape if we ignore this great salvation that was first announced by the Lord Jesus himself and then delivered to us by those who heard him speak? [4] And God confirmed the message by giving signs and wonders and various miracles and gifts of the Holy Spirit whenever he chose.   Hebrews 2:1–4

The author warned the Hebrew believers not to ignore the truth or drift away from it, but instead to recognize how important Jesus' message of salvation was compared to the Ten Commandments. With the angels, Moses gave the people God's Law. But Jesus, God's own Son, delivered the great message of salvation, confirmed by the Holy Spirit and by miracles.

Part 2—Jesus, Truly Human

The writer of Hebrews argued that Jesus was preeminent over angels, and that his message was worthy of more attention than even the Law of Moses. But angels existed long before God created human beings (Job 38:4–7). And wasn't Jesus a human being? Aren't angels more magnificent and powerful and pure and holy than human beings? The writer of Hebrews anticipated this objection, so he explained, using even more Scriptures, that even though angels are amazing, they were not given God's promises. God cares about people.

[5] And furthermore, it is not angels who will control the future world we are talking about. [6] For in one place the Scriptures say,

"What are mere mortals that you should think about them,
   or a son of man that you should care for him?
⁷ Yet for a little while you made them a little lower than the angels
   and crowned them with glory and honor.
⁸ You gave them authority over all things."

Hebrews 2:5–8a

The Hebrew believers were used to the idea that God gave human beings stewardship over animals, birds, and fish (Psalm 8:7–8, Genesis 1:28). But the writer of the letter to the Hebrews pointed out that the Scriptures taught that God gave human beings even more glory, honor, and authority than the believers realized. He explained:

⁸ Now when it [Psalm 8:6] says "all things," it means nothing is left out. But we have not yet seen all things put under their authority. ⁹ What we do see is Jesus, who for a little while was given a position "a little lower than the angels"; and because he suffered death for us, he is now "crowned with glory and honor." Yes, by God's grace, Jesus tasted death for everyone. ¹⁰ God, for whom and through whom everything was made, chose to bring many children into glory. And it was only right that he should make Jesus, through his suffering, a perfect leader, fit to bring them into their salvation.

¹¹ So now Jesus and the ones he makes holy have the same Father. That is why Jesus is not ashamed to call them his brothers and sisters. ¹² For he said to God,

"I will proclaim your name to my brothers and sisters.
   I will praise you among your assembled people."

¹³ He also said,

"I will put my trust in him,"
   that is, "I and the children God has given me."

¹⁴ Because God's children are human beings—made of flesh and blood—the Son also became flesh and blood. For only as a human being could he die, and only by dying could he break the power of the devil, who had the power of death. ¹⁵ Only in this way could he set free all who have lived their lives as slaves to the fear of dying.

Hebrews 2:8b–15

Jesus was better than angels because he could die. Angels could not die. They could not free people from the power of the devil. Jesus became a human being so that human beings could become children of God. He became incarnate—*having a human body*. The word *incarnate* comes from the Latin words *en*, meaning *in*, and *carnes*, meaning *flesh*. The doctrine of the incarnation teaches that Jesus became a human being. Paul, in Philippians, explained more about Jesus' incarnation:

⁶ Though he was God,
   he did not think of equality with God
   as something to cling to.
⁷ Instead, he gave up his divine privileges;
   he took the humble position of a slave
   and was born as a human being.

Philippians 2:6–7

After Jesus died on the cross, God honored him above everyone in heaven, on earth, and under the earth (Philippians 2:10). So the writer of Hebrews continued his comparison of Jesus with the angels:

16 We also know that the Son did not come to help angels; he came to help the descendants of Abraham. 17 Therefore, it was necessary for him to be made in every respect like us, his brothers and sisters, so that he could be our merciful and faithful High Priest before God. Then he could offer a sacrifice that would take away the sins of the people. 18 Since he himself has gone through suffering and testing, he is able to help us when we are being tested.

Hebrews 2:16–18

Because Jesus is a human being as well as the divine Son of God, he understands what we experience: the limitations of our human bodies and what it is like to feel hungry, thirsty, sleepy, tired, weak, sick, or in pain. He also understands human emotions. He can help us when we suffer or are tested. Because of this, wrote the author of Hebrews, Jesus could be a merciful and faithful High Priest for us before God. Jesus was the only one who was qualified to die on our behalf and offer the ultimate sacrifice for sin.

> **Incarnate**
> Having a human body

Topic 3—Greater than Moses

Introduction: After thoroughly explaining that Christ is greater than the angels, and why the angels could not accomplish the great salvation that Jesus obtained on the cross, the writer of Hebrews compared Moses and Jesus. He had already affirmed that Jesus' message was at least as important as the one delivered by the angels, through Moses. He repeated his warning:

MOSES, JESUS, AND ISAIAH, SCHWERIN CATHEDRAL, GERMANY

1 And so, dear brothers and sisters who belong to God and are partners with those called to heaven, think carefully about this Jesus whom we declare to be God's messenger and High Priest. 2 For he was faithful to God, who appointed him, just as Moses served faithfully when he was entrusted with God's entire house.

3 But Jesus deserves far more glory than Moses, just as a person who builds a house deserves more praise than the house itself. 4 For every house has a builder, but the one who built everything is God.

5 Moses was certainly faithful in God's house as a servant. His work was an illustration of the truths God would reveal later. Hebrews 3:1–5

What was Moses' work? First, he led the Hebrews, also called *the Israelites*, out of Egypt. Then, he gave the Hebrews the Ten Commandments that God revealed to him on Mount Sinai, and also the rest of the Torah. It contains instructions for the construction of the tabernacle, the place where God's presence would dwell with his people (Exodus 29:43). The tabernacle was an illustration of truth that God would reveal later: that each person can, through faith in Christ, have the presence of God in his or her heart. Moses made a place for God to be with the nation of Israel, but Jesus adopted us so God has sent the Spirit of his Son into our hearts (Galatians 4:6). The writer of Hebrews continued:

⁶ But Christ, as the Son, is in charge of God's entire house. And we are God's house, if we keep our courage and remain confident in our hope in Christ.

Hebrews 3:6

Not only did the writer of Hebrews compare Jesus with Moses, but he compared the believers who would receive his letter to the people of Israel who followed Moses in the wilderness. This comparison served as another warning to his readers.

⁷ That is why the Holy Spirit says,

"Today when you hear his voice,
⁸   don't harden your hearts
as Israel did when they rebelled,
    when they tested me in the wilderness.
⁹ There your ancestors tested and tried my patience,
    even though they saw my miracles for forty years.
¹⁰ So I was angry with them, and I said,

'Their hearts always turn away from me.
    They refuse to do what I tell them.'
¹¹ So in my anger I took an oath:
    'They will never enter my place of rest.'"

¹² Be careful then, dear brothers and sisters. Make sure that your own hearts are not evil and unbelieving, turning you away from the living God. ¹³ You must warn each other every day, while it is still "today," so that none of you will be deceived by sin and hardened against God. ¹⁴ For if we are faithful to the end, trusting God just as firmly as when we first believed, we will share in all that belongs to Christ. ¹⁵ Remember what it says:

"Today when you hear his voice,
    don't harden your hearts
    as Israel did when they rebelled."

¹⁶ And who was it who rebelled against God, even though they heard his voice? Wasn't it the people Moses led out of Egypt? ¹⁷ And who made God angry for forty years? Wasn't it the people who sinned, whose corpses lay in the wilderness? ¹⁸ And to whom was God speaking when he took an oath that they would never enter his rest? Wasn't it the people who disobeyed him? ¹⁹ So we see that because of their unbelief they were not able to enter his rest.

Hebrews 3:7–19

It was very important for the people of Moses' day to believe in God, but they did not. They suffered as a result of their unbelief. Therefore, the writer of Hebrews encouraged the Hebrew believers in Christ, who would receive his letter, not to follow in the steps of their ancestors. Instead, they were to have faith and encourage one another daily.

Topic 4—Sabbath Rest

Introduction: The people who followed Moses in the wilderness were unfaithful, but their descendants—the Jewish Christians in Italy—needed to remain faithful to God and his Son. The writer of Hebrews explained that faith would help those believers to receive the rest that their ancestors never obtained.

[1] God's promise of entering his rest still stands, so we ought to tremble with fear that some of you might fail to experience it. [2] For this good news—that God has prepared this rest—has been announced to us just as it was to them. But it did them no good because they didn't share the faith of those who listened to God. [3] For only we who believe can enter his rest.

Hebrews 4:1–3

What is the good news of God's rest? Writing to believers in Italy, the apostle Paul explained it this way: People are counted as righteous, not because of their work, but because of their faith in God who forgives sinners (Romans 4:5). No one can gain righteousness by working for it, but the good news is that God makes sinners right in his sight when they believe in Jesus (Romans 3:26). Jesus is the one who gives us rest (Matthew 11:28–30). And that rest is not just salvation for the here and now, and peace through our daily trials (John 14:27), but also hope for a wonderful future (Romans 8:18, Ephesians 4:4).

So, people who believe can enter God's rest. But the writer of Hebrews continued:

[3] As for the others [the ones who did not have faith], God said,

"In my anger I took an oath:
   'They will never enter my place of rest,'"

even though this rest has been ready since he made the world. [4] We know it is ready because of the place in the Scriptures where it mentions the seventh day: "On the seventh day God rested from all his work." [5] But in the other passage God said, "They will never enter my place of rest."

[6] So God's rest is there for people to enter, but those who first heard this good news failed to enter because they disobeyed God. [7] So God set another time for entering his rest, and that time is today. God announced this through David much later in the words already quoted:

"Today when you hear his voice,
   don't harden your hearts."

[8] Now if Joshua had succeeded in giving them this rest, God would not have spoken about another day of rest still to come. [9] So there is a special rest still waiting for the people of God. [10] For all who have entered into God's rest have rested from their labors, just as God did after creating the world. [11] So let us do our best to enter that rest. But if we disobey God, as the people of Israel did, we will fall.

Hebrews 4:3–11

God said. He announced. He spoke. He warned his people to hear his voice. The Bible says that we listen to God's voice by obeying his commands.

The LORD your God will delight in you if you obey his voice and keep the commands and decrees written in this Book of Instruction, and if you turn to the LORD your God with all your heart and soul.　　Deuteronomy 30:10

⁹ How can a young person stay pure?
　By obeying your word.
¹⁰ I have tried hard to find you—
　don't let me wander from your commands.
¹¹ I have hidden your word in my heart,
　that I might not sin against you.

Psalm 119:9–11

After his strong warnings to Jewish believers to listen to God's voice, the writer of the Hebrews wrote about God's Word.

¹² For the word of God is alive and powerful. It is sharper than the sharpest two-edged sword, cutting between soul and spirit, between joint and marrow. It exposes our innermost thoughts and desires. ¹³ Nothing in all creation is hidden from God. Everything is naked and exposed before his eyes, and he is the one to whom we are accountable.　　Hebrews 4:12–13

When you read God's Word, the Holy Spirit works within you to help you see yourself from God's point of view. He shows you your sin so that you can repent of it and change for the better. Studying the Bible and memorizing Scripture can be a source of comfort and a great help when you are tempted. Jesus' knowledge of Scripture helped him greatly when he was tempted (Matthew 4:1–11). Remember, Jesus was not only divine, but he was also human. Perhaps that is why the writer of Hebrews continued:

¹⁴ So then, since we have a great High Priest who has entered heaven, Jesus the Son of God, let us hold firmly to what we believe. ¹⁵ This High Priest of ours understands our weaknesses, for he faced all of the same testings we do, yet he did not sin. ¹⁶ So let us come boldly to the throne of our gracious God. There we will receive his mercy, and we will find grace to help us when we need it most.　　Hebrews 4:14–16

This Jesus was superior to the angels. His message was better than the message of Moses. Jesus died to bring eternal life to all who trust in him and stands ready to intercede for them before God. The writer of Hebrews wanted his readers to receive mercy and grace. Therefore, he urged them to stand firm and be bold in faith.

Christ, Our High Priest Lesson 17

Getting Started—The Main Ideas

Recall that the letter to the Hebrews was written by an unknown author to Jewish believers. The writer had many purposes for the letter, but its primary purpose was to encourage Jewish Christians to hold firm to their faith and convictions so they would have strength in the face of persecution.

The book's author relied on Jewish law and history to make the connection between the Hebrew Scriptures and the good news of salvation through Jesus Christ in the minds of Jewish believers. He taught that salvation through faith in the sacrificial death of God's Son was not a recent idea but was based on Scripture. He affirmed that Christ was the ultimate and final sacrifice for sin.

Salvation, or being saved from the penalty we deserve for our sin, was a well-understood concept in the Hebrew Scriptures. God provided Israel a temporary measure for people to be forgiven and reconciled with God: the sacrificial system. Animals were slaughtered by the priests in accordance with the instructions given by God to Moses, and this practice was repeated over and over. It was only through the sacrificial blood of animals that the people could hope to be forgiven for their sins and restored to a relationship with God.

After showing Jesus was superior to angels and to Moses, the author discussed the sacrificial system. He contrasted the imperfect and impermanent priesthood with Christ's perfect and heavenly priesthood.

Topic 1—Chosen by God

Introduction: The office of high priest was first given to Moses' brother Aaron and his sons following the establishment of the Mosaic covenant on Mount Sinai. The position of high priest was a messianic foreshadow (an indication of a future event) of the high priesthood of Christ.

The high priest was the intermediary between the Hebrew people and God. He offered various sacrifices for the people and for himself. On the annual Day of Atonement, Aaron, or one of his descendants, slaughtered a bull and one of two male goats for a sin offering. The other goat was called *the scapegoat*. It was kept alive but was led far into the wilderness to carry the sins away from the people (Leviticus 16:6–10). The high priest then filled an incense burner and entered the Most Holy Place where the ark of the covenant stood. He sprinkled some of the bull's blood over the ark's cover, the place of atonement, seven times. He also sprinkled the blood of the sacrificed goat over the ark (Leviticus 16:11–17). No one else was allowed inside the tabernacle when Aaron entered it for the purification ceremony in the Most Holy Place. This ceremony purified both the high priest and the congregation and made them right with God.

© Walking in Truth Grade 8

The author of Hebrews explained that no one elected himself to this position. The high priest was chosen by God and set apart as an intercessor on behalf of sinners. But before the Levitical order of priests began with Aaron as the first high priest, the Bible tells about Melchizedek, "a priest of God Most High" (Genesis 14:18). He was a type of Christ—*an Old Testament figure who exemplifies characteristics of Jesus.* Through Melchizedek, Abraham received God's blessing (Genesis 14:19–20).

AARON'S OFFERING,
CHURCH OF OUR LADY,
SAINT TRUIDEN, BELGIUM

God chose Jesus to fulfill the role of High Priest, reconciling all believers to God (1 Peter 2:4). Jesus was the only one who could fulfill the role of High Priest forever, always interceding for us before God the Father. Through the death and resurrection of Christ, believers receive spiritual blessings (Ephesians 1:3). So Hebrews says:

¹ Every high priest is a man chosen to represent other people in their dealings with God. He presents their gifts to God and offers sacrifices for their sins. ² And he is able to deal gently with ignorant and wayward people because he himself is subject to the same weaknesses. ³ That is why he must offer sacrifices for his own sins as well as theirs.

⁴ And no one can become a high priest simply because he wants such an honor. He must be called by God for this work, just as Aaron was. ⁵ That is why Christ did not honor himself by assuming he could become High Priest. No, he was chosen by God, who said to him,

"You are my Son.
    Today I have become your Father."

⁶ And in another passage God said to him,

"You are a priest forever in the order of Melchizedek."

⁷ While Jesus was here on earth, he offered prayers and pleadings, with a loud cry and tears, to the one who could rescue him from death. And God heard his prayers because of his deep reverence for God. ⁸ Even though Jesus was God's Son, he learned obedience from the things he suffered. ⁹ In this way, God qualified him as a perfect High Priest, and he became the source of eternal salvation for all those who obey him. ¹⁰ And God designated him to be a High Priest in the order of Melchizedek.

Hebrews 5:1–10

Has anyone ever told you to grow up? You may have been offended or even hurt by the remark, but it was probably well-intended. God wants us to grow in faith just as we grow physically and emotionally. Maturity in Christ comes through knowledge of Scripture and doctrine, and spiritual disciplines such as prayer, fasting, and meditation on God's Word. Notice that even though the author of the epistle worked hard to explain God's plan in the Hebrew Scriptures that was fulfilled through Christ, the people didn't always listen. So, before continuing his argument about a superior priesthood, the author advised the Hebrews to listen up.

¹¹ There is much more we would like to say about this, but it is difficult to explain, especially since you are spiritually dull and don't seem to listen. ¹² You have been

MOSES DEDICATING AARON
AND HIS SONS TO THE
LEVITICAL PRIESTHOOD

believers so long now that you ought to be teaching others. Instead, you need someone to teach you again the basic things about God's word. You are like babies who need milk and cannot eat solid food. [13] For someone who lives on milk is still an infant and doesn't know how to do what is right. [14] Solid food is for those who are mature, who through training have the skill to recognize the difference between right and wrong.

Hebrews 5:11–14

Type of Christ
An Old Testament figure who exemplifies
many of the characteristics of Jesus

Topic 2—Priest of a New Covenant

Introduction: To understand the points made by the writer of the Hebrews, it's important to remember the covenants God made with humankind and the role of the priesthood. A covenant is *a special agreement or promise.* God made several covenants with his people. Sometimes they were conditional covenants, such as the covenant God made with Moses (Hebrews were required to observe the Law). At other times they

were unconditional, like the covenant God made with Noah (never to flood the earth again) and David (he would always have a descendant on the throne). The priests played a key role in keeping the Mosaic covenant because the people were not permitted by God to offer sacrifices for their own sins.

Priests had three main duties. First, they had to maintain the temple and the sacrificial system. Second, they had to teach the people the Law. And third, they had to pray as intercessors for the nation of Israel.

Part 1—The Order of Melchizedek

Who was Melchizedek? Where did he come from? Why would Abraham give him a tenth of what he had taken in battle as an offering? What power did he have to bless Abraham? The mysterious person Melchizedek was mentioned only briefly in Genesis 14:18–20. The author of Hebrews, however, portrayed him as a type of Christ, making a point to introduce Melchizedek as a superior high priest, one without parents or a beginning or end to his life. He is a foreshadow or type of Christ because he was at once the king of the city of Salem (later this city would become Jerusalem) and a high priest. King David, in Psalm 110:4, spoke prophetically of the Messiah as a "priest forever in the order of Melchizedek." The name *Melchizedek* meant *king of justice.* Jesus alone is the King of justice for all who believe.

[1] This Melchizedek was king of the city of Salem and also a priest of God Most High. When Abraham was returning home after winning a great battle against the kings, Melchizedek met him and blessed him. [2] Then Abraham took a tenth of all he had captured in battle and gave it to Melchizedek. The name Melchizedek means "king of justice," and king of Salem means "king of peace." [3] There is no record of his father or mother or any of his ancestors—no beginning or end to his life. He remains a priest forever, resembling the Son of God.

[4] Consider then how great this Melchizedek was. Even Abraham, the great patriarch of Israel, recognized this by giving him a tenth of what he had taken in battle. [5] Now the law of Moses required that the priests, who are descendants of Levi, must collect a tithe from the rest of the people of Israel, who are also descendants

of Abraham. ⁶ But Melchizedek, who was not a descendant of Levi, collected a tenth from Abraham. And Melchizedek placed a blessing upon Abraham, the one who had already received the promises of God. ⁷ And without question, the person who has the power to give a blessing is greater than the one who is blessed.

Hebrews 7:1–7

The author of Hebrews continued to emphasize the superiority of Melchizedek's priesthood, reminding the Jewish Christians that they followed Christ because obedience to the Law could never solve the problem of sin and separation from God. No one could keep the Law; failing even in one point made the person guilty of lawbreaking (James 2:10).

⁸ The priests who collect tithes are men who die, so Melchizedek is greater than they are, because we are told that he lives on. ⁹ In addition, we might even say that these Levites—the ones who collect the tithe—paid a tithe to Melchizedek when their ancestor Abraham paid a tithe to him. ¹⁰ For although Levi wasn't born yet, the seed from which he came was in Abraham's body when Melchizedek collected the tithe from him.

¹¹ So if the priesthood of Levi, on which the law was based, could have achieved the perfection God intended, why did God need to establish a different priesthood, with a priest in the order of Melchizedek instead of the order of Levi and Aaron?

¹² And if the priesthood is changed, the law must also be changed to permit it. ¹³ For the priest we are talking about belongs to a different tribe, whose members have never served at the altar as priests. ¹⁴ What I mean is, our Lord came from the tribe of Judah, and Moses never mentioned priests coming from that tribe.

Hebrews 7:8–14

You could almost hear the Jewish believers arguing, "What are you trying to prove by saying Christ is our High Priest? Jesus cannot lay claim to the priesthood! He is not a descendant of Aaron–or even a Levite! How can Christ administer the covenant? How can he be the intercessor between God and human beings? The author went on to explain.

Part 2—Christ Is Like Melchizedek

Recall the duties of the priests: offering various sacrifices, teaching, and offering intercessory prayers for the nation. In addition, the high priest annually entered the Most Holy Place and sprinkled blood on the covering of the ark of the covenant for the forgiveness of sins. The writer of Hebrews made the point that Jesus Christ fulfilled all these duties, and he does so forever.

¹⁵ This change has been made very clear since a different priest, who is like Melchizedek, has appeared. ¹⁶ Jesus became a priest, not by meeting the physical requirement of belonging to the tribe of Levi, but by the power of a life that cannot be destroyed. ¹⁷ And the psalmist pointed this out when he prophesied,

"You are a priest forever in the order of Melchizedek."

[18] Yes, the old requirement about the priesthood was set aside because it was weak and useless. [19] For the law never made anything perfect. But now we have confidence in a better hope, through which we draw near to God.

[20] This new system was established with a solemn oath. Aaron's descendants became priests without such an oath, [21] but there was an oath regarding Jesus. For God said to him,

> "The LORD has taken an oath and will not break his vow:
> 'You are a priest forever.'"

[22] Because of this oath, Jesus is the one who guarantees this better covenant with God.

[23] There were many priests under the old system, for death prevented them from remaining in office. [24] But because Jesus lives forever, his priesthood lasts forever. [25] Therefore he is able, once and forever, to save those who come to God through him. He lives forever to intercede with God on their behalf.

SACRIFICES WERE OFFERED AT THE TABERNACLE

[26] He is the kind of high priest we need because he is holy and blameless, unstained by sin. He has been set apart from sinners and has been given the highest place of honor in heaven. [27] Unlike those other high priests, he does not need to offer sacrifices every day. They did this for their own sins first and then for the sins of the people. But Jesus did this once for all when he offered himself as the sacrifice for the people's sins. [28] The law appointed high priests who were limited by human weakness. But after the law was given, God appointed his Son with an oath, and his Son has been made the perfect High Priest forever.

Hebrews 7:15–28

Topic 3—A Superior Covenant

Introduction: Have you ever used a rotary-dial telephone? Watched a movie on a VHS tape? Turned a handle to roll down a car window? Played a 45-rpm record on a record player? Probably not. Such technology is no longer in everyday use. Technology is always changing; every device becomes obsolete when it is replaced by something newer and, hopefully, better. Nothing is ever permanent.

The author of Hebrews emphasized a new covenant with a new High Priest. Unlike the impermanence of technology, the new High Priest ministers in a heavenly tabernacle not created by human beings. Therefore, it is not subject to corruption or obsolescence. Jesus, the High Priest who serves in this tabernacle, had no beginning and has no end; he will minister and intercede for us forever.

[1] Here is the main point: We have a High Priest who sat down in the place of honor beside the throne of the majestic God in heaven. [2] There he ministers in the heavenly Tabernacle, the true place of worship that was built by the Lord and not by human hands.

³ And since every high priest is required to offer gifts and sacrifices, our High Priest must make an offering, too. ⁴ If he were here on earth, he would not even be a priest, since there already are priests who offer the gifts required by the law. ⁵ They serve in a system of worship that is only a copy, a shadow of the real one in heaven. For when Moses was getting ready to build the Tabernacle, God gave him this warning: "Be sure that you make everything according to the pattern I have shown you here on the mountain."

⁶ But now Jesus, our High Priest, has been given a ministry that is far superior to the old priesthood, for he is the one who mediates for us a far better covenant with God, based on better promises.

Hebrews 8:1–6

The Mosaic covenant—God's established "deal" with the Hebrew people before they entered the Promised Land to form a new nation—was never meant to last forever. To emphasize this fact, the writer of Hebrews quoted an Old Testament prophecy from Jeremiah 31:31–34 that anticipated the replacement of the old covenant with the new, proving to his Jewish readers that the first covenant was obsolete, replaced by another that will never pass away.

⁷ If the first covenant had been faultless, there would have been no need for a second covenant to replace it. ⁸ But when God found fault with the people, he said:

> "The day is coming, says the LORD,
>   when I will make a new covenant
>   with the people of Israel and Judah.
> ⁹ This covenant will not be like the one
>   I made with their ancestors
> when I took them by the hand
>   and led them out of the land of Egypt.
> They did not remain faithful to my covenant,
>   so I turned my back on them, says the LORD.
> ¹⁰ But this is the new covenant I will make
>   with the people of Israel on that day, says the LORD:
> I will put my laws in their minds,
>   and I will write them on their hearts.
> I will be their God,
>   and they will be my people.
> ¹¹ And they will not need to teach their neighbors,
>   nor will they need to teach their relatives,
>   saying, 'You should know the LORD.'
> For everyone, from the least to the greatest,
>   will know me already.
> ¹² And I will forgive their wickedness,
>   and I will never again remember their sins."

¹³ When God speaks of a "new" covenant, it means he has made the first one obsolete. It is now out of date and will soon disappear.

Hebrews 8:7–13

The old covenant, with its hundreds of commandments, statutes, and ordinances, was written for a hard-hearted, stubborn people. They were obligated to keep the covenant by following the Law whether they felt like it or not. The motivations to keep the Law were rewards for obedience or punishments for disobedience.

The new covenant, the author explained, relies on an internal transformation by which God's laws are written on people's hearts. Submission to God's will is a result of faith and love for him, not the result of the fear of judgment. So, the new covenant is based on a close relationship with God, our loving Abba Father, instead of a fear of God's wrath. This covenant will never be replaced!

Lesson 18 — Worship, Sacrifice, and Faith

Getting Started—The Main Ideas

In the previous lesson about the book of Hebrews, you learned that Jesus is superior to the angels and to Moses. You also learned that Jesus is a High Priest of the order of Melchizedek, an order superior to the order of the Levites, and that he is the Mediator of a new covenant, which is superior to the old covenant that God made with the Hebrew people.

In this lesson, the author of Hebrews continued his argument for the superiority of salvation through Christ. He compared the system of worship in the tabernacle, and all its rules and regulations, with that begun by Jesus, who entered the "greater, more perfect tabernacle in heaven" (Hebrews 9:11). He compared the sacrifices and blood of animals, which had to be repeated over and over again, with the sinless Christ's own sacrifice and blood, "offered once for all time" (Hebrews 9:28).

After explaining how faith in Christ fulfills promises made to Jewish ancestors, the author of Hebrews urged his readers to trust God and to hold on tightly to their hope (Hebrews 10:23). He described how the heroes of their Jewish faith, despite many trials, looked forward to the time when God would fulfill his promises through Christ.

The author of Hebrews urged believers in Christ to persevere in faith, like their heroes had, despite persecution. He encouraged his readers to recognize that God disciplines his children in love. Finally, he warned believers to show the proper reverence and awe toward God.

Topic 1—A Perfect Sacrifice

Introduction: After he died on the cross, Jesus was buried. He rose again, taught his disciples for 40 days, and ascended into heaven. What does Jesus do in heaven? Hebrews explains that Jesus continues his ministry there. Sitting at the right hand of God, in a place of honor, he is a High Priest for us. He ministers in the heavenly Tabernacle [and] mediates for us a far better covenant with God, based on better promises (Hebrews 8:1, 6). The author continued his letter by further explaining what he meant by a far better covenant.

Part 1—The Tabernacle

What was the difference between the old covenant with God and the new one? What better promises was Jesus able to mediate for all who believe in him? The answers to these questions were very important to the readers of Hebrews. Remember, they were Jewish believers in Christ who were discouraged because of the persecution they were facing. They were tempted to return to the faith of their forefathers. So the writer of Hebrews prepared to explain why believers should remain faithful to Jesus by first discussing the old covenant.

¹ That first covenant between God and Israel had regulations for worship and a place of worship here on earth.
² There were two rooms in that Tabernacle. In the first room were a lampstand, a table, and sacred loaves of

206

© Walking in Truth Grade 8

bread on the table. This room was called the Holy Place. ³ Then there was a curtain, and behind the curtain was the second room called the Most Holy Place. ⁴ In that room were a gold incense altar and a wooden chest called the Ark of the Covenant, which was covered with gold on all sides. Inside the Ark were a gold jar containing manna, Aaron's staff that sprouted leaves, and the stone tablets of the covenant. ⁵ Above the Ark were the cherubim of divine glory, whose wings stretched out over the Ark's cover, the place of atonement. But we cannot explain these things in detail now.

⁶ When these things were all in place, the priests regularly entered the first room as they performed their religious duties. ⁷ But only the high priest ever entered the Most Holy Place, and only once a year. And he always offered blood for his own sins and for the sins the people had committed in ignorance. ⁸ By these regulations the Holy Spirit revealed that the entrance to the Most Holy Place was not freely open as long as the Tabernacle and the system it represented were still in use.

Hebrews 9:1–8

The author of Hebrews emphasized that the tabernacle and the worship associated with it were temporary measures and limited in scope. The Most Holy Place could only be entered once a year. The high priest who entered it was sinful and had to offer sacrifices for his own sins and for the sins of the people. The author of Hebrews explained that the offering of sacrifices by the high priest was "an illustration pointing to the present time" (Hebrews 9:9). He used the Greek word for *illustration*, *parabolē*, the same word that is often translated into English as *parable*. A parable uses familiar things to teach important truths about God. In this case, the parable or illustration was the system of worship in the tabernacle. Sacrifices made for sins were familiar to the Hebrew people, so the author chose the tabernacle and the annual sacrifices made for sins to teach the people about God's plan of salvation through the cross. The imperfect system of annual sacrifices would foreshadow the final Sacrifice, something better to come for the people of Israel. *Foreshadow* means *to represent or be predictive of something in the future*

⁹ This is an illustration pointing to the present time. For the gifts and sacrifices that the priests offer are not able to cleanse the consciences of the people who bring them. ¹⁰ For that old system deals only with food and drink and various cleansing ceremonies—physical regulations that were in effect only until a better system could be established.

Hebrews 9:9–10

What was the better system that was to come? It was the system that the readers of this letter had been introduced to through Jesus. It was the salvation found in the Son of God.

> **Foreshadow**
> To represent or be predictive of something in the future

Part 2—The Blood of Christ

The old covenant system, with its earthly tabernacle, required the high priest to sacrifice animals and offer their blood for his own sins and for the sins of the people. The sacrifice had to be repeated annually (Leviticus 16:34). It was only one of many different sacrifices described in the law of Moses that laid out the rules and regulations the people of Israel had to follow. The yearly sacrifice covered the penalty for the sins of the previous year. But people sinned between the time their sins were forgiven and the time they could next approach God. The law of Moses described additional sacrifices they could make, many of which required the sprinkling of blood, because "the life of the body is in its blood." The writer of Hebrews knew that his audience was familiar with the rituals required by the Law, including the use of blood, so he mentioned blood in his explanation of the superiority of salvation through Jesus.

¹¹ So Christ has now become the High Priest over all the good things that have come. He has entered that greater, more perfect Tabernacle in heaven, which was not made by human hands and is not part of this created world. ¹² With his own blood—not the blood of goats and calves—he entered the Most Holy Place once for all time and secured our redemption forever.

¹³ Under the old system, the blood of goats and bulls and the ashes of a heifer could cleanse people's bodies from ceremonial impurity. ¹⁴ Just think how much more the blood of Christ will purify our consciences from sinful deeds so that we can worship the living God. For by the power of the eternal Spirit, Christ offered himself to God as a perfect sacrifice for our sins.

Hebrews 9:11–14

FRESCO OF THE LAMB OF GOD, THESSALONIKI, GREECE

The high priest in the old system could not use just any animal for his sacrifice. The animal had to be in perfect condition (Deuteronomy 15:21, Leviticus 22:20). Jesus was a perfect sacrifice because he was without sin. The prophet Isaiah said that the one on whom God would lay everyone's sins—who was led like a lamb to be slaughtered—was unjustly condemned even though he had never done anything wrong (Isaiah 53:6–7). Jesus was holy (Luke 1:35), and when John the Baptist saw him, he exclaimed, "Look! The Lamb of God who takes away the sin of the world!" (John 1:29).

So, the author of Hebrews continued speaking about Christ:

¹⁵ That is why he is the one who mediates a new covenant between God and people, so that all who are called can receive the eternal inheritance God has promised them. For Christ died to set them free from the penalty of the sins they had committed under that first covenant.

¹⁶ Now when someone leaves a will, it is necessary to prove that the person who made it is dead. ¹⁷ The will goes into effect only after the person's death. While the person who made it is still alive, the will cannot be put into effect.

FRESCO OF MOSES, VIENNA, AUSTRIA

¹⁸ That is why even the first covenant was put into effect with the blood of an animal. ¹⁹ For after Moses had read each of God's commandments to all the people, he took the blood of calves and goats, along with water, and sprinkled both the book of God's law and all the people, using hyssop branches and scarlet wool. ²⁰ Then he said, "This blood confirms the covenant God has made with you." ²¹ And in the same way, he sprinkled blood on the Tabernacle and on everything used for worship. ²² In fact, according to the law of Moses, nearly everything was purified with blood. For without the shedding of blood, there is no forgiveness.

²³ That is why the Tabernacle and everything in it, which were copies of things in heaven, had to be purified by the blood of animals. But the real things in heaven had to be purified with far better sacrifices than the blood of animals.

Hebrews 9:15–23

Jesus, the sinless Lamb, had to die to make it possible for many people to be counted righteous (Isaiah 53:11). The new covenant took effect with his blood. The writer of Hebrews continued:

²⁴ For Christ did not enter into a holy place made with human hands, which was only a copy of the true one in heaven. He entered into heaven itself to appear now before God on our behalf. ²⁵ And he did not enter heaven to offer himself again and again, like the high priest here on earth who enters the Most Holy Place year after year with the blood of an animal. ²⁶ If that had been necessary, Christ would have had to die again and again, ever since the world began. But now, once for all time, he has appeared at the end of the age to remove sin by his own death as a sacrifice.

²⁷ And just as each person is destined to die once and after that comes judgment, ²⁸ so also Christ was offered once for all time as a sacrifice to take away the sins of many people. He will come again, not to deal with our sins, but to bring salvation to all who are eagerly waiting for him.   Hebrews 9:24–28

CRUZ DE TEJEDA,
CANARY ISLANDS

The author of Hebrews wanted believers to hold on to their hope of and to eagerly wait for the second coming. In the meantime, he explained that Christ's service as priest in the heavenly tabernacle opens the way for believers to not only be forgiven of sin, but to enter the Most Holy Place as priests themselves. The apostle Peter wrote that all who trust in Christ are a chosen people . . . royal priests, a holy nation, God's very own possession [who] can show others the goodness of God (1 Peter 2:9). So, the Jewish Christians that the author of Hebrews addressed had freedom to do what their ancestors could not: They could be in God's presence without fear and serve him with joy.

¹⁹ And so, dear brothers and sisters, we can boldly enter heaven's Most Holy Place because of the blood of Jesus. ²⁰ By his death, Jesus opened a new and life-giving way through the curtain into the Most Holy Place. ²¹ And since we have a great High Priest who rules over God's house, ²² let us go right into the presence of God with sincere hearts fully trusting him. For our guilty consciences have been sprinkled with Christ's blood to make us clean, and our bodies have been washed with pure water.

²³ Let us hold tightly without wavering to the hope we affirm, for God can be trusted to keep his promise. ²⁴ Let us think of ways to motivate one another to acts of love and good works. ²⁵ And let us not neglect our meeting together, as some people do, but encourage one another, especially now that the day of his return is drawing near.

Hebrews 10:19–25

The writer of Hebrews added one more warning:

²⁶ Dear friends, if we deliberately continue sinning after we have received knowledge of the truth, there is no longer any sacrifice that will cover these sins.   Hebrews 10:26

He did not want his readers to remain as they were, in danger of drifting away from the truth (Hebrews 2:1), and of becoming deceived by sin and hardened against God (Hebrews 3:13). Instead, he wanted them to be faithful to Christ. The next part of his letter discusses faith in detail.

Topic 2—By Faith

Introduction: Chapter 11 of the book of Hebrews is often called *God's Hall of Fame*, or *the Hall of Faith*. It lists many people who were faithful to God and believed in his promises. Their stories were well-known to the Jewish Christians whom the writer of Hebrews wanted to encourage. These heroes were not only models

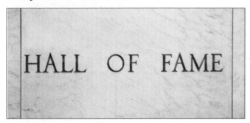

of courage and faith to be emulated; the author of Hebrews showed that they, too, had to wait for many of God's promises to come true, and so their descendants who believed should not be discouraged or feel alone. Instead, believers should reaffirm their faith in Jesus, the long-awaited Messiah their heroes had hoped for, and whose reign would bring all that was yet to come.

The author of Hebrews began by defining *faith*. Then he shared stories of God's people that are told in the book of Genesis:

¹ Faith shows the reality of what we hope for; it is the evidence of things we cannot see. ² Through their faith, the people in days of old earned a good reputation.

³ By faith we understand that the entire universe was formed at God's command, that what we now see did not come from anything that can be seen.

⁴ It was by faith that Abel brought a more acceptable offering to God than Cain did. Abel's offering gave evidence that he was a righteous man, and God showed his approval of his gifts. Although Abel is long dead, he still speaks to us by his example of faith.

⁵ It was by faith that Enoch was taken up to heaven without dying—"he disappeared, because God took him." For before he was taken up, he was known as a person who pleased God. ⁶ And it is impossible to please God without faith. Anyone who wants to come to him must believe that God exists and that he rewards those who sincerely seek him.

⁷ It was by faith that Noah built a large boat to save his family from the flood. He obeyed God, who warned him about things that had never happened before. By his faith Noah condemned the rest of the world, and he received the righteousness that comes by faith.

Hebrews 11:1–7

The stories of creation, Cain and Abel, Enoch, and Noah are all found in the first ten chapters of Genesis. The story of Abraham begins in the eleventh chapter of Genesis. The rest of Genesis tells his story and that of his descendants, beginning with his son Isaac and his grandson Jacob. It ends with the death of his great-grandson Joseph, who looked forward to the time when God would call the Hebrews back to the land he had promised to Abraham.

⁸ It was by faith that Abraham obeyed when God called him to leave home and go to another land that God would give him as his inheritance. He went without knowing where he was going. ⁹ And even when he reached the land God promised him, he lived there by faith—for he was like a foreigner, living in tents. And so did Isaac and Jacob, who inherited the same promise.

¹⁰ Abraham was confidently looking forward to a city with eternal foundations, a city designed and built by God.

¹¹ It was by faith that even Sarah was able to have a child, though she was barren and was too old. She believed that God would keep his promise. ¹² And so a whole nation came from this one man who was as good as dead—a nation with so many people that, like the stars in the sky and the sand on the seashore, there is no way to count them.

¹³ All these people died still believing what God had promised them. They did not receive what was promised, but they saw it all from a distance and welcomed it. They agreed that they were foreigners and nomads here on earth. ¹⁴ Obviously people who say such things are looking forward to a country they can call their own. ¹⁵ If they had longed for the country they came from, they could have gone back. ¹⁶ But they were looking for a better place, a heavenly homeland. That is why God is not ashamed to be called their God, for he has prepared a city for them.

¹⁷ It was by faith that Abraham offered Isaac as a sacrifice when God was testing him. Abraham, who had received God's promises, was ready to sacrifice his only son, Isaac, ¹⁸ even though God had told him, "Isaac is the son through whom your descendants will be counted." ¹⁹ Abraham reasoned that if Isaac died, God was able to bring him back to life again. And in a sense, Abraham did receive his son back from the dead.

²⁰ It was by faith that Isaac promised blessings for the future to his sons, Jacob and Esau.

²¹ It was by faith that Jacob, when he was old and dying, blessed each of Joseph's sons and bowed in worship as he leaned on his staff.

ABRAHAM OFFERS ISAAC

²² It was by faith that Joseph, when he was about to die, said confidently that the people of Israel would leave Egypt. He even commanded them to take his bones with them when they left.   Hebrews 11:8–22

The next book in the Torah that the author to the Hebrews drew his examples from is Exodus. The first chapter of Exodus tells about the Egyptians enslaving the people of Israel. It also tells how the king of Egypt wanted Hebrew baby boys to be killed.

²³ It was by faith that Moses' parents hid him for three months when he was born. They saw that God had given them an unusual child, and they were not afraid to disobey the king's command.

²⁴ It was by faith that Moses, when he grew up, refused to be called the son of Pharaoh's daughter. ²⁵ He chose to share the oppression of God's people instead of enjoying the fleeting pleasures of sin. ²⁶ He thought it was better to suffer for the sake of Christ than to own the treasures of Egypt, for he was looking ahead to his great reward. ²⁷ It was by faith that Moses left the land of Egypt, not fearing the king's anger. He kept right on going because he kept his eyes on the one who is invisible. ²⁸ It was by faith that Moses commanded the people of Israel to keep the Passover and to sprinkle blood on the doorposts so that the angel of death would not kill their firstborn sons.

²⁹ It was by faith that the people of Israel went right through the Red Sea as though they were on dry ground. But when the Egyptians tried to follow, they were all drowned.   Hebrews 11:23–29

MOSES PARTS THE RED SEA

After the Torah, which is made up of the first five books in the Bible, comes the book of Joshua, followed by other historical books that tell the story of the Israelites. The author of Hebrews drew his next examples from the Writings and the Prophets that make up the rest of the Hebrew Scriptures.

³⁰ It was by faith that the people of Israel marched around Jericho for seven days, and the walls came crashing down.

³¹ It was by faith that Rahab the prostitute was not destroyed with the people in her city who refused to obey God. For she had given a friendly welcome to the spies.

SAMSON FOUNTAIN,
SWITZERLAND

³² How much more do I need to say? It would take too long to recount the stories of the faith of Gideon, Barak, Samson, Jephthah, David, Samuel, and all the prophets. ³³ By faith these people overthrew kingdoms, ruled with justice, and received what God had promised them. They shut the mouths of lions, ³⁴ quenched the flames of fire, and escaped death by the edge of the sword. Their weakness was turned to strength. They became strong in battle and put whole armies to flight. ³⁵ Women received their loved ones back again from death.

But others were tortured, refusing to turn from God in order to be set free. They placed their hope in a better life after the resurrection. ³⁶ Some were jeered at, and their backs were cut open with whips. Others were chained in prisons. ³⁷ Some died by stoning, some were sawed in half, and others were killed with the sword. Some went about wearing skins of sheep and goats, destitute and oppressed and mistreated. ³⁸ They were too good for this world, wandering over deserts and mountains, hiding in caves and holes in the ground.

³⁹ All these people earned a good reputation because of their faith, yet none of them received all that God had promised. ⁴⁰ For God had something better in mind for us, so that they would not reach perfection without us.　　Hebrews 11:30–40

SAINTS IN PRISON

These stories of faith, courage, and dedication to God continue to inspire believers today. Imagine how they must have inspired the Hebrew believers in Christ who realized that they were part of this long line of amazing heroes, and part of God's plan! The author of Hebrews said those amazing ancestors would not reach perfection without them. How would this happen? The next part of his letter discussed what they should do.

Topic 3—God's Discipline

Introduction: Did you notice something about the last chapter of Hebrews we read? It not only gave the stories of Abel, Enoch, Noah, and many others, but the stories shared the same phrase: *by faith*. It was by faith that the

MOSAIC OF JESUS

heroes of the past accomplished wonderful things. And it was by faith, also, that Hebrew believers could join them and be perfected with them through God's plan revealed in Christ. So, the writer of Hebrews continued:

¹ Therefore, since we are surrounded by such a huge crowd of witnesses to the life of faith, let us strip off every weight that slows us down, especially the sin that so easily trips us up. And let us run with endurance the race God has set before us. ² We do this by keeping our eyes on Jesus, the champion who initiates and perfects our faith. Because of the joy awaiting him, he

endured the cross, disregarding its shame. Now he is seated in the place of honor beside God's throne. ³ Think of all the hostility he endured from sinful people; then you won't become weary and give up. ⁴ After all, you have not yet given your lives in your struggle against sin.

Hebrews 12:1–4

The Jewish Christians who received this letter faced persecution for their faith, but it was not as severe as what others would experience later. They needed to stand firm, trusting in Jesus.

⁵ And have you forgotten the encouraging words God spoke to you as his children? He said,

"My child, don't make light of the LORD's discipline,
    and don't give up when he corrects you.
⁶ For the LORD disciplines those he loves,
    and he punishes each one he accepts as his child."

⁷ As you endure this divine discipline, remember that God is treating you as his own children. Who ever heard of a child who is never disciplined by its father? ⁸ If God doesn't discipline you as he does all of his children, it means that you are illegitimate and are not really his children at all. ⁹ Since we respected our earthly fathers who disciplined us, shouldn't we submit even more to the discipline of the Father of our spirits, and live forever?

¹⁰ For our earthly fathers disciplined us for a few years, doing the best they knew how. But God's discipline is always good for us, so that we might share in his holiness. ¹¹ No discipline is enjoyable while it is happening—it's painful! But afterward there will be a peaceful harvest of right living for those who are trained in this way.

Hebrews 12:5–11

Discipline is not fun. Even Jesus did not enjoy it! Remember, even though Jesus was God's Son, he learned obedience from the things he suffered (Hebrews 5:8). So, when you are disciplined, try to have the same teachable attitude that Jesus had. The word *discipline* comes from the Latin word *discipulus* for a pupil, student, or learner. Discipline may not be fun, but it is good for us. Someone who takes the trouble to discipline you cares about you. He or she wants you to learn what you need to learn so that you can have success.

JESUS AND HIS EARTHLY
FATHER, JOSEPH

God disciplines his children because he wants each of us to develop a Christ-like character, to have a life that is full of the fruit of the Spirit, and to love him and others. The discipline that we experience is not for our individual benefit alone, so the writer of Hebrews continues:

¹² So take a new grip with your tired hands and strengthen your weak knees. ¹³ Mark out a straight path for your feet so that those who are weak and lame will not fall but become strong.

¹⁴ Work at living in peace with everyone, and work at living a holy life, for those who are not holy will not see the Lord.

Hebrews 12:12–14

A holy life does not just happen without effort. It takes discipline. It is intentional. The author of the letter to the Hebrews encouraged the believers to help each other so that they could, all together, see the Lord.

¹⁵ Look after each other so that none of you fails to receive the grace of God. Watch out that no poisonous root of bitterness grows up to trouble

you, corrupting many. ¹⁶ Make sure that no one is immoral or godless like Esau, who traded his birthright as the firstborn son for a single meal. ¹⁷ You know that afterward, when he wanted his father's blessing, he was rejected. It was too late for repentance, even though he begged with bitter tears. Hebrews 12:15–17

In the previous chapter, the author gave one example after another of praiseworthy Jewish ancestors, so that their descendants who believed in Christ would imitate their faith. But Hebrews 12:16–17 has a negative example: that of Esau. The Scriptures have both positive and negative examples for us to consider. Its portrayals of people are realistic. So, the author of Hebrews continued by providing a contrast between the Israelites at Mount Sinai and the believers who read his letter.

¹⁸ You have not come to a physical mountain, to a place of flaming fire, darkness, gloom, and whirlwind, as the Israelites did at Mount Sinai. ¹⁹ For they heard an awesome trumpet blast and a voice so terrible that they begged God to stop speaking. ²⁰ They staggered back under God's command: "If even an animal touches the mountain, it must be stoned to death." ²¹ Moses himself was so frightened at the sight that he said, "I am terrified and trembling."

²² No, you have come to Mount Zion, to the city of the living God, the heavenly Jerusalem, and to countless thousands of angels in a joyful gathering. ²³ You have come to the assembly of God's firstborn children, whose names are written in heaven. You have come to God himself, who is the judge over all things. You have come to the spirits of the righteous ones in heaven who have now been made perfect. ²⁴ You have come to Jesus, the one who mediates the new covenant between God and people, and to the sprinkled blood, which speaks of forgiveness instead of crying out for vengeance like the blood of Abel.

JESUS WITH ANGELS AND SAINTS

²⁵ Be careful that you do not refuse to listen to the One who is speaking. For if the people of Israel did not escape when they refused to listen to Moses, the earthly messenger, we will certainly not escape if we reject the One who speaks to us from heaven! ²⁶ When God spoke from Mount Sinai his voice shook the earth, but now he makes another promise: "Once again I will shake not only the earth but the heavens also." ²⁷ This means that all of creation will be shaken and removed, so that only unshakable things will remain.

²⁸ Since we are receiving a Kingdom that is unshakable, let us be thankful and please God by worshiping him with holy fear and awe. ²⁹ For our God is a devouring fire. Hebrews 12:18–29

The author of Hebrews urged believers to be faithful to God and mindful of his promises—both those of redemption and those of judgment. For just as the new covenant is greater than the old covenant, the power God will display when he shakes both heaven and Earth will be greater than we can imagine. Therefore, believers should be grateful for his mercy, worship him with reverence, and seek to please him.

Faith Lived Out

Getting Started—The Main Ideas

The epistles you have studied so far in *Christianity in Action* were named for their recipients. The epistle you will study now is the book of James, named for its writer. Most biblical scholars agree that James was the half brother of Jesus, the son of Mary and Joseph. James led the church in Jerusalem, and he addressed his letter to Jewish Christians who had left Jerusalem due to persecution. He urged them to remain true to their faith.

James' epistle is a very practical book. It was advice and instruction for the people of the first century, and it is wise advice and instruction for Christians today. Although daily life has changed a lot in two thousand years, people still face temptation, need to control their speech, and have to be reminded to live out their faith.

James began his letter by outlining some general characteristics of the Christian life (James 1:1–27). Then he wrote an exhortation to Christians to live righteously and justly in society (James 2:1–13). James went on to discuss the important relationship between faith and action, the problem of prejudice, the need to control one's speech, and the requirement to turn from evil desires and obey God.

Finally, James discussed the value of prayer and the practice of patient endurance as believers await the Lord's return.

Topic 1—Genuine Christianity

Introduction: Lately, there seem to be many substitutes for real products. Cubic zirconia is a substitute for diamonds, gold-tone jewelry is made without a speck of real gold, hamburgers are made of tofu, and vinyl is now known as *vegan leather*. Although these substitutes are convincing copies, they are still not the genuine article. Remarkably, faith can be faked too. There is a kind of faith that looks like devotion to God's will, but during times of testing, this faith proves to be worthless. James addressed the issue of fake faith in his letter, which could be considered a "how-to" manual for the authentic Christian life. James called the believers to be genuine in both faith and action.

Part 1—Introduction to James

The epistle's writer, James, was not one of Jesus' 12 disciples. In fact, it appears that he did not even believe that Jesus was the Messiah (Mark 6:1–6) until after the resurrection when he witnessed the risen Christ (1 Corinthians 15:7). That event changed James' life. He became the leader of the church in Jerusalem and, with Peter and John, was considered an apostle (Galatians 2:9).

James' letter was designed to be circulated among several groups of Jewish Christians who were now living outside Palestine, possibly because of a wave of persecution from the Jewish authorities that followed the stoning of Stephen (Acts 7). The letter was probably written in AD 49, just before the Jerusalem council, which was held in AD 50.

We know from the book of Acts that around AD 49, a dispute erupted in the church that threatened to break the unity between Jews and Gentiles. While Paul and Barnabas were in Syrian Antioch, some Jewish Christians came from Judea and began teaching the Gentile Christians saying, "Unless you are circumcised as required by the law of Moses, you cannot be saved" (Acts 15:1).

Of course, this added requirement for salvation troubled Paul and Barnabas, who had been preaching that salvation is by grace through faith alone, and not by following the Law. So, Paul and Barnabas immediately went to Jerusalem to confer with the apostles and elders, who supported Paul's position about Gentiles not needing to be circumcised to be saved. James spoke as the leader of the church when he said:

[11] "We believe that we are all saved the same way, by the undeserved grace of the Lord Jesus. . . . [19] And so my judgment is that we should not make it difficult for the Gentiles who are turning to God [by adding the requirement of circumcision]. [20] Instead, we should write and tell them to abstain from eating food offered to idols, from sexual immorality, from eating the meat of strangled animals, and from consuming blood. [21] For these laws of Moses have been preached in Jewish synagogues in every city on every Sabbath for many generations."

Acts 15:11, 19–21

James' wise and convincing words became the basis for the Jerusalem council's decision to write a letter to the believers in Antioch. It is important to understand that mention of "actions" or "good deeds" in James' epistle does not nullify the doctrine of grace. When we have received God's grace, our lives should abound in kind and loving actions.

Part 2—Faith and Confidence

Have you ever considered a problem or trouble in your life to be an opportunity? Most of the time, we dread problems and complain about what we are going through. But James told the Jewish believers to consider problems to be opportunities for great joy because enduring problems allows faith to grow. Notice that James did not say, "*if* troubles come your way," instead he said, ". . . *when* troubles of any kind come your way." Problems are part of life! But knowing that God has a purpose for us in our problems and troubles, believers can be joyful even in difficult circumstances.

[1] This letter is from James, a slave of God and of the Lord Jesus Christ.

I am writing to the "twelve tribes"—Jewish believers scattered abroad.

[2] Dear brothers and sisters, when troubles of any kind come your way, consider it an opportunity for great joy. [3] For you know that when your faith is tested, your endurance has a chance to grow. [4] So let it grow, for when your endurance is fully developed, you will be perfect and complete, needing nothing.   James 1:1–4

In discussing the wisdom Christians need to endure difficult circumstances or make hard choices, James was not talking about knowledge. Although knowledge is useful, wisdom is *the ability to make decisions that glorify God in our relationships with him, ourselves, others, and the earth.* Whenever we need wisdom, James said, we should ask God for it. He will always supply us with the wisdom we need.

Then James discussed the problem of double-mindedness, which is *having divided loyalties.* James said that Christians cannot divide their loyalties between living for God and living for themselves. A double-minded person is one who wants God's will at the same time as his or her own will. This kind of person will always be unstable.

⁵ If you need wisdom, ask our generous God, and he will give it to you. He will not rebuke you for asking. ⁶ But when you ask him, be sure that your faith is in God alone. Do not waver, for a person with divided loyalty is as unsettled as a wave of the sea that is blown and tossed by the wind. ⁷ Such people should not expect to receive anything from the Lord. ⁸ Their loyalty is divided between God and the world, and they are unstable in everything they do.

⁹ Believers who are poor have something to boast about, for God has honored them. ¹⁰ And those who are rich should boast that God has humbled them. They will fade away like a little flower in the field. ¹¹ The hot sun rises and the grass withers; the little flower droops and falls, and its beauty fades away. In the same way, the rich will fade away with all of their achievements.

James 1:5–11

Not all troubles come from the outside world. Christians face temptations from their own sinful nature. James explained that God does not tempt us to sin, but he does bless those who endure testing and resist the temptation to sin.

¹² God blesses those who patiently endure testing and temptation. Afterward they will receive the crown of life that God has promised to those who love him. ¹³ And remember, when you are being tempted, do not say, "God is tempting me." God is never tempted to do wrong, and he never tempts anyone else. ¹⁴ Temptation comes from our own desires, which entice us and drag us away. ¹⁵ These desires give birth to sinful actions. And when sin is allowed to grow, it gives birth to death.

¹⁶ So don't be misled, my dear brothers and sisters. ¹⁷ Whatever is good and perfect is a gift coming down to us from God our Father, who created all the lights in the heavens. He never changes or casts a shifting shadow. ¹⁸ He chose to give birth to us by giving us his true word. And we, out of all creation, became his prized possession.

James 1:12–18

Double-mindedness
Having divided loyalties

Part 3—Faith and Action

Wouldn't you like to have a mental "traffic light," informing you when you should say something, say nothing, or slow down before speaking? James lived long before traffic signals, but he understood that believers need to be quick in some areas of their lives yet slow in others. Being slow to speak allows time for believers to think and consider what others are saying. He explained that believers accept God's Word in their hearts and clean up their lives.

¹⁹ Understand this, my dear brothers and sisters: You must all be quick to listen, slow to speak, and slow to get angry. ²⁰ Human anger does not produce the righteousness God desires. ²¹ So get rid of all the filth and evil in your lives, and humbly accept the word God has planted in your hearts, for it has the power to save your souls.

James 1:19–21

Have you ever "followed" someone on social media? Do you "like" certain posts on your favorite websites? Do you have dozens of "friends" whom you hardly know? Isn't there a big difference between knowing about someone and really knowing him or her? James understood this concept. He knew that it was important to know about God's Word, but even more important to put it into practice.

²² But don't just listen to God's word. You must do what it says. Otherwise, you are only fooling yourselves. ²³ For if you listen to the word and don't obey, it is like glancing at your face in a mirror. ²⁴ You see yourself, walk away, and forget what you look like. ²⁵ But if you look carefully into the perfect law that sets you free, and if you do what it says and don't forget what you heard, then God will bless you for doing it.   James 1:22–25

James remarked that claiming to be religious and not controlling your speech is hypocritical. Recall that *hypocrisy* is *the behavior you have when you do something contrary to what you say or believe.* Words are a mirror of a person's heart. Actions speak louder than words.

²⁶ If you claim to be religious but don't control your tongue, you are fooling yourself, and your religion is worthless. ²⁷ Pure and genuine religion in the sight of God the Father means caring for orphans and widows in their distress and refusing to let the world corrupt you.   James 1:26–27

Topic 2—Genuine Faith

Introduction: In chapter 2, James argued against favoritism and for the necessity of kind acts. He used rhetorical questions (questions not designed to be answered) to help Jewish Christians examine their motives and behaviors, especially the practice of showing favoritism to some worshippers based on their wealth or status in society. In his letter to Christians in Rome, the apostle Paul also denounced discrimination and prejudice. He wrote:

⁹ There will be trouble and calamity for everyone who keeps on doing what is evil—for the Jew first and also for the Gentile. ¹⁰ But there will be glory and honor and peace from God for all who do good—for the Jew first and also for the Gentile. ¹¹ For God does not show favoritism.   Romans 2:9–11

To the church in Colossae, Paul wrote: in this new life, it doesn't matter if you are a Jew or a Gentile, circumcised or uncircumcised, barbaric, uncivilized, slave, or free. Christ is all that matters, and he lives in all of us (Colossians 3:11). Both Paul and James condemned favoritism. If we say that Christ is our Lord, then we must live as he requires, without prejudice and loving all people regardless of race, culture, or economic status.

Part 1—No Favoritism

[1] My dear brothers and sisters, how can you claim to have faith in our glorious Lord Jesus Christ if you favor some people over others?

[2] For example, suppose someone comes into your meeting dressed in fancy clothes and expensive jewelry, and another comes in who is poor and dressed in dirty clothes. [3] If you give special attention and a good seat to the rich person, but you say to the poor one, "You can stand over there, or else sit on the floor"—well, [4] doesn't this discrimination show that your judgments are guided by evil motives?

[5] Listen to me, dear brothers and sisters. Hasn't God chosen the poor in this world to be rich in faith? Aren't they the ones who will inherit the Kingdom he promised to those who love him? [6] But you dishonor the poor! Isn't it the rich who oppress you and drag you into court? [7] Aren't they the ones who slander Jesus Christ, whose noble name you bear?

James 2:1–7

Recall that the first Christians were Jewish. They knew what it was to obey dozens of specific laws, governing almost every aspect of their lives. However, James pointed to one law, the royal law, which is to *love your neighbor as you love yourself.* Jesus quoted the royal law in Matthew 22:39, "A second [commandment] is equally important: 'Love your neighbor as yourself.'"

James taught that when we break even one of God's laws, we are guilty of breaking them all. As Christians, we must be careful not to use this verse as a justification for sin, saying, "I can't keep God's law, so why should I even try?" James' statement shows us how much we need the grace and mercy of our loving Savior!

[8] Yes indeed, it is good when you obey the royal law as found in the Scriptures: "Love your neighbor as yourself." [9] But if you favor some people over others, you are committing a sin. You are guilty of breaking the law.

[10] For the person who keeps all of the laws except one is as guilty as a person who has broken all of God's laws. [11] For the same God who said, "You must not commit adultery," also said, "You must not murder." So if you murder someone but do not commit adultery, you have still broken the law.

[12] So whatever you say or whatever you do, remember that you will be judged by the law that sets you free. [13] There will be no mercy for those who have not shown mercy to others. But if you have been merciful, God will be merciful when he judges you.

James 2:8–13

> **The Royal Law**
> Love your neighbor as you love yourself

Part 2—Faith and Deeds

Have you ever watched a scary movie where deceased people come back to life as zombies—eerie, walking corpses? Zombies may look alive, but they are dead! The apostle James didn't know about zombies, but he expressed the idea that faith, despite the appearance of life, is actually dead unless it produces the fruit of faith—good deeds.

¹⁴ What good is it, dear brothers and sisters, if you say you have faith but don't show it by your actions? Can that kind of faith save anyone? ¹⁵ Suppose you see a brother or sister who has no food or clothing, ¹⁶ and you say, "Good-bye and have a good day; stay warm and eat well"—but then you don't give that person any food or clothing. What good does that do?

¹⁷ So you see, faith by itself isn't enough. Unless it produces good deeds, it is dead and useless.

¹⁸ Now someone may argue, "Some people have faith; others have good deeds." But I say, "How can you show me your faith if you don't have good deeds? I will show you my faith by my good deeds."

¹⁹ You say you have faith, for you believe that there is one God. Good for you! Even the demons believe this, and they tremble in terror. ²⁰ How foolish! Can't you see that faith without good deeds is useless?

²¹ Don't you remember that our ancestor Abraham was shown to be right with God by his actions when he offered his son Isaac on the altar? ²² You see, his faith and his actions worked together. His actions made his faith complete. ²³ And so it happened just as the Scriptures say: "Abraham believed God, and God counted him as righteous because of his faith." He was even called the friend of God.

James 2:14–23

Topic 3—Taming the Tongue

Introduction: In chapter 3, James presented three analogies for the tongue: it is like a bit in a horse's mouth, a rudder on a ship, and a spark that starts a blaze. The first two analogies show that the tongue can be used for good purposes. But the third analogy proves that the tongue can be evil and even dangerous.

James went on to discuss godly wisdom versus human wisdom. We make decisions on a daily basis—some minor and some with long-term consequences. For Christians, those decisions should always be made to glorify God in all we do.

Part 1—Control Your Speech

James warned the church that teachers of the Word would incur a stricter judgment from God than ordinary believers. There are three reasons for this. First, a teacher is responsible to speak the truth without bias, even when it is unpopular. Second, what a teacher says affects students' worldview. Third, teachers are expected to live the truth, not just teach it. So, you can see why accepting a call to teach requires serious consideration and prayer.

The tongue is the teacher's best tool, but a lying or uncontrolled tongue can be disastrous! Read the next section of James' epistle and pay close attention to the analogies James used for the tongue.

¹ Dear brothers and sisters, not many of you should become teachers in the church, for we who teach will be judged more strictly. ² Indeed, we all make many mistakes. For if we could control our tongues, we would be perfect and could also control ourselves in every other way.

³ We can make a large horse go wherever we want by means of a small bit in its mouth. ⁴ And a small rudder makes a huge ship turn wherever the pilot chooses to go, even though the winds are strong. ⁵ In the same way, the tongue is a small thing that makes grand speeches.

But a tiny spark can set a great forest on fire. ⁶ And among all the parts of the body, the tongue is a flame of fire. It is a whole world of wickedness, corrupting your entire body. It can set your whole life on fire, for it is set on fire by hell itself.

⁷ People can tame all kinds of animals, birds, reptiles, and fish, ⁸ but no one can tame the tongue. It is restless and evil, full of deadly poison. ⁹ Sometimes it praises our Lord and Father, and sometimes it curses those who have been made in the image of God. ¹⁰ And so blessing and cursing come pouring out of the same mouth. Surely, my brothers and sisters, this is not right! ¹¹ Does a spring of water bubble out with both fresh water and bitter water? ¹² Does a fig tree produce olives, or a grapevine produce figs? No, and you can't draw fresh water from a salty spring.

James 3:1–12

Part 2—Genuine Wisdom

If you have ever wondered how to tell a real hundred-dollar bill from a fake, here's a way to do it. Hold the bill up to the light and look at the inkwell. The Liberty Bell inside the inkwell will change from copper to green as you tilt the bill if it is real.

James may not have known about counterfeit money, but he knew a lot about fake wisdom. He called for believers to use genuine wisdom, free from selfishness and jealousy. He knew that false Christians will betray their true beliefs through what they say and how they live.

Jesus illustrated this concept, saying, "Yes, just as you can identify a tree by its fruit, so you can identify people by their actions" (Matthew 17:20). Luke told Jesus' parable this way:

⁴³ "A good tree can't produce bad fruit, and a bad tree can't produce good fruit. ⁴⁴ A tree is identified by its fruit. Figs are never gathered from thornbushes, and grapes are not picked from bramble bushes. ⁴⁵ A good person produces good things from the treasury of a good heart, and an evil person produces evil things from the treasury of an evil heart. What you say flows from what is in your heart."

Luke 6:43–45

What do your actions tell others about your faith? James wrote:

¹³ If you are wise and understand God's ways, prove it by living an honorable life, doing good works with the humility that comes from wisdom. ¹⁴ But if you are bitterly jealous and there is selfish ambition in your heart, don't cover up the truth with boasting and lying. ¹⁵ For jealousy and selfishness are not God's kind of wisdom. Such things are earthly, unspiritual, and demonic. ¹⁶ For wherever there is jealousy and selfish ambition, there you will find disorder and evil of every kind.

¹⁷ But the wisdom from above is first of all pure. It is also peace loving, gentle at all times, and willing to yield to others. It is full

of mercy and the fruit of good deeds. It shows no favoritism and is always sincere. [18] And those who are peacemakers will plant seeds of peace and reap a harvest of righteousness.

James 3:13–18

Topic 4—Submit to God

Introduction: Popular advertising slogans insist "You're worth it," "You can have it your way," "Where do you want to go today?" and "Be all that you can be." Of course, you have to buy their products to experience the personal fulfillment they imply with their ads. Human beings, by nature, seek to control others and please themselves with material possessions.

This aspect of life wasn't much different in James' day. People wanted what they did not have, and they spent time figuring out how to get it. Jealousy and discontentment caused divisions within the church. James provided the solution: watch your motives and humble yourself before God.

[1] What is causing the quarrels and fights among you? Don't they come from the evil desires at war within you? [2] You want what you don't have, so you scheme and kill to get it. You are jealous of what others have, but you can't get it, so you fight and wage war to take it away from them. Yet you don't have what you want because you don't ask God for it. [3] And even when you ask, you don't get it because your motives are all wrong—you want only what will give you pleasure.

[4] You adulterers! Don't you realize that friendship with the world makes you an enemy of God? I say it again: If you want to be a friend of the world, you make yourself an enemy of God. [5] Do you think the Scriptures have no meaning? They say that God is passionate that the spirit he has placed within us should be faithful to him. [6] And he gives grace generously. As the Scriptures say,

"God opposes the proud
but gives grace to the humble."

[7] So humble yourselves before God. Resist the devil, and he will flee from you. [8] Come close to God, and God will come close to you. Wash your hands, you sinners; purify your hearts, for your loyalty is divided between God and the world. [9] Let there be tears for what you have done. Let there be sorrow and deep grief. Let there be sadness instead of laughter, and gloom instead of joy. [10] Humble yourselves before the Lord, and he will lift you up in honor.

James 4:1–10

Humility is incompatible with sitting in judgment of others. Jesus said, "Do not judge others, and you will not be judged. For you will be treated as you treat others" (Matthew 7:1–2). James confirmed Jesus' words and added that our job as believers is not to judge others or to decide whether or not God's Law applies to us. We have no right to judge others.

[11] Don't speak evil against each other, dear brothers and sisters. If you criticize and judge each other, then you are criticizing and judging God's law. But your job is to obey the law, not to judge whether it applies to you. [12] God alone, who gave the law, is the Judge. He alone has the power to save or to destroy. So what right do you have to judge your neighbor?

James 4:11–12

James warned the believers against putting too much confidence in their plans. God is in control of today and tomorrow. Yes, we do need to plan for our future, but we need to do so humbly, remembering who oversees our lives.

James added a remark at the end of chapter 4 regarding sin. We often think that sin is only doing what is wrong, but James corrected this by adding that not doing what is right is also sinful.

[13] Look here, you who say, "Today or tomorrow we are going to a certain town and will stay there a year. We will do business there and make a profit." [14] How do you know what your life will be like tomorrow? Your life is like the morning fog—it's here a little while, then it's gone. [15] What you ought to say is, "If the Lord wants us to, we will live and do this or that." [16] Otherwise you are boasting about your own pretentious plans, and all such boasting is evil.

[17] Remember, it is sin to know what you ought to do and then not do it.

James 4:13–17

Topic 5—Patience and Prayer

Introduction: Think for a minute about times when you have had to be patient. Maybe you had to care for a younger sibling, to stay in bed because you were ill, or had to save money for a long time to buy what you had your heart set on. Everyone needs to be patient at times. People who do not have a relationship with Christ have only their natural ability to be patient in everyday frustrations. But the believer has the supernatural ability—through the Holy Spirit—to endure problems in life, even the toughest problems. In chapter 5, James exhorted the people to be patient, humble, and brave because this life is only a fraction of eternity.

[1] Look here, you rich people: Weep and groan with anguish because of all the terrible troubles ahead of you. [2] Your wealth is rotting away, and your fine clothes are moth-eaten rags. [3] Your gold and silver are corroded. The very wealth you were counting on will eat away your flesh like fire. This corroded treasure you have hoarded will testify against you on the day of judgment. [4] For listen! Hear the cries of the field workers whom you have cheated of their pay. The cries of those who harvest your fields have reached the ears of the Lord of Heaven's Armies.

[5] You have spent your years on earth in luxury, satisfying your every desire. You have fattened yourselves for the day of slaughter. [6] You have condemned and killed innocent people, who do not resist you.

[7] Dear brothers and sisters, be patient as you wait for the Lord's return. Consider the farmers who patiently wait for the rains in the fall and in the spring. They eagerly look for the valuable harvest to ripen. [8] You, too, must be patient. Take courage, for the coming of the Lord is near.

[9] Don't grumble about each other, brothers and sisters, or you will be judged. For look—the Judge is standing at the door!

¹⁰ For examples of patience in suffering, dear brothers and sisters, look at the prophets who spoke in the name of the Lord. ¹¹ We give great honor to those who endure under suffering. For instance, you know about Job, a man of great endurance. You can see how the Lord was kind to him at the end, for the Lord is full of tenderness and mercy.

James 5:1–11

People sometimes misunderstand James' warning against taking an oath, and so they will not swear an oath in a courtroom. This is not the type of oath James was talking about. In Jewish culture, people would often add emphasis to their words by swearing an oath, saying, "I swear to God this is the truth." James said not to do this because it calls on God to validate the words.

In the Sermon on the Mount, Jesus taught believers not to make a rash vow or swear an oath, saying:

³⁴ "But I say, do not make any vows! Do not say, 'By heaven!' because heaven is God's throne. ³⁵ And do not say, 'By the earth!' because the earth is his footstool. And do not say, 'By Jerusalem!' for Jerusalem is the city of the great King. ³⁶ Do not even say, 'By my head!' for you can't turn one hair white or black. ³⁷ Just say a simple, 'Yes, I will,' or 'No, I won't.' Anything beyond this is from the evil one."

Matthew 5:34–37

James repeated Christ's instruction:

But most of all, my brothers and sisters, never take an oath, by heaven or earth or anything else. Just say a simple yes or no, so that you will not sin and be condemned.

James 5:12

Real faith—faith that is lived out—endures persecution and hardships. Rather than relying on ourselves when facing problems, James called for prayer. And prayer should not be the last resort; it should be the first option

for every Christian regardless of circumstances. The church ought to pray for its people, and the elders should be called to pray for the sick.

Most Christians take time for private reflection and confession. We can also confess our sins confidentially to people who are trustworthy and prayerful, and pray for those who confide in us as well. Prayer is effective!

¹³ Are any of you suffering hardships? You should pray. Are any of you happy? You should sing praises. ¹⁴ Are any of you sick? You should call for the elders of the church to come and pray over you, anointing you with oil in the name of the Lord. ¹⁵ Such a prayer offered in faith will heal the sick, and the Lord will make you well. And if you have committed any sins, you will be forgiven.

¹⁶ Confess your sins to each other and pray for each other so that you may be healed. The earnest prayer of a righteous person has great power and produces wonderful results. ¹⁷ Elijah was as human as we are, and yet when he prayed earnestly that no rain would fall, none fell for three and a half years! ¹⁸ Then, when he prayed again, the sky sent down rain and the earth began to yield its crops.

James 5:13–18

James ended his letter on a high note, reminding believers that they shouldn't give up on fellow Christians who have strayed from the truth or left the fellowship.

¹⁹ My dear brothers and sisters, if someone among you wanders away from the truth and is brought back, ²⁰ you can be sure that whoever brings the sinner back from wandering will save that person from death and bring about the forgiveness of many sins.

James 5:19–20

Humility and Hope Lesson 20

Getting Started—The Main Ideas

In the same way that the book of James was named after its author, the epistles titled *1 Peter* and *2 Peter* were named after the person identified as their writer, Simon Peter. Simon became known as *Peter* after Jesus gave him that name, which means *rock* in Greek (John 1:42). Peter was also known as *Cephas*, which is *rock* in Aramaic. After Jesus ascended to heaven, Peter lived up to his name and became one of the most important leaders of the early church.

In his first letter, Peter sought to remind his brothers and sisters in Christ of the wonderful hope of eternal life they now had together with God's chosen people. He also wanted the believers to be holy. Their behavior would demonstrate obedience and reverence for God. Peter wanted their conduct to be a testimony to others, especially those in authority (1 Peter 2:12–15). He even urged those who were slaves to still show respect when their masters were cruel, pointing to Jesus' example of submission to God for our sake (1 Peter 2:18–21).

The believers were experiencing many trials; they were mistreated and insulted by people who did not understand their faith. Peter emphasized that God would reward the faithful who showed Christlike behavior, and that judgment would begin with God's own people. He gave the believers instructions to show love toward one another, exercise spiritual gifts, and be humble.

In his second letter, we read that Peter expected to die soon (2 Peter 1:13–15). He wanted the believers to be grounded in their faith so that they would not follow the false teachers who would come to be among them (2 Peter 2:1). He knew that when Jesus returns, no one will be spared in the day of judgment. So, Peter's second letter exhorted believers to live holy lives and to have patience.

Topic 1—The Hope of Salvation

Introduction: When Jesus was baptized, John the Baptist called him *the Lamb of God*. Andrew heard what John said and told his brother Simon that Jesus was the Messiah. He brought him to Jesus, who said, "Your name is Simon, son of John—but you will be called Cephas" (which means "Peter") (John 1:42). When Jesus began his public ministry, he specifically called Andrew and Simon to follow him. The gospel of Matthew says that Jesus saw them throwing a net into the water, for they fished for a living. Jesus called out to them, "Come, follow me, and I will show you how to fish for people!" (Matthew 4:18–19). The brothers became two of Jesus' 12 disciples.

Even though Andrew followed Jesus first, his brother was the one who took charge. Simon Peter was the most outspoken of the disciples. His name appears first when their names are listed in the New Testament (Matthew 10:2, Mark 3:15, Luke 6:14, and Acts 1:13). The Gospels tell many stories about what he did. Peter was brash, and sometimes Jesus had to rebuke him (Mark 8:33, Matthew 14:31). After Jesus was arrested, he denied even knowing Jesus (Mark 14:71). But when Jesus rose from the dead, Peter was the first apostle to enter the empty tomb (John 20:26). Even though Peter had denied him three times, the risen Jesus spoke to Peter and once more called Peter to follow him (John 20:15–19). And that is what Peter did!

THE APOSTLE PETER, CHURCH OF THE SAVIOR IN SPAIN

After Jesus ascended into heaven, Peter led the disciples while they waited for the promised Holy Spirit (Acts 1:15). On Pentecost he preached the first sermon, and 3,000 people were added to the church (Acts 2:14, 41). He was used mightily by God to work miracles and spread the gospel in Jerusalem and in other cities (Acts 3:6, 9:34, 40). After he was freed from jail by an angel, he went to another place and James became the leader of the church in Jerusalem (Acts 12:17). Peter remained active in Jerusalem, but he also preached the gospel in various cities, mostly to the Jews (Galatians 2:7–9). Eventually, according to early Christian tradition, he reached Rome. Clement, who was the bishop of Rome from AD 88 to 97, wrote that Peter was martyred for Christ.

Part 1—Introduction to 1 and 2 Peter

Peter wrote 1 Peter with Silas, who served as his secretary (1 Peter 5:12). The letter of 2 Peter refers to the first letter (2 Peter 3:1) and shows Peter believed he would soon die (2 Peter 1:14). As Peter was killed during the time that the Roman emperor, Nero, persecuted Christians in AD 64, his letters had to be written before that date. While there is no controversy regarding Peter's authorship of 1 Peter, some scholars think that 2 Peter might have been ghostwritten after his death as a way to memorialize him and continue his teaching. Whatever the case might be, the early church accepted the letter of 2 Peter into the canon of Scripture.

Neither 1 Peter nor 2 Peter is directed to a specific congregation, so they are both general epistles. Peter's first letter was written to God's chosen people who are living as foreigners in the provinces of Pontus, Galatia, Cappadocia, Asia, and Bithynia (1 Peter 1:1). These were all Roman provinces in Asia Minor in what today is the country of Turkey. Peter's second letter did not specify a particular region of the world. It was written to believers who shared Peter's faith, which includes everyone who has been born of the Spirit and become a child of God.

ROCK FORMATIONS IN TURKEY

Part 2—A Living Hope

What did Peter have to say to the many people who had become Jesus' followers throughout Asia Minor? First, he pointed out that they were chosen by God. By virtue of being chosen, they were living as foreigners. When God transforms people and makes them holy, they no longer fit in with the culture around them. Peter expressed his excitement for the believers and the wonderful blessings they would experience in Christ.

¹ This letter is from Peter, an apostle of Jesus Christ.

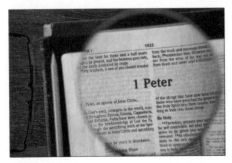

I am writing to God's chosen people who are living as foreigners in the provinces of Pontus, Galatia, Cappadocia, Asia, and Bithynia. ² God the Father knew you and chose you long ago, and his Spirit has made you holy. As a result, you have obeyed him and have been cleansed by the blood of Jesus Christ.

May God give you more and more grace and peace.

³ All praise to God, the Father of our Lord Jesus Christ. It is by his great mercy that we have been born again, because God raised Jesus Christ from the dead. Now we live with great expectation, ⁴ and we have a priceless

inheritance—an inheritance that is kept in heaven for you, pure and undefiled, beyond the reach of change and decay. ⁵And through your faith, God is protecting you by his power until you receive this salvation, which is ready to be revealed on the last day for all to see.

1 Peter 1:1–5

Praise. Mercy. Great expectation. Priceless. Pure. Peter's excitement surely encouraged the believers who first received this letter! He continued:

⁶ So be truly glad. There is wonderful joy ahead, even though you must endure many trials for a little while. ⁷These trials will show that your faith is genuine. It is being tested as fire tests and purifies gold—though your faith is far more precious than mere gold. So when your faith remains strong through many trials, it will bring you much praise and glory and honor on the day when Jesus Christ is revealed to the whole world.

1 Peter 1:6–7

MELTING GOLD IN A CRUCIBLE

When Peter wrote this, he knew that Christians were suffering as a result of their faith. He himself had already suffered tests and trials, including arrests and imprisonment (Acts 4:1–4, 12:1–11). So, when Peter said that trials prove one's faith is genuine, he knew what he was talking about. It is important to know that Peter's faith was not always strong. In fact, Jesus once said to him, "You have so little faith. Why did you doubt me?" (Matthew 14:31). But Peter the doubter, through God's grace, became a pillar of the church, as you learned in previous lessons. His words were a great comfort to those who received them. Peter added:

⁸ You love him even though you have never seen him. Though you do not see him now, you trust him; and you rejoice with a glorious, inexpressible joy. ⁹The reward for trusting him will be the salvation of your souls.

¹⁰ This salvation was something even the prophets wanted to know more about when they prophesied about this gracious salvation prepared for you. ¹¹ They wondered what time or situation the Spirit of Christ within them was talking about when he told them in advance about Christ's suffering and his great glory afterward.

FRESCO OF PROPHETS, ST. NICHOLAS CHURCH IN SLOVAKIA

¹² They were told that their messages were not for themselves, but for you. And now this Good News has been announced to you by those who preached in the power of the Holy Spirit sent from heaven. It is all so wonderful that even the angels are eagerly watching these things happen.

1 Peter 1:8–12

Instead of focusing on tests and trials, Peter wanted believers to focus on their wonderful salvation through Christ. This salvation was something that they already had. They *had* been born again; they had a precious inheritance (1 Peter 1:3–4). But salvation was something the believers *would receive* in the future too. Peter said this would happen when Jesus is revealed and rewards those who trust in him (1 Peter 1:7, 9). Salvation is incomplete without sanctification. God does not save his people so that they stay the same; he makes them into new people (2 Corinthians 5:17) and he continues working in them so they can be like Christ (Philippians 1:6). So,

Peter wanted the believers to realize what a great privilege salvation is, that it is both instantaneous and an ongoing process, and that they should live in keeping with their salvation—the topic of the next section of his letter.

Part 3—Be Holy

Peter wanted the believers to be holy. This is what he said they should do:

13 So prepare your minds for action and exercise self-control. Put all your hope in the gracious salvation that will come to you when Jesus Christ is revealed to the world. 14 So you must live as God's obedient children. Don't slip back into your old ways of living to satisfy your own desires. You didn't know any better then. 15 But now you must be holy in everything you do, just as God who chose you is holy. 16 For the Scriptures say, "You must be holy because I am holy."

1 Peter 1:13–16

The believers needed to have the right perspective. They needed to look forward and not backward. To backslide is *to slip back into undesirable ways or behavior*. It means that you return to doing bad or evil things after you had stopped doing them, or that you stop doing good and helpful things that were helping you advance. Peter wanted his brothers and sisters in the Lord to live up to what they had learned. He continued:

17 And remember that the heavenly Father to whom you pray has no favorites. He will judge or reward you according to what you do. So you must live in reverent fear of him during your time here as "temporary residents." 18 For you know that God paid a ransom to save you from the empty life you inherited from your ancestors. And it was not paid with mere gold or silver, which lose their value. 19 It was the precious blood of Christ, the sinless, spotless Lamb of God. 20 God chose him as your ransom long before the world began, but now in these last days he has been revealed for your sake.

21 Through Christ you have come to trust in God. And you have placed your faith and hope in God because he raised Christ from the dead and gave him great glory.

22 You were cleansed from your sins when you obeyed the truth, so now you must show sincere love to each other as brothers and sisters. Love each other deeply with all your heart.   1 Peter 1:17–22

Siblings in an earthly family may or may not get along, but Peter used brothers and sisters as an example of sincere love. Very few people know you as well as your siblings. They have seen you mad, sad, glad, and in every state in between. The love a brother or sister has for you is not typically based on an illusion; it is based on the real you. And God knows us more than our brothers or sisters could ever know us (Psalm 139:1–18, 23–24). Long ago, he planned to make us part of his family through Christ (Ephesians 1:4–5). So, what were the believers Peter was writing to supposed to do? They were to make love a priority in their lives.

23 For you have been born again, but not to a life that will quickly end. Your new life will last forever because it comes from the eternal, living word of God. 24 As the Scriptures say,

"People are like grass;
   their beauty is like a flower in the field.
The grass withers and the flower fades.
25 But the word of the Lord remains forever."

And that word is the Good News that was preached to you.

1 Peter 1:23–25

Topic 2—Chosen People

Introduction: Peter wrote to the believers about salvation and the precious inheritance they would receive. He also urged them to live holy lives, especially in view of eternity. As children of the Father, they needed to behave accordingly. In the next chapter of his letter, Peter continued describing the blessings of salvation and how those who are born again should live.

Part 1—Belonging to God

How should God's holy people behave toward their brothers and sisters? Peter was direct:

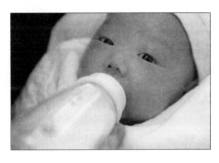

[1] So get rid of all evil behavior. Be done with all deceit, hypocrisy, jealousy, and all unkind speech. [2] Like newborn babies, you must crave pure spiritual milk so that you will grow into a full experience of salvation. Cry out for this nourishment, [3] now that you have had a taste of the Lord's kindness.

[4] You are coming to Christ, who is the living cornerstone of God's temple. He was rejected by people, but he was chosen by God for great honor.

[5] And you are living stones that God is building into his spiritual temple. What's more, you are his holy priests. Through the mediation of Jesus Christ, you offer spiritual sacrifices that please God. [6] As the Scriptures say,

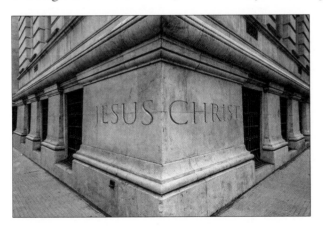

"I am placing a cornerstone in Jerusalem,
    chosen for great honor,
and anyone who trusts in him
    will never be disgraced."

[7] Yes, you who trust him recognize the honor God has given him. But for those who reject him,

"The stone that the builders rejected
    has now become the cornerstone."

[8] And,

"He is the stone that makes people stumble,
    the rock that makes them fall."

They stumble because they do not obey God's word, and so they meet the fate that was planned for them.

1 Peter 2:1–8

Peter cited the writings of the prophet Isaiah, who said that the Messiah would be "despised and rejected" and that God would then honor him for bearing our sin (Isaiah 53:3, 11–12). Christians see that the Hebrew Scriptures prophesied that many people would have a hard time with Jesus. Peter added that the reason they stumble is that they do not obey God's Word. They do not want to recognize that it is divinely inspired. Many do not want obey its commands; they would rather follow their own desires.

⁹ But you are not like that, for you are a chosen people. You are royal priests, a holy nation, God's very own possession. As a result, you can show others the goodness of God, for he called you out of the darkness into his wonderful light.

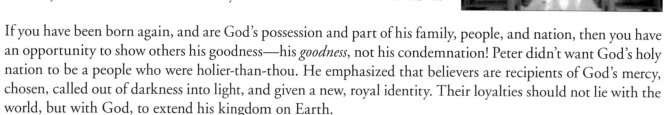

¹⁰ "Once you had no identity as a people;
now you are God's people.
Once you received no mercy;
now you have received God's mercy."

1 Peter 2:9–10

If you have been born again, and are God's possession and part of his family, people, and nation, then you have an opportunity to show others his goodness—his *goodness*, not his condemnation! Peter didn't want God's holy nation to be a people who were holier-than-thou. He emphasized that believers are recipients of God's mercy, chosen, called out of darkness into light, and given a new, royal identity. Their loyalties should not lie with the world, but with God, to extend his kingdom on Earth.

¹¹ Dear friends, I warn you as "temporary residents and foreigners" to keep away from worldly desires that wage war against your very souls. ¹² Be careful to live properly among your unbelieving neighbors. Then even if they accuse you of doing wrong, they will see your honorable behavior, and they will give honor to God when he judges the world.

1 Peter 2:11–12

Part 2—Authority

EMPEROR NERO
AD 54–68

At the time Peter wrote, Christians were seen as people who advocated things that were against the law (Acts 16:21) because they did not worship the Roman emperor, or the gods worshipped by the people around them. This meant that they could easily get in trouble with the local authorities. Peter had experienced persecution, and so had others who proclaimed the gospel of Christ. Therefore, Peter warned the believers to be careful about how they behaved around those who did not believe in Jesus.

¹³ For the Lord's sake, submit to all human authority—whether the king as head of state, ¹⁴ or the officials he has appointed. For the king has sent them to punish those who do wrong and to honor those who do right.

¹⁵ It is God's will that your honorable lives should silence those ignorant people who make foolish accusations against you. ¹⁶ For you are free, yet you are God's slaves, so don't use your freedom as an excuse to do evil. ¹⁷ Respect everyone, and love the family of believers. Fear God, and respect the king.

¹⁸ You who are slaves must submit to your masters with all respect. Do what they tell you—not only if they are kind and reasonable, but even if they are cruel. ¹⁹ For God is pleased when, conscious of his will, you patiently endure unjust treatment. ²⁰ Of course, you get no credit for being patient if you are beaten for doing wrong. But if you suffer for doing good and endure it patiently, God is pleased with you.   1 Peter 2:13–20

Peter's words are shocking to us today. He encouraged slaves to submit even to masters who were cruel. He said to submit to all human authority. But he was the same man who, on trial before Jewish authorities, said "We must obey God rather than any human authority" (Acts 5:29). Notice that this passage begins with the qualification "For the Lord's sake." The submission that Peter asked the believers—even the slaves— to model had a purpose. Peter did not want his brothers and sisters to suffer for suffering's sake, but to show others that God had transformed them into honorable people who did good and not evil.

²¹ For God called you to do good, even if it means suffering, just as Christ suffered for you. He is your example, and you must follow in his steps.

²² He never sinned,
   nor ever deceived anyone.
²³ He did not retaliate when he was insulted,
   nor threaten revenge when he suffered.
He left his case in the hands of God,
   who always judges fairly.
²⁴ He personally carried our sins
   in his body on the cross
so that we can be dead to sin
   and live for what is right.
By his wounds
   you are healed.
²⁵ Once you were like sheep
   who wandered away.
But now you have turned to your Shepherd,
   the Guardian of your souls.   1 Peter 2:21–25

WOOD CARVING OF JESUS BEING TORMENTED

What did Peter mean when he encouraged believers to follow Christ Jesus, the sinless Lamb? He wanted them to imitate the Savior's character. He wanted them to be patient and meek. He warned them not to retaliate

or seek revenge. What a turnaround this was! For Peter was the impulsive disciple who was ready to fight when the soldiers came for Jesus, and who cut off the ear of the high priest's servant (John 18:10–11). Peter knew how Jesus responded: healing the man and submitting to the authorities to fulfill the Father's plan. Jesus had courage, faith, and kindness; his followers should have the same. Peter did not encourage the faithful to be respectful and submissive out of fear, but for the Lord's sake—so that the good news of the forgiveness of sin through Jesus would spread far and wide.

Topic 3—Christ's Example

Introduction: Around the time that Peter wrote his letter, the gospel message had only been around for about 30 years. The church had multiplied far beyond Jerusalem, but believers were still very much in the minority in the Roman Empire. After all, most people found it very strange that anyone should claim there was only one God, and that he had a Son—a teacher from some rural province who'd gotten himself killed but whose followers said had been raised from the dead. Worship of multiple deities was common in the Roman Empire; the faith and way of life of Christians were not. So, Peter encouraged believers living in hostile territory to keep heaven in mind and to be holy.

ZEUS AND OTHER GODS ON
MOUNT NEMRUT, TURKEY

Part 1—A Clear Conscience

Peter continued his letter by reiterating his advice. He returned to the topic of loving your brothers and sisters. He again warned the believers not to take revenge.

⁸ Finally, all of you should be of one mind. Sympathize with each other. Love each other as brothers and sisters. Be tenderhearted, and keep a humble attitude. ⁹ Don't repay evil for evil. Don't retaliate with insults when people insult you. Instead, pay them back with a blessing. That is what God has called you to do, and he will grant you his blessing. ¹⁰ For the Scriptures say,

"If you want to enjoy life
 and see many happy days,
keep your tongue from speaking evil
 and your lips from telling lies.
¹¹ Turn away from evil and do good.
 Search for peace, and work to maintain it.
¹² The eyes of the Lord watch over those who do right,
 and his ears are open to their prayers.
But the Lord turns his face
 against those who do evil."

¹³ Now, who will want to harm you if you are eager to do good? ¹⁴ But even if you suffer for doing what is right, God will reward you for it. So don't worry or be afraid of their threats. ¹⁵ Instead, you must worship Christ as Lord of your life. And if someone asks about your hope as a believer, always be ready to explain it. ¹⁶ But do this in a gentle and respectful way. Keep your conscience clear. Then if people speak against you, they will be ashamed when they see what a good life you live because you belong to Christ. ¹⁷ Remember, it is better to suffer for doing good, if that is what God wants, than to suffer for doing wrong!   1 Peter 3:8–17

Peter encouraged the believers to be ready to share the reasons for their hope. What did believers hope for? Forgiveness of sins. A reward when Jesus returned. A precious inheritance in heaven. To share their hope, believers must keep a clear conscience. When they do so, they can evangelize freely—conscious of the love and mercy they experienced, and continue to experience, through the Lord Jesus.

¹⁸ Christ suffered for our sins once for all time. He never sinned, but he died for sinners to bring you safely home to God. He suffered physical death, but he was raised to life in the Spirit.

²² Now Christ has gone to heaven. He is seated in the place of honor next to God, and all the angels and authorities and powers accept his authority.   1 Peter 3:18, 22

Part 2—Finished with Sin

Peter emphasized that believers should not backslide but keep a clear conscience, love others, and do good to them. Living a holy life can sometimes mean that you are misunderstood; you might be insulted or mistreated. The believers Peter wrote to were suffering because of the persecution they experienced from those around them. The Christians who were slaves, in particular, were likely to suffer not just insults and injustice but actual physical harm. Peter pointed out the believers' suffering was evidence of their commitment to God.

¹ So then, since Christ suffered physical pain, you must arm yourselves with the same attitude he had, and be ready to suffer, too. For if you have suffered physically for Christ, you have finished with sin. ² You won't spend the rest of your lives chasing your own desires, but you will be anxious to do the will of God.　　1 Peter 4:1–2

Christians do not suffer only because of what others do. They also suffer in their battle against sin, and this causes them to grow (Romans 5:3–5). During the time that he was on Earth, Christ taught that those who wanted to follow him needed to be willing to suffer too:

²³ Then [Jesus] said to the crowd, "If any of you wants to be my follower, you must give up your own way, take up your cross daily, and follow me. ²⁴ If you try to hang on to your life, you will lose it. But if you give up your life for my sake, you will save it."　　Luke 9:23–24

Peter reinforced this concept in his letter, reminding the believers that they had left sinful ways, and encouraging them to remember God's coming judgment for sin.

³ You have had enough in the past of the evil things that godless people enjoy—their immorality and lust, their feasting and drunkenness and wild parties, and their terrible worship of idols.

⁴ Of course, your former friends are surprised when you no longer plunge into the flood of wild and destructive things they do. So they slander you. ⁵ But remember that they will have to face God, who stands ready to judge everyone, both the living and the dead.　　1 Peter 4:3–5

Peter continued with practical advice, repeating his admonition that believers love one another. He urged them to use their spiritual gifts to serve each other.

⁷ The end of the world is coming soon. Therefore, be earnest and disciplined in your prayers. ⁸ Most important of all, continue to show deep love for each other, for love covers a multitude of sins. ⁹ Cheerfully share your home with those who need a meal or a place to stay.

¹⁰ God has given each of you a gift from his great variety of spiritual gifts. Use them well to serve one another. ¹¹ Do you have the gift of speaking? Then speak as though God himself were speaking through you. Do you have the gift of helping others? Do it with all the strength and energy that God supplies. Then everything you do will bring glory to God through Jesus Christ. All glory and power to him forever and ever! Amen.

1 Peter 4:7–11

Topic 4—Living for God

Introduction: Have you noticed a common thread in the first three chapters of 1 Peter? The first chapter spoke of trials and testing. The second one discussed Christ's rejection and reminded the believers that Christ suffered for them. The third again focused on Jesus' example, urging believers to remain faithful even through physical suffering. Peter's focus on suffering and persecution continued in chapter 4.

Part 1—Persecution

What kind of persecution were Christians experiencing when Peter was writing? They were accused of doing wrong (1 Peter 2:12, 15). They suffered cruelty, unjust treatment, and beatings (1 Peter 2:18–20). They were insulted, slandered, and threatened (1 Peter 3:9, 14, 16). But this was not all. The book of Acts tells of instances when Christians were arrested, put on trial, fined, jailed, beaten, run out of town, or killed. Paul wrote about having false teachers follow him to subvert his work (Galatians 4:17). It should not surprise us that Peter thought it was important to discuss persecution.

¹² Dear friends, don't be surprised at the fiery trials you are going through, as if something strange were happening to you. ¹³ Instead, be very glad—for these trials make you partners with Christ in his suffering, so that you will have the wonderful joy of seeing his glory when it is revealed to all the world.

¹⁴ If you are insulted because you bear the name of Christ, you will be blessed, for the glorious Spirit of God rests upon you. ¹⁵ If you suffer, however, it must not be for murder, stealing, making trouble, or prying into other people's affairs. ¹⁶ But it is no shame to suffer for being a Christian. Praise God for the privilege of being called by his name! ¹⁷ For the time has come for judgment, and it must begin with God's household. And if judgment begins with us, what terrible fate awaits those who have never obeyed God's Good News? ¹⁸ And also,

> "If the righteous are barely saved,
>   what will happen to godless sinners?"

¹⁹ So if you are suffering in a manner that pleases God, keep on doing what is right, and trust your lives to the God who created you, for he will never fail you.

1 Peter 4:12–19

Peter's affirmation of trust in God is especially moving today, in light of the events that happened after his letter. In AD 64 the Roman emperor, Nero, blamed Christians for the great fire of Rome, which he himself was rumored to have set. Nero had Christians burned alive; also, Peter and Paul were both martyred under his rule. Paul was beheaded; Peter was crucified. Jesus had prophesied how Peter would die:

¹⁸ "I tell you the truth, when you were young, you were able to do as you liked; you dressed yourself and went wherever you wanted to go. But when you are old, you will stretch out your hands, and others will dress you and take you where you don't want to go." ¹⁹ Jesus said this to let him know by what kind of death he would glorify God. Then Jesus told him, "Follow me."

John 21:18–19

Peter followed Jesus with all his heart, and he wanted the believers to understand that doing so was a great honor. As he wrote in 1 Peter 4:16, It is no shame to suffer for being a Christian. Praise God for the privilege of being called by his name!

CRUCIFIXION OF
ST. PETER

Part 2—Humility

When Jesus appeared on Earth after the resurrection, the apostle John recorded a long conversation Jesus had with Peter on the beach. Jesus prophesied the way Peter would die. But right before that, Jesus asked Peter whether Peter loved him. He did this three times in a row. Each time, Peter said *yes*. In response, Jesus commanded Peter three times to care for his sheep or lambs (John 21:15–17), meaning the people of God (Psalm 100:3). Peter knew this was a great responsibility, and he took it seriously. In his letter to the believers in Asia Minor, he addressed others who were caring for God's people too.

[1] And now, a word to you who are elders in the churches. I, too, am an elder and a witness to the sufferings of Christ. And I, too, will share in his glory when he is revealed to the whole world. As a fellow elder, I appeal to you: [2] Care for the flock that God has entrusted to you. Watch over it willingly, not grudgingly—not for what you will get out of it, but because you are eager to serve God. [3] Don't lord it over the people assigned to your care, but lead them by your own good example. [4] And when the Great Shepherd appears, you will receive a crown of never-ending glory and honor.

1 Peter 5:1–4

Peter, an apostle, identified himself as a fellow elder. He could have been boastful about his position of authority in the church. He could have gone on and on saying he was one of Jesus' disciples, and had not only witnessed Christ's suffering but also the many miracles he performed (Acts 2:22), his transfiguration (Matthew 17:1–8), and his ascension into heaven (Luke 24:50–51). But Peter did not boast. He modeled the instruction he gave to the elders: not to lord it over others, but to be a good example (1 Peter 5:3). He continued:

[5] In the same way, you who are younger must accept the authority of the elders. And all of you, dress yourselves in humility as you relate to one another, for

"God opposes the proud
but gives grace to the humble."

[6] So humble yourselves under the mighty power of God, and at the right time he will lift you up in honor. [7] Give all your worries and cares to God, for he cares about you.   1 Peter 5:5–7

Peter affirmed that everyone should be humble, whether or not they held a position of authority. Jesus had taught Peter and the other disciples that "Whoever wants to be first must take last place and be the servant of everyone else" (Mark 9:35). Peter wanted his readers to have this same attitude and to stand firm.

[8] Stay alert! Watch out for your great enemy, the devil. He prowls around like a roaring lion, looking for someone to devour. [9] Stand firm against him, and be strong in your faith. Remember that your family of believers all over the world is going through the same kind of suffering you are.

[10] In his kindness God called you to share in his eternal glory by means of Christ Jesus. So after you have suffered a little while, he will restore, support, and strengthen you, and he will place you on a firm foundation. [11] All power to him forever! Amen.

[12] I have written and sent this short letter to you with the help of Silas, whom I commend to you as a faithful brother. My purpose in writing is to encourage you and assure you that what you are experiencing is truly part of God's grace for you. Stand firm in this grace.

[13] Your sister church here in Babylon sends you greetings, and so does my son Mark. [14] Greet each other with a kiss of love.

Peace be with all of you who are in Christ.

1 Peter 5:8–14

Peter wrote to reassure the believers that their suffering was neither unusual nor unseen by God. In the last paragraphs of his letter, he mentioned two coworkers: Silas, whom we first met in Acts as a fellow missionary (Acts 15:40), and Mark, who wrote the Gospel that bears his name. Even Peter relied on other people as he sought to serve God. Having and offering support is part of what the body of Christ does, especially in trials and troubling times.

Topic 5—Godly Living

Introduction: While we do not know exactly when 2 Peter was written, it has valuable instruction not only for those who read it in the first century, but also for us today. This letter reiterates much of what was said in 1 Peter. It also adds valuable information on our hope in Christ. It rebukes false teaching and provides more details on the events of the last days.

[1] This letter is from Simon Peter, a slave and apostle of Jesus Christ.
I am writing to you who share the same precious faith we have. This faith was given to you because of the justice and fairness of Jesus Christ, our God and Savior.

[2] May God give you more and more grace and peace as you grow in your knowledge of God and Jesus our Lord.

[3] By his divine power, God has given us everything we need for living a godly life. We have received all of this by coming to know him, the one who called us to himself by means of his marvelous glory and excellence.
[4] And because of his glory and excellence, he has given us great and precious promises. These are the promises that enable you to share his divine nature and escape the world's corruption caused by human desires.   2 Peter 1:1–4

PETER THE APOSTLE

What has God given us to be godly? According to Peter, God has given us everything we need, including wonderful and encouraging promises.

[5] In view of all this, make every effort to respond to God's promises. Supplement your faith with a generous provision of moral excellence, and moral excellence with knowledge, [6] and knowledge with self-control, and self-control with patient endurance, and patient endurance with godliness, [7] and godliness with brotherly affection, and brotherly affection with love for everyone.

⁸ The more you grow like this, the more productive and useful you will be in your knowledge of our Lord Jesus Christ. ⁹ But those who fail to develop in this way are shortsighted or blind, forgetting that they have been cleansed from their old sins.

¹⁰ So, dear brothers and sisters, work hard to prove that you really are among those God has called and chosen. Do these things, and you will never fall away. ¹¹ Then God will give you a grand entrance into the eternal Kingdom of our Lord and Savior Jesus Christ.

¹² Therefore, I will always remind you about these things—even though you already know them and are standing firm in the truth you have been taught. ¹³ And it is only right that I should keep on reminding you as long as I live. ¹⁴ For our Lord Jesus Christ has shown me that I must soon leave this earthly life, ¹⁵ so I will work hard to make sure you always remember these things after I am gone. 2 Peter 1:5–15

Peter wanted to help believers continue to be faithful. They were to realize that they would be judged for their response to the grace they had received. They could ignore it, or they could grow, please God, and reap an eternal reward. Peter affirmed the truth of the gospel.

¹⁶ For we were not making up clever stories when we told you about the powerful coming of our Lord Jesus Christ. We saw his majestic splendor with our own eyes ¹⁷ when he received honor and glory from God the Father. The voice from the majestic glory of God said to him, "This is my dearly loved Son, who brings me great joy." ¹⁸ We ourselves heard that voice from heaven when we were with him on the holy mountain.

TRANSFIGURATION OF JESUS

¹⁹ Because of that experience, we have even greater confidence in the message proclaimed by the prophets. You must pay close attention to what they wrote, for their words are like a lamp shining in a dark place—until the Day dawns, and Christ the Morning Star shines in your hearts. ²⁰ Above all, you must realize that no prophecy in Scripture ever came from the prophet's own understanding, ²¹ or from human initiative. No, those prophets were moved by the Holy Spirit, and they spoke from God. 2 Peter 1:16–21

Peter affirmed the inspiration of Scripture and that its message points us to Christ. This is what Jesus himself said (John 5:39, 46–47). The Pharisees to whom Jesus spoke refused to come to him. In contrast, 2 Peter urged believers to pay close attention to the Scriptures so that they—and we—can grow in the Lord.

Topic 6—Hope for Christians

Introduction: What do believers hope for? When he was on trial, the apostle Paul said, "My hope is in the resurrection of the dead!" (Acts 23:6). He later tied that hope to the day of judgment (Acts 24:15), to the fulfillment of God's promise of a Savior (Acts 26:6, 28:20), and to salvation (Romans 5:4). The apostle Peter referred to all these things and more in discussing what believers hope for: an inheritance (1 Peter 1:3), salvation (1 Peter 1:13), the day of judgment, and new heavens and a new Earth (2 Peter 3:12–13). Peter wanted to make sure Christians kept their sights on their glorious future, rather than on the painful present. His emphasis was necessary because the believers were being discouraged by false teachers.

APOSTLES' GATE, VALENCIA
CATHEDRAL, SPAIN

¹ This is my second letter to you, dear friends, and in both of them I have tried to stimulate your wholesome thinking and refresh your memory. ² I want you to remember what the holy prophets said long ago and what our Lord and Savior commanded through your apostles.

³ Most importantly, I want to remind you that in the last days scoffers will come, mocking the truth and following their own desires. ⁴ They will say, "What happened to the promise that Jesus is coming again? From before the times of our ancestors, everything has remained the same since the world was first created."

⁵ They deliberately forget that God made the heavens long ago by the word of his command, and he brought the earth out from the water and surrounded it with water. ⁶ Then he used the water to destroy the ancient world with a mighty flood. ⁷ And by the same word, the present heavens and earth have been stored up for fire. They are being kept for the day of judgment, when ungodly people will be destroyed.

⁸ But you must not forget this one thing, dear friends: A day is like a thousand years to the Lord, and a thousand years is like a day. ⁹ The Lord isn't really being slow about his promise, as some people think. No, he is being patient for your sake. He does not want anyone to be destroyed, but wants everyone to repent. ¹⁰ But the day of the Lord will come as unexpectedly as a thief. Then the heavens will pass away with a terrible noise, and the very elements themselves will disappear in fire, and the earth and everything on it will be found to deserve judgment.

¹¹ Since everything around us is going to be destroyed like this, what holy and godly lives you should live, ¹² looking forward to the day of God and hurrying it along. On that day, he will set the heavens on fire, and the elements will melt away in the flames. ¹³ But we are looking forward to the new heavens and new earth he has promised, a world filled with God's righteousness.

¹⁴ And so, dear friends, while you are waiting for these things to happen, make every effort to be found living peaceful lives that are pure and blameless in his sight.
2 Peter 3:1–14

Have you ever been impatient while waiting for something to happen? It can be easy to give up hope or become discouraged when what we are awaiting takes much longer than anticipated. Peter knew this. He constantly reminded believers to live holy lives so as to be worthy of the coming reward and all they hoped to receive through Christ. Peter also urged the believers to make good use of their opportunities to share the good news with others (1 Peter 3:15–16). Peter had been called by Jesus to fish for people (Mark 1:17); he cared about the lost. So he said, Remember, our Lord's patience gives people time to be saved (2 Peter 3:15). He continued:

ST. PAUL, ROME, ITALY

This is what our beloved brother Paul also wrote to you with the wisdom God gave him— ¹⁶ speaking of these things in all of his letters. Some of his comments are hard to understand, and those who are ignorant and unstable have twisted his letters to mean something quite different, just as they do with other parts of Scripture. And this will result in their destruction.
2 Peter 3:15–16

God gave us the Bible for our benefit, but it is a complicated book. It is not always clear or easy to interpret or apply.

© Walking in Truth Grade 8

Almost two millennia have passed since the Bible's newest parts were written. Our culture and context are very different from those of its first readers! Yet even in the first century, people had difficulty understanding what God's Word said. That is why we should recognize that there is no shame in seeking help when we have questions or doubts about what the Scriptures say or what is meant by a particular passage. We all need to approach God's Word with humility, remembering its power.

Peter concluded his letter with exhortation and praise:

[17] You already know these things, dear friends. So be on guard; then you will not be carried away by the errors of these wicked people and lose your own secure footing. [18] Rather, you must grow in the grace and knowledge of our Lord and Savior Jesus Christ.

All glory to him, both now and forever! Amen.

2 Peter 3:17–18

Lesson 21 Love, Faith, and the Last Days

Getting Started—The Main Ideas

Although he never referred to himself by name, we know that John, who called himself *the disciple whom Jesus loved*, wrote the three epistles named for him that we have in our Bible. He also wrote the gospel of John and the book of Revelation. You will find John's epistles just before the book of Jude, and the book of Revelation is the last book in the New Testament. John's epistles are grouped with Hebrews, James, 1 and 2 Peter, and Jude as general epistles.

FRAGMENTS OF 1 JOHN ON PAPYRUS

John's epistles were written between AD 85 and 90 (estimated dates vary), quite some time after many of the other New Testament books. John wrote the letters as an old man. He was probably living in Ephesus before his exile to the Island of Patmos, where he wrote the book of Revelation. He had seen the church grow and expand during his life, but then he saw the next generation of Christians begin to become complacent in standing for the truth of the gospel. In the book of Revelation, John addressed the problem of being "lukewarm" for the faith—showing marginal commitment to God and his Word.

The letter of 1 John and the book of Revelation present sharp contrasts. As you read 1 John and the book of Revelation, look for the contrast between light and darkness, truth and error, God and Satan, life and death, love and hate, and victory and defeat.

Topic 1—The Light

Introduction: Most of the eyewitnesses to Jesus' life and ministry had died by the time John wrote his letters. He may have been the only survivor of Jesus' 12 disciples. Despite hardship and persecution, the church had thrived and grown by the end of the first century. But some of the second- or third-generation Christians started to have questions about what they had been taught about Jesus. Gentile Christians had a hard time accepting the fact that Jesus was a human being, as well as God the Son, because of the false teachings prominent in the Greek world. One heresy (false teaching) was *gnosticism—a worldview that taught physical matter was evil and the spirit was good*, so Jesus could not have been a human being. John warned believers against such heresy in the strongest possible terms. The intent of his letters was to put believers, whom he often called his *dear children*, back on track with their faith.

Part 1—Introduction to the Epistles of John

Recall that the city of Ephesus, where John lived and wrote his epistles, was a center for pagan worship. The temple to Artemis (Diana) dominated the landscape. The church was situated in a place where polytheism flourished, and worship of the Greek and Roman gods was the dominant religion. Yet believers had become comfortable with the worldview of the prevailing culture. They listened to false teachers who denied the reality of sin. They wanted to be Christians without the need to confess and repent of their sins, forgetting that sin breaks the relationship of harmony with God.

RUINS IN EPHESUS

Part 2—Walking in the Light

John began his letter explaining that Jesus is the Word of life who existed from the beginning:

[1] We proclaim to you the one who existed from the beginning, whom we have heard and seen. We saw him with our own eyes and touched him with our own hands. He is the Word of life. [2] This one who is life itself was revealed to us, and we have seen him. And now we testify and proclaim to you that he is the one who is eternal life. He was with the Father, and then he was revealed to us. [3] We proclaim to you what we ourselves have actually seen and heard so that you may have fellowship with us. And our fellowship is with the Father and with his Son, Jesus Christ. [4] We are writing these things so that you may fully share our joy.   1 John 1:1–4

John declared that God *is* Light—all light and zero darkness. He is all clean, with no dirt, shame, or impurities; all right, with nothing wrong; all truth, with nothing false. Light can be trusted to lead us because it always dispels darkness. Jesus said, "I am the light of the world. If you follow me, you won't have to walk in darkness, because you will have the light that leads to life" (John 8:12).

When people claim they do not sin, even if they truly believe their own claim, they are lying to themselves. God declares that all people are born with a sinful nature and sin against him by what they say, do, and think. Saying that sin does not exist is calling God a liar! John continued:

[5] This is the message we heard from Jesus and now declare to you: God is light, and there is no darkness in him at all. [6] So we are lying if we say we have fellowship with God but go on living in spiritual darkness; we are not practicing the truth. [7] But if we are living in the light, as God is in the light, then we have fellowship with each other, and the blood of Jesus, his Son, cleanses us from all sin.

[8] If we claim we have no sin, we are only fooling ourselves and not living in the truth. [9] But if we confess our sins to him, he is faithful and just to forgive us our sins and to cleanse us from all wickedness. [10] If we claim we have not sinned, we are calling God a liar and showing that his word has no place in our hearts.   1 John 1:5–10

Topic 2—Love One Another

Introduction: Saying that we do not sin is fooling ourselves, but saying that we cannot do anything about our sin is also foolish. Some first-century believers fell prey to the false teaching that since it is impossible to stop sinning, they shouldn't even try! When John talked about sin, it is important to understand the distinction between committing a sin (but repenting for it) and living an unrepentant lifestyle that flaunts disobedience to God. John wrote that anyone who lives contrary to God's commandments is a liar and does not really know God at all.

Part 1—A New and an Old Command

[1] My dear children, I am writing this to you so that you will not sin. But if anyone does sin, we have an advocate who pleads our case before the Father. He is Jesus Christ, the one who is truly righteous. [2] He himself is the sacrifice that atones for our sins—and not only our sins but the sins of all the world.

³ And we can be sure that we know him if we obey his commandments. ⁴ If someone claims, "I know God," but doesn't obey God's commandments, that person is a liar and is not living in the truth. ⁵ But those who obey God's word truly show how completely they love him. That is how we know we are living in him. ⁶ Those who say they live in God should live their lives as Jesus did.

1 John 2:1–6

When Jesus walked on Earth, he was in constant opposition to the religious leaders who taught obedience to the letter of the Law as the way to salvation. Of course, obeying the Mosaic law with all its minor statutes was impossible. Jesus emphasized the spirit of the Law over the letter—the Law was given to people because they did not naturally love God or others. Jesus summed up the Law in a few sentences: ³⁷ "'You must love the LORD your God with all your heart, all your soul, and all your mind.' ³⁸ This is the first and greatest commandment. ³⁹ A second is equally important: 'Love your neighbor as yourself.' ⁴⁰ The entire law and all the demands of the prophets are based on these two commandments" (Matthew 22:37–40). John reminded the believers of Jesus' words:

⁷ Dear friends, I am not writing a new commandment for you; rather it is an old one you have had from the very beginning. This old commandment—to love one another—is the same message you heard before. ⁸ Yet it is also new. Jesus lived the truth of this commandment, and you also are living it. For the darkness is disappearing, and the true light is already shining.

1 John 2:7–8

John used *light* as a metaphor for having a relationship with God through faith. He addressed his admonition to all believers: live in the light!

⁹ If anyone claims, "I am living in the light," but hates a fellow believer, that person is still living in darkness. ¹⁰ Anyone who loves a fellow believer is living in the light and does not cause others to stumble. ¹¹ But anyone who hates a fellow believer is still living and walking in darkness. Such a person does not know the way to go, having been blinded by the darkness.

¹² I am writing to you who are God's children
    because your sins have been forgiven through Jesus.
¹³ I am writing to you who are mature in the faith
    because you know Christ, who existed from the beginning.
I am writing to you who are young in the faith
    because you have won your battle with the evil one.
¹⁴ I have written to you who are God's children
    because you know the Father.
I have written to you who are mature in the faith
    because you know Christ, who existed from the beginning.
I have written to you who are young in the faith
    because you are strong.
God's word lives in your hearts,
    and you have won your battle with the evil one.   1 John 2:9–14

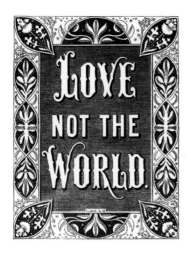

John probably wanted to shout the next admonitions from the hilltops: Do not love the world! The world is not your home! Recall that Peter wrote in his epistle: Believers are "temporary residents" (1 Peter 1:17). They should always remember that they are pilgrims or exiles in this world.

[15] Do not love this world nor the things it offers you, for when you love the world, you do not have the love of the Father in you. [16] For the world offers only a craving for physical pleasure, a craving for everything we see, and pride in our achievements and possessions. These are not from the Father, but are from this world. [17] And this world is fading away, along with everything that people crave. But anyone who does what pleases God will live forever. 1 John 2:15–17

Part 2—The Antichrist

John warned his readers about the last days—the time between Jesus' first and second comings. This is the time we live in today. During this time, antichrists—false teachers whose goal is to deceive Christians into turning away from their faith—will come to deceive Christians. These false teachers are backed by Satan, who is in the full-time business of deception. Jesus described Satan as " . . . a murderer from the beginning. He [Satan] has always hated the truth, because there is no truth in him. When he lies, it is consistent with his character; for he is a liar and the father of lies" (John 8:44). Satan's business plan goes back to the garden of Eden, where he deceived Adam and Eve, and his destructive intentions have not changed.

Finally, just before Christ returns, one great Antichrist will arise (Revelation 13; 19:20). We do not need to be afraid that we won't recognize this antichrist because we can discern a false teacher by his heretical words and by the power of the Holy Spirit living within us.

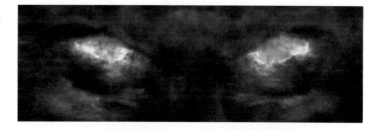

[18] Dear children, the last hour is here. You have heard that the Antichrist is coming, and already many such antichrists have appeared. From this we know that the last hour has come. [19] These people left our churches, but they never really belonged with us; otherwise they would have stayed with us. When they left, it proved that they did not belong with us.

[20] But you are not like that, for the Holy One has given you his Spirit, and all of you know the truth. [21] So I am writing to you not because you don't know the truth but because you know the difference between truth and lies. [22] And who is a liar? Anyone who says that Jesus is not the Christ. Anyone who denies the Father and the Son is an antichrist. [23] Anyone who denies the Son doesn't have the Father, either. But anyone who acknowledges the Son has the Father also.

[24] So you must remain faithful to what you have been taught from the beginning. If you do, you will remain in fellowship with the Son and with the Father. [25] And in this fellowship we enjoy the eternal life he promised us.

[26] I am writing these things to warn you about those who want to lead you astray. [27] But you have received the Holy Spirit and he lives within you, so you don't need anyone to teach you what is true. For the Spirit teaches you everything you need to know, and what he teaches is true—it is not a lie. So just as he has taught you, remain in fellowship with Christ. 1 John 2:18–27

Now that he had taught believers how to recognize antichrists, John turned his attention to how to recognize God's children. They are the courageous and steadfast believers who know and do what is right in God's sight. The children of God live lifestyles of righteousness and love their brothers and sisters in Christ, but false believers do not live righteous lifestyles and do not love other believers.

²⁸ And now, dear children, remain in fellowship with Christ so that when he returns, you will be full of courage and not shrink back from him in shame.

²⁹ Since we know that Christ is righteous, we also know that all who do what is right are God's children.

1 John 2:28–29

> **Antichrists**
> False teachers whose goal is to deceive
> Christians into turning away from their faith

Topic 3—Children of God

Introduction: Recall that there were heresies rampant in the early church. One of these heresies, gnosticism, said that because the body was bad and the soul was good, Jesus could not have had a human body. Paul, Peter, and John all denied this philosophy in their epistles. However, the idea that the body was not important because it would pass away had worked its way into the church. Some believers decided that since the body was only a shell for the soul, it really didn't matter much what they did with their body. John warned the believers that they, body and soul, were God's children! It *did* matter what they did with their bodies, and they were to keep themselves pure, living lives with integrity.

¹ See how very much our Father loves us, for he calls us his children, and that is what we are! But the people who belong to this world don't recognize that we are God's children because they don't know him. ² Dear friends, we are already God's children, but he has not yet shown us what we will be like when Christ appears. But we do know that we will be like him, for we will see him as he really is. ³ And all who have this eager expectation will keep themselves pure, just as he is pure.

⁴ Everyone who sins is breaking God's law, for all sin is contrary to the law of God. ⁵ And you know that Jesus came to take away our sins, and there is no sin in him. ⁶ Anyone who continues to live in him will not sin. But anyone who keeps on sinning does not know him or understand who he is.

⁷ Dear children, don't let anyone deceive you about this: When people do what is right, it shows that they are righteous, even as Christ is righteous. ⁸ But when people keep on sinning, it shows that they belong to the devil, who has been sinning since the beginning. But the Son of God came to destroy the works of the devil. ⁹ Those who have been born into God's family do not make a practice of sinning, because God's life is in them.

So they can't keep on sinning, because they are children of God. ¹⁰ So now we can tell who are children of God and who are children of the devil. Anyone who does not live righteously and does not love other believers does not belong to God.

1 John 3:1–10

Do you love surprises? You may not love the "surprise" John warned his followers about. He said that if we love God, people outside the church may find reasons to hate us. But, if we love our brothers and sisters in Christ, it does not matter what the world thinks of us because we have passed from death into eternal life.

¹¹ This is the message you have heard from the beginning: We should love one another. ¹² We must not be like Cain, who belonged to the evil one and killed his brother. And why did he kill him? Because Cain had been doing what was evil, and his brother had been doing what was righteous. ¹³ So don't be surprised, dear brothers and sisters, if the world hates you.

¹⁴ If we love our brothers and sisters who are believers, it proves that we have passed from death to life. But a person who has no love is still dead. ¹⁵ Anyone who hates another brother or sister is really a murderer at heart. And you know that murderers don't have eternal life within them.

1 John 3:11–15

John spoke of real love as giving up our lives for our brothers and sisters. He meant that we should look to the needs of others and put them first, demonstrating love, concern, and compassion. We should even be willing to die for them if necessary. Real love is an action, not a feeling. How do you show real love for others?

¹⁶ We know what real love is because Jesus gave up his life for us. So we also ought to give up our lives for our brothers and sisters. ¹⁷ If someone has enough money to live well and sees a brother or sister in need but shows no compassion—how can God's love be in that person?

¹⁸ Dear children, let's not merely say that we love each other; let us show the truth by our actions. ¹⁹ Our actions will show that we belong to the truth, so we will be confident when we stand before God. ²⁰ Even if we feel guilty, God is greater than our feelings, and he knows everything.

²¹ Dear friends, if we don't feel guilty, we can come to God with bold confidence. ²² And we will receive from him whatever we ask because we obey him and do the things that please him.

²³ And this is his commandment: We must believe in the name of his Son, Jesus Christ, and love one another, just as he commanded us. ²⁴ Those who obey God's commandments remain in fellowship with him, and he with them. And we know he lives in us because the Spirit he gave us lives in us.

1 John 3:16–24

Topic 4—Love and Faith

Introduction: Many people struggle with assurance of their salvation. They doubt whether they have enough faith or have done enough good works. Or they may think about how sinful they are or get stuck thinking that God cannot forgive or accept them. What a tragedy! The great joy of the message of salvation is that Jesus accomplished everything for us. He paid our debt in full and sent his Spirit to assure us of our salvation.

Because assurance of salvation is so important, John admonished believers to stop living in fear of judgment, and instead live a life of confidence.

Part 1—The Way of Love

Remember that everyone has big questions. One of those questions is: What is God like? John answered that question by saying, "God is love." The word for God's love in Greek is *agape*. This is the complete and unselfish love that God has for us.

⁷ Dear friends, let us continue to love one another, for love comes from God. Anyone who loves is a child of God and knows God. ⁸ But anyone who does not love does not know God, for God is love.

⁹ God showed how much he loved us by sending his one and only Son into the world so that we might have eternal life through him. ¹⁰ This is real love—not that we loved God, but that he loved us and sent his Son as a sacrifice to take away our sins.

¹¹ Dear friends, since God loved us that much, we surely ought to love each other. ¹² No one has ever seen God. But if we love each other, God lives in us, and his love is brought to full expression in us.   1 John 4:7–12

John reminded the believers that the Holy Spirit living in their hearts was proof that they were saved. Paul indicated that the Holy Spirit is God's guarantee that we are God's own people (Ephesians 1:14). We can trust in God's love.

¹³ And God has given us his Spirit as proof that we live in him and he in us. ¹⁴ Furthermore, we have seen with our own eyes and now testify that the Father sent his Son to be the Savior of the world. ¹⁵ All who declare that Jesus is the Son of God have God living in them, and they live in God.   1 John 4:13–15

What does it mean to live like Jesus? Should we wear a robe and sandals, head out to the streets, and preach to the people? No, that was not what John was saying. Living like Jesus means that we value others as image-bearers of God, love others as sinners for whom Christ died, and serve others as Jesus served—in humility, giving God glory and honor. We have no fear of condemnation because we love God, and he lives in us.

¹⁶ We know how much God loves us, and we have put our trust in his love.

God is love, and all who live in love live in God, and God lives in them. ¹⁷ And as we live in God, our love grows more perfect. So we will not be afraid on the day of judgment, but we can face him with confidence because we live like Jesus here in this world.

¹⁸ Such love has no fear, because perfect love expels all fear. If we are afraid, it is for fear of punishment, and this shows that we have not fully experienced his perfect love. ¹⁹ We love each other because he loved us first. ²⁰ If someone says, "I love God," but hates a fellow believer, that person is a liar; for if we don't love people we can see, how can we love God, whom we cannot see? ²¹ And he has given us this command: Those who love God must also love their fellow believers.   1 John 4:16–21

Part 2—Victory through Faith

John taught believers how to recognize the antichrists and how to recognize true children of God. But how can we be sure that we are God's children? John provided a straightforward answer: everyone who believes that Jesus is the Christ is a child of God, loving God and keeping his commandments.

¹ Everyone who believes that Jesus is the Christ has become a child of God. And everyone who loves the Father loves his children, too. ² We know we love God's children if we love God and obey his commandments. ³ Loving God means keeping his commandments, and his commandments are not burdensome. ⁴ For every child of God defeats this evil world, and we achieve this victory through our faith. ⁵ And who can win this battle against the world? Only those who believe that Jesus is the Son of God.

1 John 5:1–5

Sometimes nonbelievers think that the Christian life is tiring. They know that Christians seek to obey God, and they think this is a big burden and a hassle. But God's commandments can be summarized as loving God and loving our neighbor; they are not supposed to be burdensome! Remember that when Jesus was on Earth, he invited people to follow him, saying:

²⁸ "Come to me, all of you who are weary and carry heavy burdens, and I will give you rest. ²⁹ Take my yoke upon you. Let me teach you, because I am humble and gentle at heart, and you will find rest for your souls. ³⁰ For my yoke is easy to bear, and the burden I give you is light."

Matthew 11:28–30

Christ came to Earth so that we could be reconciled with God and with one another. Through faith, we can live a life of joy, peace, and victory. John continued, encouraging his readers to believe in Jesus:

⁶ And Jesus Christ was revealed as God's Son by his baptism in water and by shedding his blood on the cross—not by water only, but by water and blood. And the Spirit, who is truth, confirms it with his testimony. ⁷ So we have these three witnesses— ⁸ the Spirit, the water, and the blood—and all three agree. ⁹ Since we believe human testimony, surely we can believe the greater testimony that comes from God. And God has testified about his Son. ¹⁰ All who believe in the Son of God know in their hearts that this testimony is true. Those who don't believe this are actually calling God a liar because they don't believe what God has testified about his Son.

¹¹ And this is what God has testified: He has given us eternal life, and this life is in his Son. ¹² Whoever has the Son has life; whoever does not have God's Son does not have life.

1 John 5:6–12

John wanted his readers to hold on to that life, to hold on to Jesus. He concluded his letter with one more admonition: Dear children, keep away from anything that might take God's place in your hearts (1 John 5:21).

John also wrote two other letters: the epistles of 2 John and 3 John. These are very brief and cover some of the same topics that John discussed in 1 John.

Topic 5—End Times

Introduction: Besides his epistles and gospel, John wrote the book of Revelation. Scholars believe that the seven churches of Asia to whom John addressed the book were experiencing persecution. Rome had destroyed the temple in Jerusalem in AD 70 and executed James, Jesus' half brother, and Peter. Other apostles were martyred as well. John survived as an exile on Patmos, a rocky island in the Mediterranean Sea, and wrote Revelation there (Revelation 1:9–11).

FRESCOES AT ST. JOHN THE THEOLOGIAN'S MONASTERY ON PATMOS

Part 1—Introduction to Revelation

Near the end of his life, John, possibly the last eyewitness of the incarnate Christ, had a vision of the glorified Christ, the last days, and Christ's return. Jesus revealed to John what must take place in the future—judgment, tribulation, and the ultimate triumph of God over Satan and all evil. John wrote Revelation in response to Jesus' command to write a book for the churches in Asia Minor (Revelation 1:11).

The epistle, or book, of Revelation is a literary genre called an apocalypse—*an uncovering of something that had been hidden.* Although the word appears only once in the book of Revelation, it could apply to the entire book. In the New Testament, the Greek word *apokalypsis* was used by the apostle Paul in Ephesians when he wrote that the truth of salvation for all nations is now revealed (Ephesians 3:3).

Revelation was not the only apocalyptic writing of the period. It was just one of the Jewish and Christian writings of 200 BC to AD 150. Apocalyptic literature is usually a narrative, or a story, that uses symbols to tell about the end times, when God will destroy the ruling powers of evil and raise the righteous to life. But narratives are not always written in strict chronological order; sometimes there is a flashback or a flash-forward. Because John wrote Revelation in this type of literary form, the events he prophesied about are not all in order. Christians have puzzled over how to interpret John's imagery and symbols for a long time. Most agree that the message of the book is that at the end of time, God will reward the faithful with eternal life, but that those who refuse to believe in Jesus will face eternal punishment.

John also wrote about a new heaven and a new earth. All believers will live with Jesus forever in perfect peace. Those who have already died will be raised to life. These promises for the future give us hope and comfort.

Though the book of Revelation is difficult to understand, God promises that it brings a blessing to the reader (Revelation 1:3). It is important to study the book humbly, being careful not to read into it, but researching what we do not understand and asking God for wisdom in applying its teaching to our life.

We will look at two very small sections of the book. In the first chapter of Revelation, John shared the vision he had of Jesus. In the last chapter, John described the new Jerusalem coming down from heaven. These beautiful visions give us hope and comfort for the future.

> **Apocalypse**
> The uncovering of something
> that had been hidden

Part 2—John's Vision

In the very first chapter of the Gospel of John, the beloved apostle wrote, we have seen his glory, the glory of the Father's one and only Son (John 1:14). And do you remember how John's first epistle began? He talked about seeing Jesus with his own eyes, and that he wrote about it to share his joy (1 John 1:4). In Revelation, John shares a vision he had of the Lord Jesus Christ in much more detail for us to rejoice and be blessed.

[1] This is a revelation from Jesus Christ, which God gave him to show his servants the events that must soon take place. He sent an angel to present this revelation to his servant John, [2] who faithfully reported everything he saw. This is his report of the word of God and the testimony of Jesus Christ.

[3] God blesses the one who reads the words of this prophecy to the church, and he blesses all who listen to its message and obey what it says, for the time is near.

[4] This letter is from John to the seven churches in the province of Asia.

Grace and peace to you from the one who is, who always was, and who is still to come; from the sevenfold Spirit before his throne; [5] and from Jesus Christ. He is the faithful witness to these things, the first to rise from the dead, and the ruler of all the kings of the world.

All glory to him who loves us and has freed us from our sins by shedding his blood for us. [6] He has made us a Kingdom of priests for God his Father. All glory and power to him forever and ever! Amen.

[7] Look! He comes with the clouds of heaven.
    And everyone will see him—
    even those who pierced him.
And all the nations of the world
    will mourn for him.
Yes! Amen!

[8] "I am the Alpha and the Omega—the beginning and the end," says the Lord God. "I am the one who is, who always was, and who is still to come—the Almighty One."

Revelation 1:1–8

John could have made a big deal out of his background and relationship with Christ, but he did not. He simply called himself "a brother and partner in suffering" (Revelation 1:9). He continued his letter with humility, telling how he was exiled to Patmos and how he kept up his practice of worshipping in the Spirit. Maybe he was kneeling in prayer when the Lord took hold of him and brought him into the spiritual realm. John was terrified and fell down as if dead! He had no language to describe the heavenly things he was seeing, so he had to rely on earthly terms to communicate what he saw. As you read, notice how many times John used the term "like."

[9] I, John, am your brother and your partner in suffering and in God's Kingdom and in the patient endurance to which Jesus calls us. I was exiled to the island of Patmos for preaching the word of God and for my testimony about Jesus. [10] It was the Lord's Day, and I was worshiping in the Spirit. Suddenly, I heard behind me a loud voice like a trumpet blast. [11] It said, "Write in a book everything you see, and send it to the seven churches in the cities of Ephesus, Smyrna, Pergamum, Thyatira, Sardis, Philadelphia, and Laodicea."

¹²When I turned to see who was speaking to me, I saw seven gold lampstands. ¹³And standing in the middle of the lampstands was someone like the Son of Man. He was wearing a long robe with a gold sash across his chest. ¹⁴His head and his hair were white like wool, as white as snow. And his eyes were like flames of fire. ¹⁵His feet were like polished bronze refined in a furnace, and his voice thundered like mighty ocean waves. ¹⁶He held seven stars in his right hand, and a sharp two-edged sword came from his mouth. And his face was like the sun in all its brilliance.

¹⁷When I saw him, I fell at his feet as if I were dead. But he laid his right hand on me and said, "Don't be afraid! I am the First and the Last. ¹⁸I am the living one. I died, but look—I am alive forever and ever! And I hold the keys of death and the grave.

¹⁹"Write down what you have seen—both the things that are now happening and the things that will happen. ²⁰This is the meaning of the mystery of the seven stars you saw in my right hand and the seven gold lampstands: The seven stars are the angels of the seven churches, and the seven lampstands are the seven churches.

Revelation 1:9–20

John continues by writing down specific messages that the Son of God gives to the seven churches. After that, the book of Revelation continues for many chapters, discussing wars, trials, and tribulations that people will experience in the end times and at the last judgment. But if we trust in Christ, we do not need to be afraid. John has shown us who Jesus is, and we can affirm: I know the one in whom I trust, and I am sure that he is able to guard what I have entrusted to him until the day of his return (1 Timothy 1:12).

Part 3—The Heavenly City

John wrote the book of Revelation toward the end of his life. What had he lived through? Recall that Jesus chose John, along with his brother James, to be one of his 12 disciples (Mark 3:17). John had traveled with and learned from the Lord, seen him killed, and seen his empty tomb. John saw Christ ascend to heaven and saw the Holy Spirit come with fire to empower the church. He witnessed the persecution that resulted in the death of his brother (Acts 12:2). He saw the Roman emperor Nero blame Christians for the fire that ravaged Rome in AD 64 and the intense persecution that followed, including the deaths of Peter and Paul.

Yet John also saw the church grow from 120 believers on the day of Pentecost to a movement that had followers not only in Jerusalem, but in cities as far away as Ephesus, Corinth, Rome, and even Alexandria. Scholars estimate that by the time John was writing on Patmos, there were more than 40 churches established in the Roman Empire.

John knew Jesus had taught that his kingdom was not an earthly kingdom (John 18:36). And in writing the vision that Jesus gave him, John described a city he called *Babylon the Great*, which represented the earthly and sinful powers of the world aligned against God. He then contrasted this city to Jerusalem.

¹Then I saw a new heaven and a new earth, for the old heaven and the old earth had disappeared. And the sea was also gone. ²And I saw the holy city, the new Jerusalem, coming down from God out of heaven like a bride beautifully dressed for her husband.

³ I heard a loud shout from the throne, saying, "Look, God's home is now among his people! He will live with them, and they will be his people. God himself will be with them. ⁴ He will wipe every tear from their eyes, and there will be no more death or sorrow or crying or pain. All these things are gone forever."

⁵ And the one sitting on the throne said, "Look, I am making everything new!" And then he said to me, "Write this down, for what I tell you is trustworthy and true." ⁶ And he also said, "It is finished! I am the Alpha and the Omega— the Beginning and the End. To all who are thirsty I will give freely from the springs of the water of life. ⁷ All who are victorious will inherit all these blessings, and I will be their God, and they will be my children.

Revelation 21:1–7

John was given a guided tour of the new Jerusalem! Wouldn't you like to see if for yourself?

¹ Then the angel showed me a river with the water of life, clear as crystal, flowing from the throne of God and of the Lamb. ² It flowed down the center of the main street. On each side of the river grew a tree of life, bearing twelve crops of fruit, with a fresh crop each month. The leaves were used for medicine to heal the nations.

³ No longer will there be a curse upon anything. For the throne of God and of the Lamb will be there, and his servants will worship him. ⁴ And they will see his face, and his name will be written on their foreheads. ⁵ And there will be no night there— no need for lamps or sun—for the Lord God will shine on them. And they will reign forever and ever.

⁶ Then the angel said to me, "Everything you have heard and seen is trustworthy and true. The Lord God, who inspires his prophets, has sent his angel to tell his servants what will happen soon."

Revelation 22:1–6

Jesus spoke to John and to us, his readers, assuring us that his second coming would be soon:

⁷ "Look, I am coming soon! Blessed are those who obey the words of prophecy written in this book."

⁸ I, John, am the one who heard and saw all these things. And when I heard and saw them, I fell down to worship at the feet of the angel who showed them to me. ⁹ But he said, "No, don't worship me. I am a servant of God, just like you and your brothers the prophets, as well as all who obey what is written in this book. Worship only God!"

¹⁰ Then he instructed me, "Do not seal up the prophetic words in this book, for the time is near. ¹¹ Let the one who is doing harm continue to do harm; let the one who is vile continue to be vile; let the one who is righteous continue to live righteously; let the one who is holy continue to be holy."

¹² "Look, I am coming soon, bringing my reward with me to repay all people according to their deeds. ¹³ I am the Alpha and the Omega, the First and the Last, the Beginning and the End."

¹⁴ Blessed are those who wash their robes. They will be permitted to enter through the gates of the city and eat the fruit from the tree of life. ¹⁵ Outside the city are the dogs—the sorcerers, the sexually immoral, the murderers, the idol worshipers, and all who love to live a lie.

¹⁶ "I, Jesus, have sent my angel to give you this message for the churches. I am both the source of David and the heir to his throne. I am the bright morning star."

In this chapter, Jesus is described in many different ways. He is the Alpha and Omega, First and Last, the Beginning and the End, the Heir to David's throne, the bright morning Star, and the Lamb of God. But there is another description that is also implied in this passage: Jesus is the Bridegroom, and the church is his bride (Ephesians 5:25–27). John continued:

¹⁷ The Spirit and the bride say, "Come." Let anyone who hears this say, "Come." Let anyone who is thirsty come. Let anyone who desires drink freely from the water of life. ¹⁸ And I solemnly declare to everyone who hears the words of prophecy written in this book: If anyone adds anything to what is written here, God will add to that person the plagues described in this book. ¹⁹ And if anyone removes any of the words from this book of prophecy, God will remove that person's share in the tree of life and in the holy city that are described in this book.

²⁰ He who is the faithful witness to all these things says, "Yes, I am coming soon!"

Amen! Come, Lord Jesus!

²¹ May the grace of the Lord Jesus be with God's holy people.   Revelation 22:7–21

Walking in Truth Grade 8 Student Textbook Index

abiogenesis 59, **60**
affliction 161
agnosticism 17
antichrists 243, **244**
apocalypse 248
apologetics 19
apostle 126, 138
archaeology 104
atheism 16, 90

backslide 228, **229**
biology 56, 114
biogenesis 60

causal argument 37, **39**
Christian psychology 77
Christianity 5, 113
church 84, 91
Colossae 159
contentment 149, 156, 184
Corinth 190
creation 7, 39, 101
cultural moral relativism 45, **46**
culture 9, **10**

deism 23
deliverance 39
design argument 65, **66**
discipline 213
double-mindedness 217
doctrine 158, 179
doxology 142

Ephesus 137, 240
epistemology 35

epistle 170
ethics 44, **45**, 114
evolution 57
external evidence 104, **105**

faith 33, **34**, 118, 210–212, 219–220
fall, the 7, 101
family 84, 89, 146, 164
foreshadow 201, **207**

general revelation 17, **18**
gnosticism 240

heresy 178, 240
higher consciousness 113
history 98, 115
hypocrisy 128, **129**, 218

incarnate 194, **195**
Incarnation, the 153, 193–195
information theory 63
intelligent design 59
intercede 180, **181**
internal evidence 102

judgment 39, 237–238, 251

leadership 181–184, 235

macroevolution 61, **62**
marriage 146
Marxism 6, 46, 85, 88, 101, 112

Walking in Truth Grade 8 Student Textbook Index

materialism 36, 73
mentor 178
metaphysics 36
metanarrative 6–7, 101
microevolution 62
mind argument 75
miracle 39, **40**
monotheism 16
moral absolutes 47, **48**
moral argument 49, **50**
moral relativism 45, **46**

natural selection 62
naturalism 112
Neo-Darwinism 58, **59**
New Jerusalem, the 250
new spirituality 6, 46, 101, 113

pantheism 17
parable 207
pastoral epistles 178
peer pressure 128, **129**
persecution 170, 174–175, 231, 234
Philippi 149
philosophy 31, 114
polytheism 17
popular culture 9, **11**
postmodernism 6, 46, 86, 88, 101, 112
preconception 100, **101**
preeminent 191, **193**
psychology 71, **72**, 114
psychological materialism 73, **74**
psychological spiritualism 73, **74**
psychological supernaturalism 73, **74**

redemption 8, 101
religion 5
restoration 8, 101
resurrection, proofs for 106

royal law, the 219

Sabbath 197
science 37, **38**
second coming, the 167, 172–176, 185, 251
secularism 6, 46, 85, **87**, 88, 100, 111–112
seven disciplines 11, 113–116
sexual sin 145, 164, 171
situation ethics 45, 52
slavery 165, 230–231
sociology 84, 115
special revelation 18, **19**
spiritual gifts 143, 233
spiritualism 36, 73
state 84, 230
submission 137, 146, 222
supernaturalism 37, 73
supremacy of Christ 160, **161**, 191

theism 16
theology 16, 113
Thessalonica 167
Trinity 23
truth 34
type of Christ 200, **201**

wisdom 31, **33**, 217, 221–222
worldview 3, 111
worldview tests 111

Credits

The New Jerusalem (Tapestry of the Apocalypse) (Page 8)
Credit: Kimon Berlin
https://creativecommons.org/licenses/by-sa/3.0/legalcode

John Lennox (Page 65)
Credit: Christliches Medienmagazin pro
https://creativecommons.org/licenses/by-sa/2.0/legalcode

Pontius Pilate Stone (Page 105)
Credit: Marion Doss
https://creativecommons.org/licenses/by-sa/2.0/deed.en

Four Evangelists in Mont Saint-Michel (Page 118)
Credit: Jebulon
https://creativecommons.org/licenses/by-sa/3.0/legalcode

St Timothy window, St Nicholas, Halewood (Page 168)
Credit: Rodhullandemu
https://creativecommons.org/licenses/by-sa/4.0/legalcode